The Age of Attila.

THE
AGE
OF
ATTILA

Fifth-Century Byzantium and the Barbarians

BY C. D. GORDON

Foreword by Arthur E. R. Boak

Dorset Press
New York

This edition published by Dorset Press,
a division of Marboro Books Corp.,
by arrangement with The University of Michigan Press.

1992 Dorset Press

ISBN 0-88029-788-3

Printed and bound in the United States of America

M 9 8 7 6 5 4 3 2

To R. K. G.

Illi debetur et a me gratia maior.

Foreword

by Arthur E. R. Boak

DURING THE FIFTH CENTURY the writing of contemporary history in the western part of the Roman world was limited virtually to the compilation of meager chronicles. In the East on the other hand, a sequence of historians writing in Greek maintained the literary tradition of the Classical and Hellenistic periods and consciously sought to link the present with the past by adding to the works of their predecessors substantial narratives of their own times. Thus, they recorded the death throes of the Western Empire and the desperate yet in the end successful struggle for survival by its Eastern counterpart.

Unfortunately, the remains of these fifth-century histories consist of fragments of varying length preserved in works of writers of a later age. But such as they are, they constitute an indispensable source for our interpretation of the history of the critical period in which they were written. Professor Gordon has made the bulk of the fragments available for the first time in English translation. He has supplied an introduction that facilitates their interpretation and linked them together with short supplementary narratives in such a way as to present a fairly continuous account of the outstanding military and political developments from the death of the Emperor Theodosius I in 395 to the conquest of Italy by Theodoric the Ostrogoth in 493.

Since these fragments were preserved by later writers of the Eastern Empire, who quoted them for various reasons, it is only natural that they should be passages which deal for the most part with persons or episodes that affected the East rather than the West. But this emphasis on the East probably reflects the original character of the Greek histories of the fifth century, for their authors wrote from the standpoint of residents of the Eastern Empire and tended to treat at greater length the happenings of which they had more direct and more detailed information. Events in the West seem to have been discussed in proportion to their importance for the East, especially for the relations existing between the two empires.

The theme which dominates the secular history of the period is the struggle of the Romans against the barbarians— if we may use the latter term to describe all of the foreign enemies of the two empires, even though many of them had made considerable advances in civilization, particularly under stimulus of their contacts with the Romans themselves. We see both empires beset from within as well as from without. Along their northern frontiers from Britain to the Caucasus tribes were poised for assault upon the imperial defenses whenever the slightest hope of being able to break through appeared. Within the frontier line of defense were other peoples who had settled there with Roman assent as autono- mous military allies supported by Roman subsidies, but whose rulers sought to win better lands and ever greater independ- ence for their followers at the expense of their nominal over- lords. In addition, there were both individuals and sizable bands under their own chiefs enrolled in the imperial armies— for the most part composed of barbarian mercenaries, many of whom held the highest military commands under the emperors and only too often sought to take over control of the government. The historians do not disguise the fact that the empires depended for their existence upon barbarian arms and that their main problem was how to make use of and at the same time control their mercenaries and allies.

Although most of these barbarians were of Teutonic origin, potentially the greatest menace to East and West alike dur- ing the earlier and middle parts of the fifth century came from the Huns, particularly when they were firmly united under the rule of Attila (445–53). These terrible warriors not only drove other barbarians to seek refuge within the empires and forced still others to follow them in their attacks upon the Romans, but they themselves raided far and wide on Ro- man territory and imposed crushing tribute on the West as well as on the East. And yet we find bands of Huns serving as mercenaries under the Roman standards. In one of the lengthier fragments we have a vividly drawn picture of Attila at the height of his power—and of the barbaric splendor in which he lived—from the pen of the historian and official Priscus, who visited him as a member of an embassy sent by the Eastern emperor, Theodosius II. From Priscus and other writers one gains the impression that on various occasions Attila could have overrun either or both empires had he pressed his attacks against them. That he refrained seems to have been due partly to a wish to preserve such a rich source of tribute in gold, partly to a mistrust of the influence of the civilized urban life led by those whom he considered to be his military inferiors. His sudden death in 453 was a factor of major importance in the survival of the empire in the East.

Against the background of the barbarian pressure these historians describe a condition of almost incredible weakness and confusion in the imperial governments themselves. We see weak and incompetent emperors, dominated by corrupt and ambitious favorites, unable to distinguish between useful and ruinous policies, rewarding loyalty with treachery, success with assassination. The palaces are hotbeds of intrigue—ministers against generals, members of each service against their colleagues, with palace eunuchs playing a sinister role. Honest and efficient public servants are so rare as to be singled out for exceptional praise. Standards of public conduct certainly had not improved with the Christianizing of the empire. Little is said directly of economic conditions, but the huge sums of gold paid by the Eastern Empire as tribute to the Huns are faithfully recorded, and we are told of the ruin of many persons under the heavy exactions of avaricious finance ministers. And the defense which Priscus offers of the administration of justice in the East is by no means as convincing to modern ears as he claims that it was to a Roman refugee living among the Huns.

The fragments have a dramatic quality because they deal with the great personalities whose aims and actions were determining the course of events. Foremost among these are the three outstanding barbarian chieftains: Alaric the Visigoth, Attila the Hun, and Theodoric the Ostrogoth, with whom we should perhaps associate Gaiseric the Vandal. Others also, although somewhat less prominent, played roles of great significance. Such were the barbarians Stilicho and Ricimer, the Romans Constantius and Aëtius, and even the grand chamberlains Eutropius and Chrysaphius. We see, too, the influential part taken in public affairs by women of the imperial households, for example, by the much-married Galla Placidia in the West and by the Empress Pulcheria and the intriguing Verina in the East.

One looks in vain for any discussion of the reasons for the fall of the empire in the West or the survival of its Eastern counterpart. But for the first, the factual narrative is self-explanatory. An inept military policy, ineffectual rulers, a lack of native military manpower, all in the face of unceasing barbarian attacks, made the collapse inevitable. As for the East, we see that the extinction of the dynasty of Theodosius the Great gave an opportunity for the appointment of a series of forceful energetic emperors, that a source of military strength with which to combat the Teutonic mercenaries was found within the Empire, that two indomitable foes, Alaric and Theodoric, were diverted from the East to the West, and that the capital of the Empire in the East, Constantinople, proved an impregnable refuge and base for military operations. All these factors were of prime importance for the survival of the East. Yet chance, too, played its part in the providential death of the most formidable of the enemies of the Empire, Attila the Hun.

Preface

THE FIFTH CENTURY of our era saw far-reaching political changes in the Mediterranean world. When the century began the Roman Empire controlled directly very nearly the whole area it had dominated at its widest extent, and, though under two rulers, was still a single entity from Yorkshire to the Upper Nile and from Portugal to the Caucasus. When the century ended all western Europe and western Africa were under the control of more or less independent Teutonic kings. Many thousands of these Teutons had been settled in restless semidependence within the empire before 400, and after 500 many of their kingdoms were still nominally held at the discretion of the ruler of Constantinople—Africa, Italy, and parts of Spain were even subsequently brought for a time again under direct Roman rule by Justinian in the sixth century. Nevertheless, the western regions of the empire were in this century very largely permanently alienated from the dominions which the Roman emperor could say he really ruled.

It is a great loss that not one competent contemporary historian for the period has been preserved intact. As a result the modern investigator is forced to rely on ecclesiastical historians of dubious veracity who only incidentally mention secular affairs, on very sketchy chroniclers, many of them of a later date, on a subsidiary literature primarily nonhistorical, and on tantalizing fragments of historical writings the chief part of which has been long lost.

The dearth of adequate source material and the virtual absence of any source material whatever with pretentions to literary merit have long turned historians away from this century. Certainly, the writings of Julian the Apostate and Ammianus in the fourth century and of Procopius and Justinian's legal works in the sixth have attracted scholarship toward their centuries to the comparative neglect of the fifth. Furthermore, the spectacle of decay and defeat which this century

presents is not one that has appealed to ages prior to our own
—which in many respects is better able than most to understand the spirit of the fifth century.

But today the rapid decline in the knowledge of Latin and
Greek has cut off even the educated reader from this fascinat-
ing period, so similar to our own. He must rely on such
epitomes as general histories provide—and even they are not
so common as they might be—or on learned works based on
authors he cannot check. To remedy this to a slight extent
the translations on which this book is based give the reader
with little or no Greek, a chance to see for himself how the
writers nearest to the events described their age and its mo-
mentous tragedies. With very few exceptions (noted in Appendix B) all the passages here translated have, to the best of
my knowledge, never appeared in full in English or any
other modern language, though paraphrases and summaries of
most of them are, of course, included in general histories of
the period.

I have tried to tell the story of this tragic period as nearly
as possible in the words of contemporary or near contemporary
authors, linking the pitiful fragments of history left to us by
only such connective and introductory material from many
scattered sources of less general interest as seemed necessary
to give a coherent and complete narrative. The choice of
authors I have translated is fairly obvious considering the
custom of that age of one historian continuing the work of
his predecessor. In that way Olympiodorus, Priscus, and
Malchus overlap very little and together give a continuous
history of most of the century. To them I have added the short
summary of Candidus which throws additional light on the
court history of Leo's and Zeno's reigns. All these men were
more or less contemporaries of the events they describe, but
the last author, Joannes Antiochenus, lived considerably later
and my excuse for including the excerpts from his work per-
taining to the years from 408–91 is that, as most scholars agree,
he made wide use of the other authors, often indeed, it seems,
copying them verbatim. Thus his work probably contains

more extracts from Priscus, Malchus, and Candidus than are
printed with those authors' known remains.

The best-known and most studied aspect of fifth-century
civilization is that concerned with religion and church affairs.
For that reason I have virtually ignored these matters, not
because they were unimportant but because being well publi-
cized they do not need further elucidation in a book primarily
concerned with the interplay of barbarian and Roman. And
the ecclesiastical writers, historians and others, are in most
cases readily available in English translations. For the same
reasons this book also ignores most other aspects of life in
this period—economics, private life, the arts, constitutional
problems, law, and so on—except insofar as they impinge on
the history of the courts and the dealings with the barbarians.
I use the word barbarian rather loosely perhaps, as including
all whom a civilized native of Constantinople would so consider and name. Most of them, of course, were invaders from
beyond the frontiers, but the wild Isaurian mountaineers may
also, I hope, be included in the term without undue criticism.

The specific sources for the fragments translated are given
in Appendix A. The most common are Constantine Porphy-
rogenitos' compilation of historical excerpts dealing with
embassies to and from the barbarians, the "library" of the
bibliophile Photius who read and summarized hundreds of
books in the ninth century, and the dictionary of Suidas, a
kind of encyclopedia compiled in the tenth or the eleventh
century. The fragments have been collected by several hands
and are most readily accessible in the compilations of Niebuhr
in the *Corpus Scriptorum Historicorum Byzantinorum*, of
Müller in the *Fragmenta Historicorum Graecorum* (*F.H.G.*),
Vol. IV and V, and of L. Dindorf in *Historici Graeci Minores*,
Vol. I. For Olympiodorus, Priscus, Malchus, and Candidus,
I have followed this last text and for Joannes Antiochenus,
not included in Dindorf, I have used the *F.H.G.* Most of the
emendations suggested by various authorities in both of these
works have been adopted and any deviations from these noted.

All passages that are translations of the Greek are printed

in the type used for this sentence. I have also indicated in
the margin the fragment number used by Dindorf or Müller
(in the case of Joannes Antiochenus): P. stands for Priscus,
M. for Malchus, O. for Olympiodorus, C. for Candidus, and
J.A. for Joannes Antiochenus. In Appendix A I have also
indexed all fragments in the text.

Most proper names, except for those too well known to be
thus treated, have been simply transcribed. For this reason I
have used the terms "Scythian" and "Hun," "Hellene" and
"Greek," where the original uses them, in order to maintain
the distinctions. Priscus, for instance, uses the term "Scythian" as a generic name for all the northern nomads, including the Huns, who are a specific race. The only outstanding
exception to this is that I have translated Ister by Danube.
There has been occasional difficulty regarding the translation
of Greek titles of officials into the more familiar Latin or
English forms.

The notes—with few exceptions of interest only to a spe-
cialist—are for the most part cross references, references to
other ancient and a very select few modern works, or deal with
matters of text. Appendix A does not attempt to defend the
dates assigned to each fragment, although they have been determined with recent work on the subject in mind and are
as accurate as care can make them. Appendix B gives only
the briefest outline of modern opinions on the usefulness of
the various authors, but does attempt to argue the cases. The
geographical index will, I hope, prove useful to everyone
with a reasonably good historical atlas.

The chronological table is not designed for completeness
nor to give a chart of the historical forces at work in this century, but to show the framework within which the events
described are to be found; for this reason little reference is
made to religious or social events.

The genealogical tables are based on those in Bury's *Later
Roman Empire* (1923 edition)—with some changes, addi-
tions, and omissions—to show more clearly the relationships
between husbands and wives and do not, in places, indicate
the relative ages of children in a family.

I am deeply grateful to the late Dr. W. D. Woodhead, formerly head of the Department of Classics, McGill University, for generous advice and encouragement in the preparation of the translations and for having read them all in manuscript. And to Dr. A. E. R. Boak for many helpful suggestions generously given, for removing many ambiguities of fact and language, and for help in determining the shape the book has taken, my debt is very great indeed and his kindness has been very much appreciated. Needless to say, any inaccuracies or infelicities are to be blamed on me alone, but without this kind help these would have been far more numerous.

Contents

Chronological Table
of the Fifth Century

395 THEODOSIUS I died. HONORIUS emperor of the West (395–423) and ARCADIUS emperor of the East (395–408)

408 THEODOSIUS II (the Younger) became emperor in Constantinople. He ruled until 450

410 Rome captured by the Visigoth Alaric

412 Visigoths settled in Gaul

422 Minor war with Persia

423–25 Joannes usurper in the West; overthrown by Aspar and Ardaburius

425 VALENTINIAN III became emperor of the West. Placidia regent (425–37)

429 Vandals, who had entered the empire in 406 and settled in Spain, crossed to Africa under Gaiseric (427–77)

433 Attila became king of the Huns, and Aëtius returned as a power in the Western Empire

441 War with Persia quickly settled in the face of Attila's first serious invasion of the Eastern Empire

447 Second invasion by Attila

448 Embassy of Maximinus and Priscus to Attila

450 THEODOSIUS II died; MARCIAN became emperor

451 Battle of Chalons; Attila repulsed from Gaul. Council of Calchedon

452 Attila invaded and devastated northern Italy and retired

453 Death of Attila

454 Aëtius assassinated. Attila's empire broken up after the battle of Nedao with Goths and others

455 VALENTINIAN III assassinated; MAXIMUS emperor; Rome sacked by Vandals. MAXIMUS overthrown and replaced by AVITUS (455–56) as emperor of the West. Ricimer became a great power in the West

457 MARCIAN succeeded by LEO I in the East. Aspar became a great power at Constantinople. MAJORIAN came to the western throne and reigned 457–61. Failure of expedition against Gaiseric

461–65 SEVERUS emperor of the West

467–72 ANTHEMIUS emperor of the West

468 Great combined expedition against Gaiseric failed

471 Aspar overthrown in the East. Theodoric the Ostrogoth began to be a threat to the East

472 Ricimer died

472–73 OLYBRIUS emperor of the West

473–74 GLYCERIUS emperor of the West

474 LEO died; succeeded by ZENO the Isaurian (474–91)

473–78 NEPOS emperor of the West, ending his reign in Dalmatia

474–76 ROMULUS AUGUSTULUS last emperor of the West

475–76 Revolt of Basiliscus in the East, reigned 20 months as usurper

476 Odovacar became king in Italy

484–88 Revolt of Illus in the East

493 Theodoric having left the East in 488 became king in Italy

GENEALOGICAL TABLES

(Emperors' Names in Capitals)

THE HOUSE OF THEODOSIUS

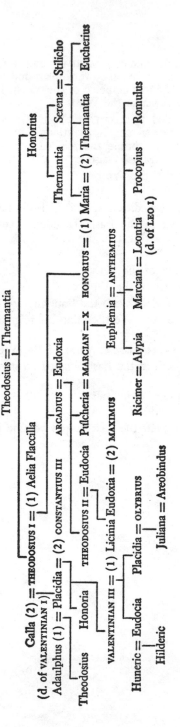

THE HOUSE OF LEO

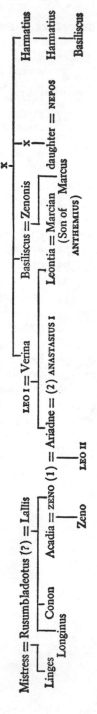

chapter **1**

Imperial Government

THEODOSIUS THE GREAT died early in 395, the last ruler of a united Roman Empire—as great in extent as that left by Augustus. His two sons divided the empire between them, Arcadius in the East and Honorius in the West, and never again did a single government control the whole Mediterranean world. For centuries two languages had divided this world and more recently the stagnation of trade, preoccupation with differing threats on opposite frontiers, and religious disputes had intensified the division. Though in the minds of contemporaries there still existed a single monolithic oecumene with twin capitals, to all intents and purposes the historian now has to deal with two separate nations, closely related to one another by historical ties and even, in the upper ranks of government for a few generations, by family ties, but each generally concerned exclusively with its own pressing internal and external problems and going its own way politically. It is not surprising, therefore, to find in the history of the fifth century, the Eastern Empire diverting barbarian threats from itself westward against its sister empire and seldom lifting a finger to help in the defense of the West in its dying agonies.

To understand how the courts at Constantinople and in Italy faced the crisis of the fifth century—the barbarian attack from the north—a general picture of the government and military machinery is necessary. (All references to government and military officials in our historians are listed in the index.)

Christianity had achieved its final triumph with Theodosius so that the emperor besides his supreme temporal power was henceforth also the sacred representative of Christ on earth and as such in a very special way divorced from ordinary mankind. His palace and everything about him was "sacred"; those who approached him had to kneel in reverence, his person was holy, and he was addressed as *Dominus*, Lord. He was supreme commander of all the armies and, though in theory subject to the dictates of the traditional law and the Church, in practice he was able to change or amplify the law by edict and to control the bishops of the Church.

And yet he was still, as under the principate, an elected official; this was no hereditary monarchy. In practice, of course, the ruler chose his successor by associating him in the supreme power with the titles of Augustus or Caesar, and the senate and army and, later, the Church merely ratified this choice at inauguration ceremonies. The choice usually fell to the ruler's son, if any, or to a relative by blood or marriage. The army had the final say on who should rule and for how long, as is shown by the frequency of military backing for usurpers in this period; but it is also noticeable that most would-be usurpers were connections of the man they were trying to supersede.

In order to enhance the awe of the population and escape the buffetings of misfortune and blame, the emperors made themselves somewhat mysterious figures, hidden behind the palace walls, inaccessible and remote, and shielded from the public by innumerable bureaucrats and palace officials.

The senate had become a largely hereditary and purely honorary body of nobles, a sort of House of Lords, without real power, but its members were highly respected and by virtue of individual offices frequently very powerful. For the sons of senators the praetorship was the indispensable office through which admittance to the senate was gained. The praetors' only duty was the exhibition of games or construction of public works—frequently very heavy financial burdens. Eight praetors were chosen by the senate each year. Higher officials of the bureaucracy, often men who had worked their way up from humble origins, could also be

named to the senate without the burden of the praetorship
being required by the emperor.

If the senatorship was largely a mere honor so also were a
series of other titles of rank. The consulship was still the
supreme dignity; a consul's duties were similar to those of
the praetors, but financially he was often helped by the state.
Besides the two regular consuls each year not infrequently a
consul suffectus would be named, a man who received the
title and rank without the actual office. Next to men of
consular rank came the patricians, who had no office or
function at all. They were men who, for outstanding services
to the state, had been raised to this high dignity by the emperor. The titles of illustris, spectabilis, and clarissimus, in
descending order, were also purely honorary, but, at least by
the end of the fifth century, all holders of these titles were
classed as senators, though only the illustres could actually
take part in the deliberations of the senate. Nobilissimus was
a more restricted title, confined to the royal family. It was
lower than the designation of Caesar and temporarily
dropped out of use during the fifth century.

More powerful than the senate in the government was the
consistorium or Imperial Council which was constantly
called on by the ruler for advice. The quaestor presided over
this council, which included the financial ministers, the
master of offices, the resident praetorian prefect and masters
of soldiers, and probably other high officials, assisted by a
large body of secretaries and clerks.

The supreme legal minister (the quaestor sacri palatii)
drafted the laws and imperial answers to petitions and generally supervised the emperor's business.

The important and powerful master of offices (magister
officiorum) supervised several rather diverse departments in
the civil service and the palace. Separate masters of bureaus
reported directly to the emperor from the separate secre-
tarial bureaus (scrinia), but the master of offices himself
controlled and supplied these bureaus. He was responsible
for court ceremonial, the general supervision of foreign af-

fairs and the reception of foreign ambassadors, the imperial
post system (cursus publicus), and the secret service (the
schola of agentes in rebus). These last—also called magistriani from the head of the department controlling them—
acted as couriers or messengers for confidential business as
well as spies on other officials in the capital and in the
provinces. The master of offices also supervised state arsenals
and had some control over frontier military commanders,
but the imperial bodyguards—the scholae palatii—were the
only force directly subject to him. They were divided into
seven cohorts or scholae (five in the West) stationed in and
around the capital and commanded by officers of the rank
of count (comes).[1]

There were two chief financial ministers each with his
own staff, but the exact division of their responsibilities, re-
membering the emperor's all-embracing power, is hard to
define. These were the minister of finance (comes sacrarum
largitionum) who supervised the raising of taxes and other
revenues, government monopolies and factories, and the
mints; and a sort of minister of the privy purse (the comes
rerum privatarum) who managed all imperial funds, imperial
lands, and the personal and crown property of the emperor.

So far we have been dealing with civil officials who helped
manage the affairs of the empire as a whole, but there was
also a huge body of officials concerned, at least in theory,
with the management of the palace itself. At the head of
this body was a grand chamberlain, usually a eunuch, known
as the praepositus sacri cubiculi. With his subordinates he
controlled the palace servants and attendants and even the
imperial estates and so, coming into closer personal contact
with both the emperor and empress than any other official,
frequently wielded enormous power. As a eunuch he was
almost invariably despised, but, as a man having the sov-
ereign's ear, also widely feared and courted. The relationships of this man with his fellow chamberlains (the primicerius sacri cubiculi, the castrensis sacri cubiculi—in control
of palace servants—and comes sacrae vestis—in charge of
the royal wardrobe) are very uncertain. Indeed, at times the

exact position of historical figures is indefinite from the
Greek habit of translating the titles by phrases like "sword
bearer" or "bed chamber attendants." It has been suggested
for instance that the very powerful Rasputin-like Chrysaphius, Theodosius II's chamberlain, was not a praepositus
but a primicerius with the functions of a bodyguard (or
spatharius, from the Greek word spatha, a "broadsword").[2]
The primicerius was probably independent of the praepositus
and the others his subordinates; certainly the thirty ushers
(silentiarii) who formed the guard of honor in the palace
were controlled by him. Often the empress had her own
chamberlain (praepositus).

All higher officers of the civil service or palace staff as
well as all military officers both in the capital and in the
provinces were issued, on appointment, a diploma drawn up
by a chief personnel officer (the primicerius notariorum),
who noted the exact precedence each had in the complex
hierarchy of honors and dignity at court.

So much for the central government. The empire was
divided into four large prefectures: of the Gauls, of Italy, of
Illyricum, and of the East—the first two subject to the
Western and the last two to the Eastern emperor. Each
prefecture was under a praetorian prefect, of whom the
prefects of Italy and the East were the highest ranking
officials in the empire and were sometimes referred to as
praesens, attending the emperor himself. A prefect issued
edicts concerning his prefecture, supervised its finances,
coinage, and grain supply, and acted as administrator of
justice—assisted in this last duty by a legal adviser called
an assessor. The prefectures were divided into dioceses
under vicarii, and these were subdivided into provinces
each under a governor—variously referred to as praeses,
proconsul, or procurator. These officials were not infrequently recruited from among men of humble origins in
the civil service, and we hear of men from the secret service
rising to a provincial governorship.

The cities of Rome and Constantinople were not under
the jurisdiction of any praetorian prefect, but each had a

prefect of the city (praefectus urbanus). He was head of
the senate and his functions were purely civil; he was chief
criminal judge, police commissioner, and in charge of the
water supply and the provisioning of the city.

One of the great contrasts between the government of
the Autocracy and the Principate was the separation of
military and civilian authority. There were exceptions to
this rule, as in Isauria, at times in Egypt, [3] and in the capital
with regard to certain forces of bodyguards, but the two
branches were usually kept strictly apart. The armed forces
at this time consisted of two classes of troops, a mobile
field army for use on any threatened border or against any
internal trouble, and garrison troops permanently stationed
on the frontiers. In the East the armies were commanded
by five masters of soldiers (magistri militum). Two of these
(magistri militum praesentales, or in praesenti) attended
the emperor at Constantinople and had precedence over
the others who were in charge of the large military districts
of Thrace, Illyricum, and the East (Orientis). Under these
were counts (comites) in charge of the local field forces
and dukes (duces) in charge of the frontier garrison troops.
In the West the system was somewhat different. There the
armies were divided between two masters in praesenti, one
in charge of the cavalry (equitum) and the other of the
foot soldiers (peditum). Very frequently, however, the
master of infantry was made the superior of his brother
general by being given supreme charge of both branches
with the title of master of both services (magister utriusque
militiae) or simply master of soldiers. The counts and
dukes in the West had positions similar to those in the East.

Apart from these forces there were various kinds of bodyguards stationed in the capitals. We have already seen the
scholae under the master of offices, but in addition to these
there were the candidati, who also were in close attendance
on the emperor, and the domestici. These last were both
horse and foot and while usually stationed at the court
could be sent elsewhere. They were under the command of
a count of domestics (comes domesticorum) who was in-

dependent of the master of soldiers and probably subject to the minister of the privy purse (comes rerum privatarum). In any case we find them at times apparently being used to collect taxes, which shows a connection with a financial officer.[4] The palatini, in spite of their name, were not in any sense a part of the bodyguard at the capital, but merely an elite corps forming a privileged part of the field forces kept closer to the capitals than other troops.

One difficulty in identifying such officials, civil and military alike, is the frequent vagueness and avoidance of the correct Latin designation of which almost all Byzantine historians are guilty. In addition many military titles like count (comes) or even master (magister) were conferred as honorary titles on foreign leaders to win their respect or loyalty, but without always implying specific duties.

The masters of soldiers were obviously men of very great power and corresponding rank at court, and it is striking to find at this time so many of them of foreign, usually German, extraction. The "foreignization" of the armies had been going on for a long time, but the preponderance of Germanic influence dates particularly from the time of Constantine the Great in the first quarter of the fourth century. Many German tribesmen were enrolled in the regular armies of the empires, and whole tribes were also enlisted under their own chieftain (phylarch). These were the so-called foederati, a term which was always rather vague and ambiguous. The chief of an allied tribe received an annual sum of money supposed to be the pay for the troops he commanded, but payments to tribes beyond the frontier as bribes to purchase immunity from attack had the same name (annonae) as payments to the tribes settled within the empire, and it was only a face-saving gesture to call them foederati—allies in the true sense. During the fifth century the term foederati also came to be applied to miscellaneous foreign mercenaries commanded by Roman officers and forming a distinct section of the imperial forces. O.fr.7,11   The name "bucellarius," in the days of Honorius, was applied not only to the Roman soldiers but also to certain Goths. Also the name "foederati" was applied to a diverse and heterogeneous corps. The historian says dry bread was called "bucellaton" and so supplies a comic nickname to the soldiers, since from this they are called "bucellarii."

The only important exception to the almost complete dominance of the military service by Germanic troops and generals was the employment of Isaurians in the latter half of the century as a counterpoise to them. This people from the backward and still almost barbaric southern interior of Asia Minor, almost alone of the old peoples of the empire, could still furnish large numbers of warlike and efficient soldiers when called on to do so. Because of them the Eastern Empire did not have to rely so heavily on the Germans and as a partial consequence escaped the fate of the West.

In subsequent chapters we shall see how the empire dealt with the major threats from across the Rhine and Danube; the scanty references to the much less important threats on other frontiers may be briefly collected here. The nation foremost in Byzantine eyes for the longest time was undoubtedly the empire of Persia or, as they often called it erroneously, Parthia. In contrast to other eras the relationship between the two empires in this century was remarkably free from conflict, probably because both were too preoccupied with other threats to trouble each other. Certainly, the Huns were a common danger for many years. There was a brief outbreak of hostilities in 422 and again in 441, both almost immediately patched up, and the Romans in most years continued a fourth-century agreement by which they paid a fixed sum annually to the Persians, ostensibly to help in the defense of the Caspian Gates against the Huns. Though several incidents occurred that might have led to hostilities all were quickly smoothed over.

P.fr.31   About 464 when Perozes [Peroz] was reigning in Persia (453–82) an embassy came from the monarch of the Persians with an accusation concerning men of his nation who were fleeing to the Romans and concerning the

Magi. These were Persians of the priestly class who from ancient times had dwelt in the land of the Romans, particularly in the province of Cappadocia. They asserted that the Romans desired to keep the Magi from their native customs and laws and from the holy rites of their deity, that they constantly troubled them, and that they did not allow the fire, which they call unquenchable, to burn according to their law. The Persian religion was a form of Sun or Fire worship and Mazda was a sun god. Further, they said, the Romans, by supplying money, ought to give attention to the fortress of Iouroeipaach situated at the Caspian Gates, or else ought to send soldiers to guard it. It was not right that Persians alone should be burdened with the expense and with the guarding of the place. If the Romans did not give help the outrages of the races dwelling round about would easily fall not only on the Persians but also on the Romans. It was fitting, they said, that the Romans should help with money in the war against the Huns, who were called Kidarites, or Ephthalites,[5] since they would have the advantages if the Persians were triumphant, in that the nation would not be allowed even to cross into the Roman dominion.

The Romans answered that they would send someone to confer with the Parthian monarch concerning these points. They said that there were no fugitives among them nor had they troubled the Magi about their religion. And as for guarding the fortress of Iouroeipaach and the war against the Huns, since the Persians had undertaken these on their own behalf, they did not justly demand money from them . . . Constantius was sent to the Persians. He had attained the dignity of a third prefecture[6] and in addition to consular rank had obtained patrician honors.

P.fr.32   Constantius remained at Edessa, a Roman city on the border of the land of the Persians, since the Parthian monarch for a long time continually postponed admitting him.

P.fr.33   After Constantius, the envoy, had waited a time on his embassy in Edessa, as was told, the monarch of

the Persians received him into his country and ordered him
to come to him while he was busy, not in the cities, but
on the borders between his country and that of the Kidarite
Huns. He was engaged in war with them on the pretext
that the Huns had not brought the tribute which the former
rulers of the Persians and Parthians had imposed. Perozes'
father, Isdigerdes, had been refused the payment of the
tributes and had resorted to war. This war he had passed to
his son along with the kingship, so that the Persians, being
worn out with fighting, desired to resolve the differences
with the Huns by treachery. So Perozes, for this was the
name of the ruler of the Persians, sent to Kunchas, the
leader of the Huns, saying that he would gladly make peace
with him, and wished to conclude a treaty of alliance, and
would betroth his sister to him, for it happened that he
was very young and not yet the father of children.

When Kunchas had received these proposals favorably
he married, not the sister of Perozes, but another woman
adorned in royal fashion. The monarch of the Persians
had sent this woman and promised that she would share in
royal honors and prosperity if she revealed nothing of
these arrangements, but that if she did tell of the deceit she
would pay the death penalty. The ruler of the Kidarites,
he said, would not stand having a maidservant for a wife in
place of a nobly born woman. Perozes having made a treaty
on these conditions did not long enjoy his treachery against
the ruler of the Huns. The woman, since she feared that
sometime the ruler of the race would learn from others
what her fortune was and submit her to a cruel death,
revealed what had been practiced on him. Kunchas praised
the woman for her honesty and continued to keep her as
his wife,[7] but wishing to punish Perozes for his trick, he
pretended to have a war against his neighbors and to need
men—not soldiers suited for battle, for he had an infinite
number of these—who would prosecute the war as generals
for him. Perozes sent three hundred men to him from his
elite corps. Some of these the ruler of the Kidarites killed,
and others he mutilated and sent back to Perozes to an-

nounce that he had paid this penalty for his falsehood. So
again war had flamed up between them, and they were fighting
obstinately. In Gorga, therefore, for this was the name of
the place where the Persians were encamped, Perozes received Constantius. For several days he treated him kindly
and then dismissed him, having made no favorable answer
concerning the embassy.

P.fr.25   In the eastern Black Sea area the land of
the Christian Lazi was for long a bone of contention. In
the years 465–66 the Romans went to Colchis to war against
the Lazi, and then the Roman army packed up for return
to their own land. The emperor's court prepared for another fight and held council whether they should carry
on the war by proceeding by the same route or the route
through Armenia, which bordered on the country of the
Persians, first having won over the monarch of the Parthians
with an embassy. It was considered impracticable for them to
sail along the difficult lands by sea, since Colchis was harbor-
less. Gobazes, the king of the Lazi, sent an embassy to the
Parthians and also one to the emperor of the Romans. The
monarch of the Parthians, since he was engaged in war
against the Huns, called Kidarites, threw out the Lazi who
had fled to him. This monarch (*monarchos* as distinct from
basileus, the Roman emperor) was Perozes.

P.fr.26   The Romans answered the envoys sent by
Gobazes that they would cease from war if Gobazes laid
aside his sovereignty or deprived his son of his royalty, for
it was not right, according to ancient custom, that both
should be rulers of the land. And so Euphemius proposed
that either man should reign over Colchis, Gobazes or his
son, and that war be stopped there. He held the position
of master of offices and, having a reputation for intelligence
and skill in arguments, had had the management of the
affairs of Emperor Marcian assigned to him, and had been
that ruler's guide in many good counsels. He took Priscus
the historian as a partner in the cares of his command.[8]

When the choice was given him, Gobazes chose to withdraw from his sovereignty in favor of his son, himself laying

down the insignia of his rule. He sent men to the ruler of
the Romans to ask that, since a single man was now ruling
the Colchians, he should no longer in anger take up arms
on his account. The emperor ordered him to cross into
the land of the Romans and explain what seemed best to
him. He did not refuse to come, but demanded that the
emperor should hand over Dionysius, a man who had formerly been sent to Colchis because of disagreements with
the same Gobazes, as a pledge that he would suffer no
serious harm. Whereupon Dionysius was sent to Colchis,
and they made an agreement regarding their differences.

P.fr.34   After the burning of the city under Leo,
Gobazes with Dionysius came to Constantinople, wearing
a Persian robe and attended by a bodyguard in the Medic
manner. Those who received him at the palace blamed him
at first for his rebellious attitude and then, showing him
kindness, sent him away, for he won them over by the
flattery of his speeches and the symbols of the Christians
brought with him.

P.fr.37   The Persians did not interfere in these Lazic
affairs because they were almost constantly being attacked
by the eastern Hunnish tribes. For instance, about 467
the Saraguri, having attacked the Akatiri and other races,[9]
marched against the Persians. First they came to the Caspian
Gates, and, finding a Persian fortress established in them,
turned to another route. Through this they went against
the Iberians and ravaged their country and then overran
the lands of the Armenians. And so the Persians, who were
alarmed at this inroad on top of the old war with the
Kidarites which was engaging their attention, sent an embassy to the Romans and demanded money or men for the
defense of the fortress of Iouroeipaach. They said—what
had often been said by their ambassadors—that since they
were undertaking the fighting and were not allowing the
oncoming barbarian tribes to have admittance, the land of
the Romans remained unravaged. When they received the
reply that each ought to fight for his own territory and to

care for his own fortress, they retired again with nothing accomplished.

Other troubles arose from time to time because of other Caucasian races who appealed now to the Romans and now to the Persians and therefore came under the domination of now one and now the other empire. Souannia and Iberia were two of these petty principalities.

P.fr.41   In 468 there was a very grave disagreement between the nation of the Souanni and the Romans and Lazi; the Souanni were fighting in particular against Sema, leader of the Lazi under. . . .[10] Since the Persians also wished to go to war with the king of the Souanni on account of the fortresses captured by them, he sent an embassy demanding that auxiliaries be sent to him by the emperor from among the soldiers guarding the frontiers of the Armenians who were tributary to the Romans. Since these were nearby he would thus have a ready help and not be in danger while waiting for those who were far off, nor be burdened by the expense if they came in time. The war, as had happened before, might be continually postponed if this should be done, for when aid had been sent under Heracleius, the Persians and Iberians who were at war with him were at that time embroiled with other nations. So the Souannian king had dismissed the allied force, being troubled about the supply of their provisions, but when the Parthians returned against him again he recalled the Romans.

The Romans announced that they would send help and a man to lead this force. Then an embassy came from the Persians too, declaring that the Kidarite Huns had been conquered by them and that they had taken the city of Balaam by siege. They disclosed this victory and boasted in barbaric vein that they would willingly show the mighty force which they had. But the emperor at once dismissed them when their news had been announced, since he considered the events in Sicily to be of greater concern.[11]

J.A.fr.214(9)   In spite of the Persian king's boast his troubles with the Huns were not over. Perozes, the king of the

Persians, who reigned after his father Isdigerdes, lived sixty years and died in the war against the neighboring Huns in January 484. After the lapse of four years [12] Cabades took the kingship, but, by a plot of certain important officials, he too was removed from the leadership and shut up in a fort. Escaping secretly, he reached the Huns called Kadisenes and through their help again seized the kingship and slew those who had plotted against him. These Kadisene Huns are probably the same or nearly allied to the Kidarite and Ephthalite Huns.[13] Cabades, or Kawad, reigned 488-97 and 499-531, and under him serious wars broke out again with the Roman Empire of the East in the sixth century.

On the Syrian frontier the Saracens, sometimes referred to as Arabs, were closely allied with the Persian problem. They were largely nomadic brigands who for many years played the Persians off against the Romans to their own advantage by offering their services to the rival empires in turn, but their sporadic raids were not, in this century, a serious threat at any time.

P.fr.20   About 451 Ardaburius, the son of Aspar, was waging war at Damascus against the Saracens. When Maximinus, the general, and Priscus, his secretary, arrived there they found him negotiating for peace with the ambassadors of the Saracens.

Ardaburius, a man of noble mind, had stoutly beaten off the barbarians who often overran Thrace. The Emperor Marcian gave him the Eastern army command as master of soldiers in the East as a reward for his valor. When he had pacified this region the general turned to relaxation and effeminate ease. He took pleasure in mimes and jugglers and all the delights of the stage, and passed the whole day in such shameful pursuits, heedless of the reputation his actions gave him.

Marcian was a good emperor, but he soon died (457), and Aspar, of his own unhindered will, appointed Leo to be his successor.

M.fr.1   In 473 again, in the seventeenth year of the reign of Leo the Butcher, so called because of his ruthless destruction of Aspar and his family in 471, everything seemed in complete and utter confusion. A certain Christian priest among the tented Arabs, whom they called Saracens, arrived on the following mission. The Persians and Romans had made a treaty in 422 when, in Theodosius' time, the great war had broken out between them, to the effect that neither would accept the Saracens as allies if any of them proposed to raise the standard of revolt.[14]

Among the Persians was a certain Amorkesos [Amiru 'l Kais] of the race of Nokalius. Either because he was not attaining honor in the Persian land or for some other reason, he thought the Roman Empire better, and, leaving Persia, he went to the part of Arabia bordering on Persia. Advancing from there he made forays and wars, not against any Romans but always against the Saracens he met. As he advanced little by little his power increased by reason of these raids. He seized an island belonging to the Romans, Jotabe by name, and, throwing out the Roman tithe collectors, he held it himself, seizing its tribute and gaining no little wealth from it.

Amorkesos seized other villages nearby and asked to become an ally of the Romans and a commander of the Saracens under Roman rule against Persia. He sent Peter, a bishop of his company, to Leo, the emperor of the Romans, to see if he could ever gain his point by persuading the emperor of these matters. When Peter had arrived and made his representations to the emperor, the latter accepted his arguments and straightway sent for Amorkesos to come to him.

In this respect he acted very ill-advisedly, for if he intended to appoint Amorkesos commander he ought to have made this appointment while he was far away so that he might always appreciate the might of the Romans and come submissively before any Roman commanders and heed the greeting of the emperor. At a distance the emperor would have seemed to be superior to other humans. Instead, he first led him through cities which he would see full of luxuriousness and unaccustomed to arms. Then, when he

reached Byzantium, he was readily received before the
emperor, who caused him to share the royal table and, when
the senate was meeting, had him join with that council. The
most shameful disgrace for the Romans was that the emperor, pretending to have persuaded Amorkesos to become
a Christian, ordered that he be seated with precedence over
the patricians. Finally, when he had privately received a
certain very valuable gold and mosaic picture, he dismissed
him having repaid him with money from the state funds [15]
and ordered such of the others as were in the senate to
bring him gifts. The emperor not only left him firmly in
possession of the island which I mentioned, but also handed
over to him many villages. By granting these concessions
to Amorkesos, and making him phylarch of the tribes he
had asked for, he sent him away a proud man, who was not
going to pay tribute to those who had made him welcome.
The island was recovered in 498.[16]

O.fr.37   Once Diocletian had brought the tribes
south of Egypt under Roman domination they remained
generally peaceful. They were people who stirred Roman
curiosity. Early in the century Olympiodorus the historian who came from this region wrote about them. He
says that while he was living at Thebes and Syene for the
sake of investigating them, the chiefs and priests of Isis and
Mandulis among the barbarians at Talmis (called Blemmyes) wished to meet him, because of his reputation. "They
took me," he says, "as far as Talmis itself so that I might
investigate those regions which are five days distant from
Philae, as far, indeed, as the city called Prima, which of
old was the first city of the Thebaid that one reached when
coming from barbarian territory. Hence it was called Prima
by the Romans, that is 'First' in the Latin language; and
even now it is still so named, although for a long time it
has been occupied by the barbarians, with four other towns
—Phoenico, Chiris, Thapis, and Talmis"—in accordance
with the arrangements of Diocletian which moved the
boundary northward. In these districts, he says, he learned
that there were emerald mines,[17] from which the stone was

supplied in abundance to the kings of Egypt. "But these," he says, "the priests of the barbarians forbade me to see. Indeed, this was impossible to do without royal permission."

O.fr.33   The desert too remained a matter of wonder. The same author tells many strange tales about the Oasis and its fine atmosphere, and says that not only none there have epilepsy—called the sacred sickness because in their fits the victims were thought to be communing with the gods—but that those who come there are freed from the disease on account of the fine quality of the air. Concerning the vast extent of sand and the wells dug there, he says that, having been dug to a depth of two hundred, three hundred, or sometimes even five hundred cubits—300 to 730 feet—they gush forth in a stream from the opening. The farmers who perform the community labor draw water in turn from the wells, to water their native soil. The fruit is always heavy on the trees, and the wheat, better there than any other wheat and whiter than snow, and sometimes the barley too, is sown twice a year, and the millet always three times. They water their fields every third day in summer and every sixth day in winter, so that the fertility is maintained. There are never clouds. He also tells about the water clocks made by the natives. He says that [the Oasis] was formerly an island separated from the mainland and that Herodotus calls it the Isles of the Blessed.[18]

Herodorus, who wrote a history of Orpheus and Musaeus, calls it Phaeacia. He proves that it was an island both from the evidence of the discovery of sea shells and the oysters molded in the stones of the mountains which stretch from the Thebaid to the Oasis, and, second, because sand always pours out and fills up the three Oases. (He says that there are three Oases, two great ones, one further out in the desert and the other closer in, situated opposite each other, about one hundred miles apart, and a third smaller one separated by a great distance from the other two.) He states as proof of its having been an island that fish are often seen being carried by birds, and at other times the remains of fish, so it is conjectured that the sea is not far from the place. He says that Homer derived his descent from the Thebaid near this place. This was the oasis of El Kargeh, "seven days' journey from Egyptian Thebes" according to Herodotus' approximately correct estimate. The oasis of Ammon, modern Siwah, was much farther away.[19] The other great oasis is either Karafra north of El Kargeh or Dakhla to the west.

P.fr.21   A brief rebellion broke out in 451 along the southern border, but was easily handled by the local Roman official, Florus.[20] The Blemmyes and Nubades or Nobatae, having been conquered by the Romans, sent ambassadors to Maximinus from both their races to conclude a treaty of peace. They said they would keep the peace conscientiously as long as Maximinus remained in the region of Thebes. When he did not allow them to make peace for that length of time, they said that they would not take up arms during his lifetime. When he did not agree to the second proposals of the embassy either, they proposed a hundred years' treaty. In this treaty it was agreed that the Roman captives should be freed without ransom whether they had been captured in this or another attack, that cattle which had been driven off should be handed back, that compensation should be paid for those consumed, that nobly born hostages were to be given by them as security for the truce, and that in accordance with an ancient law they were to have unhindered admittance to the shrine of Isis, though the Egyptians retained the care of the river boat in which the statue of the goddess was placed and ferried across. At a specified time the barbarians carry the image across to their own land, and having received oracles from it they bring it back safe again to the island.

It seemed fitting to Maximinus, therefore, to settle these agreements in the temple at Philae. Other men were sent for this purpose, and those of the Blemmyes and Nubades who had proposed the treaty came to the island. When the agreements were written down and the hostages handed over—these were from the ruling families and the sons of rulers, a thing which had never before happened in this war, for never had the sons of Nubades or Blemmyes been hostages among the Romans—Maximinus became sick and died. As soon as the barbarians learned of Maximinus' death they recovered the hostages, took them away, and overran the country.

P.fr.22   These troubles on the frontier were intensified by more serious religious disturbances in the capital. The local patriarch, Dioscorus, was removed from his see by the Council of Calchedon in October 451 for his Eutychian heresies, despite the fact he had played a leading part in the Council of Ephesus three years previously. Besides, Dioscorus was condemned to live in the city of Gangra in Paphlagonia, and Proterius was named bishop of Alexandria by the common vote of the synod. When he occupied his appointed throne a great tumult arose among the people who seethed in differences of opinion. Some demanded Dioscorus, as is natural on such occasions, and others more spiritedly clove to Proterius, so that many irreparable troubles befell them. Priscus, the rhetorician, writes in his history that at this time he arrived at Alexandria from the province of Thebes, and saw the mob advancing against the governors. When a military force tried to stop the riot the people threw stones. They put the troops to flight and besieged them, and when they retired to the temple formerly devoted to Seraphis they burned them alive.

When the emperor learned of these events he dispatched two thousand newly enlisted troops, and with a fair wind they landed in the great city of Alexandria on the sixth day. Such a rapid journey was only possible with the Etesian winds of July. Then, since the soldiers drunkenly abused the wives and daughters of the Alexandrians, events much more terrible than before took place. Finally, the mob, assembled in the Hippodrome, asked Florus, the commander of the military forces and in charge of the civil administration, to institute again the distribution of grain which he had taken from them, and the baths and spectacles and whatever else he had deprived them of on account of the disorders which

had taken place. And so Florus at the emperor's [21] suggestion appeared before the people and promised to do this,
and the rioting soon stopped.

This flareup in Alexandria reminds us that in this century,
at the very time when the empire was being dangerously
hard-pressed from the north it was also having to face serious
internal dissensions caused largely by three separate things
—religious factionalism, economic difficulties, and the ambitions of unscrupulous and powerful figures at the courts.
In the fourth century the great religious dispute arose about
the heresy of Arianism, which denied that Christ was co-
eternal with the Father. Though this doctrine was condemned at the Council of Nicaea in 325 and soon died out
in the empire, it had spread to the Germanic tribes and
for two centuries or more tended to increase friction between
them and the orthodox imperial courts. In the next centuries the important theological disputes centered around
the exact relationship of the humanity and divinity in
Christ, one faction tending to deny that Christ was ever
a real man and the other supporting the indissoluble com-
bination of the human and divine in him. Even among
the latter group the exact formula for expressing the union
of the two natures of Christ caused many bitter quarrels
intensified by the rivalry for precedence of the patriarchs
of Alexandria, Antioch, Constantinople, and the pope in
Rome.

At Calchedon in 451 the Fourth Ecumenical Council
attempted to reconcile the divergent views and though it
agreed on a formula, it could not reconcile the powerful
bishops to one another nor the Eastern patriarchs to beliefs
largely dictated by the pope. Soon renewed conflict arose
led by the Monophysites in Egypt, who upheld the single
nature of Christ as opposed to the doctrine of two natures
adopted at Calchedon, and the dispute, often accompanied
by violence, spread throughout the East in spite of vigorous
persecution. Under the usurper Basiliscus it even reached
to the imperial throne itself. In 481 in a further attempt to
restore peace Zeno issued his Henotikon, a letter to the

church in Egypt, in which by ignoring the formula of Calchedon he sought to suggest that the Monophysites and their rivals could agree to the older Nicaean Creed and forget their other differences. This dictation to the Church by the Eastern emperor was, of course, not acceptable to the pope; the Henotikon reconciled the moderate Monophysites and secured ecclesiastical peace in the East for thirty years but only at the cost of a schism with the West.

The economic difficulties faced by the courts were due to a complex group of causes, manpower shortages, overtaxation, ravishment of large areas by invasion or rebellion, payments of large subsidies to enemies beyond the frontiers, and the enormous inequalities of wealth. The whole coinage system of this period is full of difficulties, but it is sufficient here to deal only with gold. After Constantine's reforms the standard Roman coin—variously called the solidus, aureus, nomisma, or simply "piece of gold"—was valued at 72 to the Roman pound or, since the Roman pound equaled .72 of a modern pound, 100 to the modern pound. Gold in 1958 was $35.00 an ounce, and with 12 ounces to the pound (Troy weight), a pound of gold was worth $420. (The occasional use of the out-of-date "talent" indicates about 5.8 pounds of gold.) Thus, a solidus would be worth $4.20 in gold and a Roman pound $302.40. We also find frequent mention of the centenarium, which was not a coin but simply indicated 100 Roman pounds of gold or $30,240. The ratio of gold to silver fluctuated between 1:14 to 1:18.

A more difficult question is the purchasing power of gold or the real value in food, shelter, and so on of these sums. Bury has estimated that a unit of gold in the fifth century would purchase thrice as much as in 1900.[22] If that is true it would buy at least ten times as much as today. We have little concrete evidence about prices in this period and what we do have is conflicting or at least shows great variation in prices between different periods and places and in different situations. Thompson points out that eight solidi or about $33.60 would buy nearly 100 modii, 25 bushels, of wheat which would amount to $1.34 per bushel.[23] This seems rather high; a few years later a solidus would buy 60 modii which would mean a price of $.28 per bushel. This is stated as a mark of the prosperity of Theodoric's kingdom in Italy, but what the farmers (in days before price support programs) thought about this price we are not told.[24] On the other hand, in exceptional circumstances, probably when in 416 the Goths and Vandals were both in Spain and the Goths were blockaded in Taragonne by the Romans to force them to peace terms,[25] there was runaway inflation.

O.fr.29 *The Vandals call the Goths Trouli, because, crushed by hunger, the latter brought from the Vandals a trula of wheat for one aureus. The trula does not hold a third of a sextarius. As a sextarius was less than a pint, there were something like 200 trulae to a bushel, and wheat brought the astounding amount of $840 a bushel.*

Taxation, a subject that hardly concerns us here, fell very heavily on ordinary people, especially the small farmers. The most arduous of their burdens was a tax in kind (annona), originally to supply the army but by this century also to support the huge bureaucracy. This tax (*annona militaris* or *to stratiotikon siteresion*) might be called the Army Food Stuffs Quota. That taxation did not fall heavily on the privileged aristocracy, who could either evade it or pass it on to the tenants on their estates, is borne out by references to huge fortunes.

O.fr.44 *Each of many Roman households received revenues of about forty centenaria of gold from their possessions, not counting the grain and wine and all other goods in kind which, if sold, would have amounted to a third of the gold brought in. The houses of the second class in Rome, after the foremost ones, had revenues of ten or fifteen centenaria. Probus, the son of Olympius,[26] spent twelve centenaria of gold when exercising his praetorship in the time of the usurper Joannes. Symmachus, the orator, a senator of moderate wealth, before Rome was captured in 410 expended twenty centenaria when his son Symmachus was exercising the praetorship. Maximus, one of the wealthy men, laid out forty centenaria for the praetorship of his son. The* praetors used to celebrate the solemn festivals for seven days.

O.fr.43   In fact the ancient capital of the empire still gave as a whole an impression of wealth at the beginning of our period. Each of the great houses of Rome had in itself everything that a moderate town could have, a hippodrome, fora, temples, fountains, and divers baths; wherefore the historian exclaims,

"One house a city is; the city hides ten thousand towns." There were also immense public baths. Those called the Baths of Antoninus, now the Baths of Caracalla, had 1600 seats of polished marble for the use of the bathers, and those of Diocletian had nearly double the number. The wall of Rome, measured by Ammon the geometrician at the time the Goths made their earlier attack on Rome, was shown to have a length of twenty-one miles. Ammon made a mistake, though, for the walls of Aurelian, repaired by Honorius at the time of Alaric's attack in 408–10, were only twelve miles long.

The third cause of internal trouble, revolts and rebellions on the part of ambitious officials and the almost continuous court intrigues, will be amply illustrated in the following chapters. It is enough to point out here the fact that most of these troubles were inspired or carried out by the powerful barbarian generals within the empire.

chapter **2**

The Dynasty of Theodosius I and the Barbarians in the West

THE reigns of Arcadius and Theodosius II in the East and of Honorius and Valentinian III in the West span the whole first half of the fifth century, but to imagine that the governments were in any real sense dominated by any of these four weak monarchs during their respective reigns would be a complete misreading of history. The real power at the courts was in the hands of a succession of powerful ministers —many of Germanic origin—who used it or abused it largely for their own ends and managed their nominal masters by flattery and the courts by almost continuous intrigue. Unlike their behavior in the later years of the century, these powerful generals did not aim for the most part at setting up their own puppet emperors but only at eliminating rivals of their own kind.

On the death of Theodosius the Great the first such struggle occurred between Rufinus, a Gaul, at that time praetorian prefect of the East, and Stilicho, a man of Vandal extraction who had been comes domesticorum, magister militum praesentalis, and magister utriusque militiae in Italy. Stilicho had married Serena the niece of Theodosius, who left his young sons under his unofficial protection.

O.fr.2   *Concerning Stilicho, Olympiodorus tells what great power he attained—appointed guardian of the children, Arcadius and Honorius, by their father Theodosius the Great—and how he married Serena when Theodosius betrothed her to him. After this Stilicho made the Emperor Honorius his son-in-law, as husband first of his daughter Maria and, after her death in 408, of his other daughter,*

25

Thermantia, and so was raised even further to the highest
pitch of power. He successfully waged many wars for the
Romans against many tribes. Finally, by the murderous and
inhuman avidity of Olympius, whom he himself had intro-
duced to the emperor, he met his death by the sword.

This man, nominally only a general of the Western
armies, was in fact the chief military figure of both empires,
and before the year of Theodosius' death was out he had
secured the murder of his Eastern rival Rufinus. But he
came into renewed and continued conflict with the Eastern
court over which empire should control Illyricum, the most
valuable reservoir of military manpower in either empire
at this period. Stilicho naturally tried to bring it under his
jurisdiction in the West and so made enemies for himself
in the East.

Arcadius, a youth of seventeen or eighteen on coming to
supreme power in Constantinople, was a feeble-minded and
ineffectual ruler easily dominated by strong personalities
at the court. Hence his reliance first was on Rufinus, then
briefly on Stilicho, then on Gaïnas, the leader of Ostrogothic
forces, and in civil affairs on the eunuch Eutropius. Gaïnas
was particularly dangerous to the security of the state and,
after he had destroyed Eutropius, the Huns under Uldin and
German troops under the Goth Fravitta eventually had to
be called in to destroy him. Meanwhile, the Eastern Empire
was ravished by the Visigoths under Alaric in the Balkan
lands and by a wild Hunnish invasion from the East. By
400 the Germanic danger to the East had been temporarily
removed, only to be followed by a series of even more violent
conflicts between the Empress Eudoxia and John Chrysos-
tom, the patriarch of Constantinople, and by serious troubles with Isaurian brigands in the southern part of Asia
Minor. The chief power of the government was in the hands
of Anthemius, the praetorian prefect of the East.

When Arcadius died in 408 he left a young son of seven
to succeed him as Theodosius II, but for six years the government was in the capable hands of Anthemius as regent. In
414 Pulcheria, Theodosius' elder sister and a woman of de-

cisive and vigorous character destined to dominate the court for nearly half a century, was proclaimed Augusta and took over the reins of government in the name of her brother.

J.A.fr.191 On account of his extreme youth Theodosius was not able to make decisions or to wage war. He wrote his signature for those who desired it—especially for the eunuchs of the palace by whom everyone was being ravaged of his possessions, so to speak. Some while still living made over their property, and some sent their wives to other men and had their children forcibly taken from them, being unable to oppose the commandments of the emperor. The Roman state was in the hands of these men. The chief of these eunuchs was Antiochus, who had great power as tutor to the young emperor until he was removed by Pulcheria.

J.A.fr.192 We have two brief descriptions of Theodosius as a young man. The Emperor Theodosius, saying that he enjoyed their pleasures, turned his mind toward liberal books, and to Paulinus and Placitus, who read them with him, he freely granted great offices and wealth.

J.A.fr.193 Because he was shut up in the palace, he grew to no great size; he became so thoughtful that he used to make trial of many matters with those he met and was so patient that he could endure nobly cold and burning heat. His forbearance and friendliness conquered all men, so to speak. The Emperor Julian, although proclaiming himself a philosopher, did not bear anger against the Antiochenes who had approved of him but did torture Theodorus. Theodosius, on the other hand, proclaiming that he enjoyed the syllogisms of Aristotle, practiced his philosophy in action and wholly put aside anger, violence, grief, pleasure, and bloodshed. Once when a bystander asked him why the unjust should not be put to death, he answered, "Would that it were possible even to restore the dead to life!" If anyone was brought before him who had committed deeds worthy of capital punishment, a reminder of his love of mankind caused that man's death penalty to be rescinded.[1]

J.A.fr.194 Two pictures of the emperor in later life are not so flattering. Theodosius, who inherited his office

from his father, Arcadius, was unwarlike. He lived in cowardice and gained peace by money, not arms. He was under
the control of his eunuchs in everything. They contrived to
bring affairs to such a pitch of absurdity that, though Theodosius was of noble nature, they beguiled him, to put it
briefly, as children are beguiled with toys, and united in
accomplishing nothing worthy of note. Though he reached
the age of fifty years, they prevailed on him to persevere
in certain vulgar arts and in wild beast hunting, so that
they, and Chrysaphius in particular, held control over the
empire. Pulcheria took vengeance on this man after her
brother's death.

Theodosius received his office from his father, and because he was unwarlike, lived in cowardice, and won peace
by money not arms, he brought many evils on the Roman
state. Having been brought up under the influence of the
eunuchs, he was well disposed to their every command,
so that even the most important men needed their help.
They made many innovations in political and military
affairs, while the men able to manage these matters were
absent from their posts, supplying gold instead, because of
the greed of the eunuchs. And so piracy broke out on the
part of Sebastian's troops and troubled the Hellespont and
Propontus. Sebastian, the son-in-law of Boniface, who was
banished from the West by Aëtius in 434,[2] was master of
soldiers (magister utriusque militiae) in the West in 433.

The chief foreign difficulties faced by the Eastern Empire
under Theodosius were with the Huns and will be dealt
with later. We must now turn to affairs in the West and
the more immediate dangers faced by that region.

Honorius was even younger than Arcadius on his father's
death and relied even more heavily on the powerful help
of Stilicho and others. Related to the royal family both
through his wife and his daughters, Stilicho's position could
not easily be challenged, and for thirteen years he loyally
supported his master and won high honors for himself in
the process. At first his chief problem had to do with
the Visigoths. This tribe fleeing before the expanding

Hunnish power had crossed into the empire in 375 and settled there by treaty. In 378 they had revolted and wiped out a Roman army and killed the Emperor Valens at Hadrianople. After many years Theodosius the Great had succeeded in settling them in Lower Moesia and had used them in Italy against the usurper Eugenius in the last year of his life, a campaign in which they suffered severe losses. At about this time the tribe, whch had never had a single king, united under Alaric. In 395 they rebelled and spread devastation through Thrace and Macedonia and even threatened Constantinople until Stilicho faced them in Thessaly. Arcadius, under Rufinus' influence, called off any attack on them, the Eastern troops under Stilicho's command being handed over to Gaïnas, and the Vandal retired to consolidate his power in Italy and the West.

Alaric was thus left a free hand in Greece, through whose ancient cities he marched as a conqueror and plunderer. Stilicho in 397 sailed to Greece to attack him, but was again thwarted in his design by Arcadius through fear of acknowledging that the prefecture of Illyricum was in the Western domain. For the next year he was engaged in putting down a Moorish rebellion in Africa, and in 400 he attained the high honor of the consulship. Alaric in the meantime had settled in Epirus with some recognition of his position from Arcadius and for four years apparently remained quiet. In 401, however, he suddenly seized the chance of invading Italy when the Western armies were distracted by an incursion of Vandals and other barbarians under Radagaisus across the upper Danube. Stilicho having dealt with Radagaisus returned to face the Goths in northern Italy. The fighting was indecisive, but by diplomacy Alaric was induced to leave the peninsula and to guard the Illyrian lands for the Western Empire. It was at this time of peril that the court was moved to the easily defended marsh city of Ravenna.

Though the danger from Alaric and the Visigoths had been temporarily averted even greater disasters were imminent for the Western Empire. The provinces of the

upper Danube in these years had suffered both from the
barbarians settled within them and from those without,
and their defense in the welter of difficulties faced by the
government had been virtually abandoned. Late in 405 a
vast host of Ostrogoths led by Radagaisus crossed the
frontier and penetrated northern Italy and were only
ultimately defeated and massacred at Fiesole by the aid of
the Huns.

O.fr.9   *Of the Goths who followed Radagaisus the
foremost, amounting to 12,000, were called "optimates";
Stilicho made allies of these when he had overwhelmed
Radagaisus.*

To achieve this victory, however, almost all available
troops had to be withdrawn from Britain and the Rhine
frontier, thus opening the way to accumulating disasters
in both places. In the next year a huge host of German
tribes crossed the Rhine almost unopposed—Burgundians,
Vandals, Sueves, and Franks. Instead of opposing them
or trying to protect the Gauls Stilicho was again involved
with the Eastern Empire over the perennial dispute about
Illyricum.

O.fr.5   *Alaric, while Stilicho was still living, received
forty centenaria as pay for his soldiery.* This was compensation for holding Illyricum for Honorius, but when the payment was approved by the senate one disgusted senator is
said to have cried out, "This is not peace, it is a pact of
slavery." [8]

O.fr.12   This pact was finally confirmed in 408, but
in the meantime Britain had been lost to a usurper who
took advantage of the great invasion of the Rhine and
Stilicho's preoccupation with Illyricum. There was no doubt
discontent there with the rule of the Vandal Stilicho and
with the lack of attention his government paid to the
defense of Britain against the Picts. In 407 *Constantine,
being raised to the supreme power, sent an embassy to
Honorius, with his defense that he ruled unwillingly and
under compulsion of the soldiers, and he asked recognition
and association in the honors of the imperial office. The*

emperor, because of his current difficulties in 409 and because Constantine held certain members of the Theodosian family captives, for a while accepted this imperial association, and the two were consuls together in this year. Constantine had been proclaimed in the provinces of Britain and brought to power by a revolt of the soldiers there. Indeed, in the provinces of Britain, before the seventh consulship of Honorius in 407, they had stirred the army there to revolt and proclaimed a certain Marcus supreme ruler. When he was killed by them, Gratian was set up in his stead, and after about four months, he also became distasteful to them and was slain. Constantine was then raised to the position of supreme commander. He appointed Justinus and Neovigastes[4] as generals and, leaving the Britains (that is, the province of Britain), crossed with his forces to Bononia, the city of that name on the coast and the first in the territories of the Gauls. He waited there and, having won over all Gaul and the Aquitanian soldiery, he became master of Gaul as far as the Alps between Italy and Gaul. This man had two sons, Constans and Julian; he appointed Constans Caesar, and later, during the same period, he named Julian nobilissimus. Since Constantine did not apparently interfere much with the marauding Vandals and other Germans his control over Gaul at this time and of Spain later cannot have been very real in most areas.

These accumulating disasters reacted on Stilicho, already unpopular with the pagan Roman nobility. He was undermined in the emperor's estimation by the slanders of Olympius, a palace official, later if not already the master of offices, and his own troops were induced to mutiny. Arrested, he was put to death. Though all-powerful in the West for many years, he was more responsible than any other for the ill will between the empires which laid the way open for the terrible and permanent breaches in the imperial defenses and the resulting devastations. For forty years after his death no man of German extraction in the West or East held a comparable position.[5]

With Stilicho's death the foreign soldiers in Italy deserted the imperial armies to join Alaric, and only a handful under the Goth Sarus remained behind. Olympius, now the dominant figure at court, was faced with the double problem of Alaric and Constantine, with neither of whom was he able to cope. Alaric asked for a subsidy in order to remain in Noricum and was refused.

O.fr.6   He attacked Italy in 408, threatening Rome itself, where the senate gave way to panic. *After the death of Stilicho, his wife, Serena, was also put to death by throttling, since she was thought the cause of Alaric's attack on Rome. Before her death but after that of Stilicho their son, Eucherius, was put to death.* Serena was in Rome at the time, and it was thought that her death would cause Alaric to withdraw knowing he had no sympathizers inside the walls.

O.fr.4   *During the siege of Rome there was cannibalism among the inhabitants.* But the siege went on until Alaric was bought off with 5000 pounds of gold, 30,000 pounds of silver, 4000 silk tunics, 3000 scarlet died skins, and 3000 pounds of pepper. To raise these enormous sums both public and private ornaments were melted down. Furthermore, Alaric was promised a permanent peace and hostages to secure it. He waited in Etruria for these terms to be fulfilled. In 409 Alaric's brother-in-law, Athaulf or Adaulphus, entered Italy with reinforcements to join him, and the government of Olympius failed to stop him. This cost the minister his position for the time being.

When all efforts to placate the Goth failed during a year of negotiation, Alaric marched on Rome and occupied it without a struggle and there set up his own puppet emperor, Attalus, the prefect of the city. After the removal of Olympius a man known variously as Jovius or Jovian became, as praetorian prefect of Italy, the chief minister of Honorius. He failed to secure peace with Alaric, but was still the logical one to conduct negotiations with Attalus when he moved on Ravenna.

O.fr.13   *Attalus, being emperor in opposition to Honorius, pitched his camp near Ravenna. Jovian, a prefect* and patrician, was sent to him, as though to an emperor, from the Emperor Honorius, and also Valens, a master of soldiers, the quaestor Potamius, and Julianus, the primicerius notariorum (chief secretary). These men made known to Attalus that they had been sent by Honorius to treat concerning an association of rule. He refused, but agreed that Honorius, without suffering harm, should live on an island or some other place of his own choosing. Jovian despairing of saving Honorius and going over to the camp of Attalus was pleased with this answer and in reply even told him to cripple the Emperor Honorius in one limb. Attalus reproved Jovian for this, saying that there was no precedent for mutilating an emperor who, of his own free will, had laid aside his kingship. Jovian, making frequent embassies and gaining nothing thereby, remained at Attalus' court and was called Attalus' patrician. On the other hand, at Ravenna, power came into the hands of Eusebius, the praepositus, who after a while met his death by clubbing in the presence of the emperor because of his wanton insults of Allobichus (or Hellebich), Honorius' master of soldiers. This was done by public decree. After some time, Attalus was removed from his office for not obeying Alaric. The dispute was over the question of whether the Goths should be sent to secure Africa, which under Heraclian had remained loyal to Honorius. Alaric desired this, but Attalus opposed it and sent a small Roman force under a certain Constans to win the province over by diplomacy. This force was defeated, and at the same time Honorius in Ravenna was reinforced by troops from the East.

These reversals for Attalus caused Jovian to switch sides once more, so that the usurper's deposition was brought about particularly by the efforts of Jovian, who had before betrayed the embassy of Honorius. Attalus remained by choice in private life with Alaric. Then, to complete his story, he afterward became emperor again and was again deposed. This happened in 415 when he was set up at Arles by Adaulphus, Alaric's successor, during the later dispute over Placidia. He was shortly thereafter abandoned by the Goths, captured in 416, graced a Roman triumph in 417, and still *later, when he approached the neighborhood of Ravenna, he had the fingers of his right hand cut off and was banished from the country to the island of Lipara.*

During the negotiations following the deposition of Attalus, Alaric's camp was attacked by a Gothic force under Sarus. This man had been one of Stilicho's followers and one of the few who remained loyal after Stilicho's death. He remained aloof from the fighting till 410 when, for reasons unknown, he suddenly made his foolish assault during the truce, an act which Alaric logically suspected had been ordered by Honorius. This time the Gothic king resolved to show no mercy to the ancient capital.

O.fr.3   *Alaric, the phylarch of the Goths, whom Stilicho summoned to Illyricum as a guard for Honorius (for his father Theodosius had assigned this district to his rule),*[6] *because of Stilicho's murder and because he did not get what had been promised to him, besieged and plundered Rome. He carried from it incalculable money and made prisoner the half-sister of Honorius, Placidia, who was living in Rome. (Before capturing the city he proclaimed as emperor one of the nobles of Rome, Attalus by name, who was then occupying the prefecture of the city.) This he did for the reasons mentioned and because of Sarus, a Goth and commander of a small force (his army did not exceed two or three hundred men) and besides an heroic man and unbeatable in battle. Because the Romans had made this man their ally, as he was hostile to Alaric, they made Alaric their implacable foe.*

Rome was given over to complete pillage and fire, and the sack lasted three days. The news of the capture of the ancient capital caused profound shock and consternation all over the Roman world. For the first time men began to see that the foundations of their life were crumbling, and there were mutual recriminations of pagan and Christian. Neglect of ancestral observances, the pagans said, had brought about divine punishment, and the Christians in turn blamed the disaster on the wicked continuance of pagan-

ism in Rome. So disturbed were men's minds that in answer
to their fears St. Augustine in Africa composed *The City of
God* to remind the faithful that the downfall of the temporal
city was of little importance compared with the eternity of
the kingdom of heaven.

O.fr.15   From Rome Alaric led his host south with
the aim of crossing to Sicily and hence to Africa. *From
Rhegium, the metropolis of Bruttium, Alaric was desirous
of crossing to Sicily. He was kept away, the historian says,
for a consecrated statue standing there prevented the crossing. It had been consecrated, according to tradition, by the
ancients as a means of turning aside the fire of Mount Etna
and of preventing the attack of barbarians by sea. In one foot
there was an ever-burning fire and in the other perpetual
water. When it was destroyed Sicily received damage both
from the fire of Etna and from the barbarians. Asclepius,
a man appointed as steward of the possessions of Constantius and Placidia in Sicily, overturned the statue, as a Christian gesture against paganism.*

Actually, a storm destroyed the fleet.[7] Before the end of
the year Alaric died at Cosenza, and his body was buried
in a stream whose waters were diverted for the purpose, in
order that his grave might never be desecrated.

*O.fr.10   When Alaric had died of disease, Adaulphus,
his wife's brother, was set up as his successor.* The new king
delayed some fourteen or fifteen months in Italy and then
marched north along the west coast, crossed the Alps in
412, and settled for the time being in southern Gaul.

Meanwhile, that whole province had for six years been at
the mercy of the hordes of German tribesmen who had
broken through the frontier in 406. The Vandals crossing
the upper Rhine had devastated southern and eastern Gaul
and moved steadily southwestward toward the Pyrenees.
On the middle Rhine the Burgundians attacked, plundered,
and finally settled in the region to which they gave their
name. Farther north it was the Franks who moved into
Belgica and northern Gaul. Into this confused situation,
to further confuse it, came the British usurper Constan-

tine, as we have seen, and though he is reported to have
defeated the barbarians he brought no real security to the
area nor did he drive any of the invaders out. He at least
seized Arles for his capital, then the most prosperous city
in Gaul, and repelled the first efforts made to dislodge him
—an attack led by Sarus.

Constantine's next move was against Spain in 408. His
son Constans and his captain Gerontius conquered the
province in 409, and the former was recalled and created
Augustus. In the same year Honorius, hard pressed by Alaric,
was forced to recognize Constantine as a colleague in the
empire. The Spanish troops guarding the passes of the
Pyrenees revolted and opened the way for the Asdings and
Silings, Sueves and Alans, who had been oppressing Aquitania for two years, to pour into this new unviolated land.

O.fr.30   When the Vandals overran Spain, the Romans fled into walled cities, and so great was the famine that
they were reduced to cannibalism. One woman who had four
children ate them all, making the excuse for each the nourishment and preservation of the remaining ones, until, having
eaten them all, she was stoned to death by the people. When
Constans blamed Gerontius for the debacle and returned to
supersede him, Gerontius too rebelled and made a pact
with the barbarians, ceding much of the land to them.

O.fr.16   When the usurper Constantine and his son
Constans (who at first was Caesar and then was appointed
emperor) were overwhelmed and took to flight, the general
Gerontius, satisfied by peace with the barbarians, proclaimed
his son Maximus emperor, a man who had held a post in
the corps of bodyguards, the domestici. At the beginning of
410 there were thus six emperors, Honorius and Theodosius
II, Attalus in Rome, Constantine, Constans, and Maximus.
Then Gerontius pursued Constans, brought about his destruction in 411 at Vienne, and dogged the footsteps of his
father Constantine until he shut him up and besieged him
in Arelate.

While this was happening, Constantius and Ulphilas,
the master of cavalry who had succeeded Allobichus, were

sent against Constantine by Honorius and they besieged
Arelate, where Constantine was staying with his son Julian.
Gerontius, who had started the siege, fled before Honorius'
generals and the siege changed hands. After three months
Constantine's barbaric allies were defeated near the city
and the siege ended. Constantine fled to an oratory and was
ordained a priest when oaths were given for his safety. The
gates of the city were opened to the besiegers and Constantine with his son was sent to Honorius. Bearing a grudge
against them because Constantine had put to death his
relations, Honorius, contrary to the sworn oaths, ordered
their execution while they were still thirty miles from
Ravenna.

Gerontius had fled when Ulphilas and Constantius approached. Because he had commanded his private troops with
a firm hand they plotted against him. They set fire to his
house, but he fought bravely against his opponents, with
one assistant, a man of the Alan race, one of his servants.
Finally, he killed his wife and the Alan at their request and
then slew himself. His son Maximus, learning of these things,
fled to the barbarian allies.

O.fr.8   Meanwhile, the management of affairs at
the court of Honorius had passed through several hands.
On Stilicho's death, as we have seen, Olympius, who had
plotted against Stilicho, became master of offices and was then
removed from that office in 409, again installed in it, and
again removed. Finally, having left that office, he was beaten
with clubs at the order of Constantius, who had married
Placidia in 417, and perished, after having his ears cut off.
And so at the end justice overtook that evil-working man and
he did not go unpunished. Jovian momentarily took over the
first place only to give way to Eusebius and he in turn to
Allobichus.

O.fr.14   Allobichus after a short while paid the
penalty for having made away with the praepositus Eusebius,
being put to death with the consent of the emperor and in
his presence. Constantine, the usurper, learning of the
death of Allobichus while proceeding to Ravenna in order

to make a treaty with Honorius, turned back afraid. Allobichus had probably worked for the compact between the
emperors of Gaul and Italy and had become suspect, therefore, of favoring Constantine. His death deterred the latter
from his designs on Italy.

O.fr.23   Constantius, the next man to take the leadership of affairs, was an extremely attractive character and a
capable general. He succeeded Valens as master of soldiers
in 412 [8] and for the next ten years was Honorius' chief
military support—as Stilicho had been before him. Having
at one time been consul designate, he became consul at
Ravenna in 414 and Constans held office with him at Constantinople. A meet and sufficient supply of gold was found
for the cost of his consulship among the goods of Heraclian,
who had been killed while making preparations for revolt.
Not so much, however, was found as was expected—not
more than twenty centenaria of gold—though his immovable
property came to 2000 pounds. This man had been the
executioner of Stilicho in 408 and had been rewarded with
the post of count of Africa, a province he loyally held for
Honorius against Alaric and Attalus. But "tyranny," as the
Byzantine historians called usurpation of the crown, was
so much in the air at this period that he too revolted in
413, in the very year of his consulship. He landed in Italy
and was promptly defeated. On his return to Africa he found
himself alone and was caught and executed in the same
year. Constantius was the general who beat him and received
all this estate in one requisition from Honorius. On his
progresses Constantius went with downcast eyes and sullen
countenance. He was a man with large eyes, long neck, and
broad head, who bent far over toward the neck of the horse
carrying him and glanced here and there out of the corners
of his eyes so that he showed to all, as the saying goes, "an
appearance worthy of a tyrant." At banquets and parties,
however, he was so pleasant and witty that he even contended with the clowns who often played before his table.
This was the man, then, who captured the usurper Constantine at Arelate.

O.fr.17   But Constantine's fall was only the signal
for the rise of a new usurper in Gaul. *Jovinus at Mogun-*
tiacum in the other (i.e., Upper) Germany, a town which
had been plundered by Germans in 407, *was proclaimed*
as a usurper by the efforts of Goar the Alan and Guntiarius,
who bore the title of phylarch of the Burgundians. Goar was
one of those who had led the invasion of 406, but for a
while he had loyally served Honorius and remained king
of the Alans for many years. *Adaulphus was advised by*
Attalus to join the rebel and he did, along with his army.
Jovinus was embarrassed by the presence of Adaulphus and
oddly enough blamed Attalus for inducing him to come.
Sarus was about to come to Jovinus, but when Adaulphus
learned this he went to meet him first, taking with him
10,000 troops, though his adversary had with him only
eighteen or twenty men. Sarus displayed heroic deeds,
worthy of record, and they make him prisoner with lassoes [9]
only with difficulty; later they put him to death. He had
stood aloof from Honorius because, when one of his at-
tendants—Belleridus—had been put to death, there was no
explanation of the execution from the emperor and no
punishment of the murder.

O.fr.19   This incident caused a further rift between
Adaulphus and Jovinus, and the next move intensified it.
Jovinus, contrary to the advice of Adaulphus, appointed
his own brother, Sebastian, emperor and so incurred the
enmity of Adaulphus, who then sent ambassadors to Ho-
norius, promising the heads of the usurpers and that he
himself would make peace. When the men returned and
oaths were sworn, the head of Sebastian was sent to the
emperor. Jovinus, besieged by Adaulphus at Valentia,
finally surrendered and was sent to the emperor. Dardanus,
the praetorian prefect of Gaul, slew him, once he had him in
his power in 413 in Narbo. Both heads were set up outside
Carthage, [10] *where those of Constantine and Julian, cut off*
formerly, and those of Maximus and Eugenius, who had
been involved in a rebellion under Theodosius the Great
and had finally come to this end, had also been set up.

For his help in overthrowing Jovinus, Adaulphus was looked on with more favor by Honorius and his court, but the presence of Galla Placidia, the half sister of the emperor, at the Gothic camp remained a continuing source of friction for several years. There is evidence that Placidia herself was reasonably content with her lot and not eager to return. Nevertheless, Adaulphus agreed to restore the royal woman in exchange for grain to be supplied by the Romans and the ceding of a Gallic homeland to him. Those promises, because of the cutting off of the African grain supplies by the revolt of Heraclian, could not be fulfilled and hunger stalked the Gothic army.

O.fr.20,21   *Placidia was demanded from Adaulphus out of regard for Constantius, who later also married her. But when the promises to Adaulphus were not kept, and especially the promise to supply grain, he did not surrender the woman and prepared to break the peace and make war. When Adaulphus was asked for Placidia he demanded in turn the appointed grain. Though there was a shortage of the supplies they had promised to give, they nonetheless agreed to supply them if they got Placidia. The barbarian answered in like terms, and proceeding to the city of Massilia he was in hopes of taking it by trickery. There, Boniface, a most noble man, struck and wounded him, and barely escaping death he retired to his own camp, leaving the city full of joy and praising and acclaiming Boniface.*

O.fr.22   The Gothic king did, however, succeed in capturing Narbo, which he made his headquarters, and other towns in western Gaul and Aquitania. Early in 414 he determined to bolster his position by marrying the apparently willing Placidia himself. *Adaulphus, preparing for his marriage to Placidia, made even heavier demands when Constantius demanded her, so that when his demands were not met he might seem to have detained her with good reason.*

O.fr.24   *The marriage of Adaulphus to Placidia was celebrated in the beginning of the month of January at the city of Narbo, in the house of a certain Ingenius, a lead-*

ing man of that city at the urging and advice of Candid-
ianus.[11] Placidia was installed there in a bridal chamber
adorned in the Roman manner and with royal dress, and
Adaulphus sat beside her, having put on the toga and other
Roman dress. At this time, along with other wedding gifts,
Adaulphus gave her fifty handsome youths dressed in silken
clothes, each carrying in his hands two huge platters one
of which was full of gold and the other full of priceless
stones. These had come from Rome, having been taken
as booty by the Goths in the sack of the city. Then wedding
hymns were sung, Attalus singing first and then Rusticius
and Phoibadius. The wedding was celebrated amid the
rejoicing and acclamation alike of the barbarians and Romans there.

Under the influence of his remarkable bride Adaulphus
became steadily more favorably inclined toward the Romans and tried to reach a firm agreement with them. Only
when all else failed did he once more resort to the expedient (and precedent of Alaric) of setting up Attalus as
emperor. When Constantius attacked him and severely
afflicted his people with starvation the Goth moved into
Spain and established his capital at Barcelona. Attalus was
abandoned to his fate as we have already seen.

O.fr.26   When a son was borne by Placidia to
Adaulphus in Barcelona, to whom he gave the name Theodosius, he adopted an even greater friendliness toward the
Romans. This boy was a grandson of Theodosius the Great,
and his very name shows Adaulphus' feelings at this time.
He is even reported to have said, "I hope to be handed
down to posterity as the initiator of a Roman restoration." [12]
But Constantius and those around him so opposed him
that the desires of Adaulphus and Placidia remained un-
fulfilled. When their son died, they grieved over him
greatly and buried him, laying him away in a silver coffin
in a certain church near Barcelona. Then, in 415 Adaulphus
was killed while busy inspecting his private horses, as was
his custom, in the stable. One of the Goths of his household, Dubius, who had watched his opportunity to avenge

an ancient grudge, slew him. Formerly, this man's master, a king of part of the Gothic land had been overthrown by Adaulphus, who had taken Dubius from him and made him his servant. So he, avenging his first master, killed his second. On his deathbed Adaulphus ordered his brother to give Placidia back, and, if they possibly could, to procure the friendship of the Romans for themselves. But Singerich, the brother of Sarus, rather by scheming and force than by natural succession or law, became his successor. He slew the children who had been borne to Adaulphus by a former wife, seizing them by force from the protection of Bishop Sigesarus, and out of spite against Adaulphus he ordered the queen, Placidia, to walk on foot before his horse along with the other prisoners. Having ruled for seven days he was killed and Valia was set up as leader of the Goths and ruled till 418.

For the time being Roman rule was restored to all of Gaul except Burgundy, and there is even good reason for believing that Britain, abandoned at the time of Constantine's usurpation and seriously hurt by Saxon attacks in 408, was again brought under Roman control for the remainder of Honorius' reign. Spain, on the other hand, was still in the hands of the various German tribes, and the new Visigothic king was not disposed to follow Adaulphus' pro-Roman policies. He first tried to lead his people to Africa, but his fleet was wrecked and he was forced to open negotiations with Honorius.

O.fr.31   Euplutius, the magistrianus, was sent to Valia, who had the title of phylarch of the Goths, in order to make a treaty of peace and receive back Placidia. He got her back without trouble. When grain had been sent to Valia to the amount of 600,000 measures [13] Placidia was handed over to Euplutius and sent back to Honorius, her brother, in 416.

In the next few years Valia fought the Vandals, Alans, and Sueves who had entered the peninsula in 409, devastating it far and wide, and then settling in various districts. The Asding Vandals and Sueves became allies (foederati),

as were the Visigoths, the Siling Vandals were virtually
wiped out, and the Alans, after the death of their king,
joined the Asdings, now ruled by Gunderic. As a reward
for these successes the Visigoths were granted a permanent
home in Aquitania along with the large cities of Bordeaux
and Toulouse; there they settled as allies in name, of the
Empire, owning two-thirds of the land but in practice ruling
a virtually independent kingdom.

O.fr.35   In 418 before these arrangements could be
completed, when Valia, the chieftain of the Goths, died,
Theodoric received the rule. This man, the grandson of
Alaric, carried the new agreement into effect and became
the staunch ally of the Romans and their chief savior in
the great fight against Attila in 452.

O.fr.34   In the meantime at Ravenna the fine soldier Constantius was moving from strength to strength.
He had triumphed over the usurpers Constantine and
Heraclian and proved himself the only efficient leader in the
government. So in 417 when Emperor Honorius had entered
on his eleventh consulship and with Constantius for the
second time, they arranged the marriage of Placidia to
Constantius. She, meanwhile, strongly refusing him, made
Constantius angry at her attendants. Finally, on the day he
entered on his consulship Emperor Honorius, her brother,
taking her by the hand, handed her over completely against
her will to Constantius, and the marriage was solemnized
in most splendid fashion. A child was later born to them
whom they called Honoria, and later still in 419 a son to
whom they gave the name Valentinian. This boy, while
Honorius was still alive, became a nobilissimus, for Placidia
compelled her brother to grant this. After the death of
Honorius and after the overthrow of the usurpation of
Joannes, he was accepted as emperor at Rome.

Constantius held the empire jointly in 421 with Honorius,
who appointed him rather unwillingly. Placidia was named
Augusta, her brother and her husband making the appointment. A proclamation which announced the emperorship of
Constantius was then sent to Theodosius who, as a nephew

of Honorius, ruled the eastern parts of the empire. But this proclamation remained unaccepted. Distress came over Constantius, and he regretted the emperorship because it was no longer possible for him to come and go safely, where and how he wished, and because as emperor he could no longer enjoy the pastimes which he had been accustomed to enjoy. Finally, after a seven months' reign, just as his dream had told him—"Six are accomplished, the seventh is beginning"—he died of pleurisy. With him also died his campaign against the East with which he was busy, because they had not approved his association in the imperial power.

O.fr.39   Constantius was an Illyrian by race from the city of Naissus in Dacia, who passed through many campaigns from the time of Theodosius the Great and later, as was narrated, entered into the imperial office. Before he was married to Placidia he was praiseworthy and superior to bribery. But when he was united with her he became avaricious. After his death petitions against him, on the part of those who had been wrongfully deprived of their possessions, flowed into Ravenna from all sides. The easygoing nature of Honorius, however, and Placidia's relationship to him rendered their demands, as also the power of justice, fruitless.

O.fr.40   So great had grown the affection of Honorius for his own sister—because of which her husband, Constantius, departed his life—that their immoderate passion and their continuous kissing on the mouth brought them under a shameful suspicion in the eyes of many people. But by the efforts of Spadusa and Elpidia, Placidia's nurse, to both of whom she paid great attention—and with the help of Leontius her steward—such enmity arose between them that riots often broke out in Ravenna. A host of barbarians surrounded her both because of her marriage to Adaulphus and because of her union with Constantius. Blows were given on either side. Finally, because of the inflaming of this enmity and the hatred which counteracted their former love, when her brother proved the stronger Placidia was banished to Byzantium in 423 with her children. Boniface alone kept faith with her and from Africa, which he ruled, sent whatever money he could and hastened to offer other services. Later, he contributed everything toward the restoration of the empress.

O.fr.41   A few months later, Honorius, being attacked by dropsy, died on the sixth day before the Kalends of September (August 27) 423. He had been a weak and ineffectual ruler whose reign witnessed the first permanent breaching of the Roman defenses in the West and the settlement of large Germanic kingdoms on imperial soil, the capture and sack of Rome for the first time in 800 years, and the terrible devastation of almost all the Western lands. He was only lucky to have survived these threats and the numerous usurpers until he died a natural death. *They sent a letter announcing the death of the emperor to the East, but, while this was being sent, a certain Joannes seized the power and ruled as a usurper. While his proclamation was taking place, it was said about him, as though it was derived from some oracle, "He falls, he doesn't stand." The mob, as though to undo the utterance, exclaimed in reverse, "He stands, he doesn't fall."*

This man so suddenly raised to the imperial throne was an obscure civil servant who had only reached the position of primicerius notariorum (chief secretary) but he was supported by Castinus, the master of soldiers, and by the young Aëtius. Having lived among the Huns, Aëtius obtained their backing for Joannes to oppose the forces of legitimacy marshaling in the East, for Theodosius belatedly recognized the claims of the boy Valentinian to the Western throne and was preparing to send him and his mother Placidia back to take over power there.

O.fr.42   Also supporting Placidia was another remarkable man who had already distinguished himself in the West. Boniface had valiantly defended Massilia, as we have seen, against Adaulphus in 413 and in 422 had been sent to defend Africa against the Moors. *Boniface was a heroic man who often fought valiantly many barbarians, some-*

times attacking with a few troops, sometimes with many,
and occasionally even engaging in single combat. To speak
plainly, he set Africa completely free from many barbarians
and diverse tribes. A lover of justice and contemptuous of
bribes, he performed a deed of the following kind. A certain
countryman who had a wife in the full bloom of youth
found out that she was being seduced by one of the barbarian auxiliary soldiers. He begged help of Boniface, bewail-
ing his disgrace. Boniface, having learned the distance to
the place and the name of the field in which the acts of
seduction were taking place, dismissed the suppliant and
ordered him to return on the following day. Then, eluding
the eyes of all, he hurried to the field, about eight miles
distant, where, finding the barbarian lying with the adulteress,
he cut off his head and returned home the same night.
When the husband came, according to his orders on the
following day, Boniface handed over the barbarian's head
to him and asked him if he recognized it. The man was at
once astounded by the spectacle and struck dumb, but
when he recognized the head he gave many thanks for the
justice done him, and departed happily. Such was the man
who held the important province of Africa loyal to the house
of Theodosius and who was destined to play an important
role in subsequent events.

O.fr.46   The history of Olympiodorus ends with
the successful expedition against Joannes. Placidia was sent
back with her children from Constantinople by Theodosius against the usurper. She received back the title and
honor of Augusta and Valentinian the title of nobilissimus,
and so the previous refusal to recognize her and her son
in the East was withdrawn. With them was sent an army and
Ardaburius, a commander of both forces, with his son Aspar
and, third, Candidian. Helion, the master of offices, sent
by Theodosius to Thessalonica, in that same city put the
robes of a Caesar on Valentinian, though he was only five
years old. As they were descending into Italy, Ardaburius
was captured by the soldiers of the usurper and sent to
him, becoming his apparent friend, but he actually seized

the chance of his captivity to undermine the loyalty of
Joannes' supporters. His son (Aspar), as well as Placidia,
was despondent and distressed. However, Candidian captured
many cities, and by his eminent distinction dispelled their
distress and revived their spirits. The usurper Joannes was
then slain, and Placidia and her son the Caesar entered
Ravenna. Helion, the master and patrician, took Rome and
when all assembled there clothed Valentinian, now seven
years old, in the imperial robes on October 23, 425.

J.A.fr.195   A slightly different and more detailed account comes to us from another source. When Joannes the
chief of the royal secretaries, not content with the good
fortune of his own office, seized the imperial power, he
sent an embassy to Theodosius to demand that he be accepted as emperor. The emperor threw these men into a
fortress and sent the general Ardaburius, who had fought
the Persian war of 422. He reached Salona and sailed for
Aquileia, but he experienced the opposite of good luck—
rather the divine will, as was afterward revealed. Unfortunately, a storm blew up which put him into the hands of
the usurper, who by his capture hoped to compel the emperor to choose him as co-emperor. Theodosius was in
anguish, as also was Aspar, the son of Ardaburius, and
despair gripped the Roman forces. God sent a messenger
in the guise of a shepherd to show the Roman army and its
leader, Aspar, the way. He led them right through the
marsh surrounding Ravenna—for the usurper was staying
in this city—where no one is ever before recorded to have
passed. Crossing the impassable barrier in this way and
finding a feasible route by dry land, they discovered the
gates open and became masters of the city. When they had
put Joannes to death they made their actions known to
the emperor, who gave thanks to God, and considered
which of the easterners he should declare emperor.[14]

J.A.fr.196   When the fighting was all over Aëtius
arrived in Italy with 60,000 Huns. He was won over by
Placidia to her service, and the Huns were induced to
retire with a large stipend. Aspar and his father returned to

their posts in the East, but Placidia still had two generals, to one of whom, Boniface, she turned over Libya, and the other, Aëtius, she kept nearby. Aëtius was jealous and wrote to Boniface, "The empress is opposed to you, and the evidence for this is that she will summon you for no reason. If, therefore, she orders you to come, do not obey, for she will slay you." Then he approached the empress and said that Boniface was preparing a rebellion. "You may be convinced of this," he said, "for if you summon him, he will not come." When the empress wrote to him to come, he handed Libya over to the Vandals [15] and was not persuaded to come, thinking the disclosures made to him by Aëtius were true. Later, when men were sent to him and a treaty was made, the deception was discovered. The empress was all the more well disposed toward him, and she loathed Aëtius for having acted recklessly in this, though he had not been able to do any harm. She was never able to recover Libya from Boniface.[16]

The mutual hostility of the two generals was not to be resolved before one or the other completely triumphed, and their rivalry led to new troubles for the harassed Western lands. The real power at the court of Ravenna, if not in the government as a whole, lay in the hands of the Augusta Placidia just as in the East, too, Pulcheria was the strong character at court and the real power behind Theodosius. The first man Placidia chose to be her supreme military commander was neither Boniface nor Aëtius, possibly fearing that by choosing one she would stir up trouble for herself with the other, but Felix. He was master of soldiers for four years (425–29) and consul in 428, but he does not seem to have taken the field. On the other hand Aëtius was very active.

Flavius Aëtius was a native of Moesia on the lower Danube and in his youth had been a hostage with Alaric and later with the Huns, since his father had been a prominent general himself. It was on his shoulders that the fortunes of the West were to rest for the next twenty-eight years, and very capable shoulders they usually proved, belonging to a man who well deserved the praise of his contemporaries. His wife was—typically of the age—a Goth and his son, Carpileon, in 425 was sent as a hostage to the Huns, like his father before him. Aëtius' first task was the protection of the Gallic provinces against the encroachments of the Visigoths and in the north the pressure of the Franks. With the aid of Hunnish auxiliaries he won successes against both tribes in 427–28 and so was able to supplant Felix in 429 and have him put to death the next year.

In the meantime in 429 the Vandals in Spain succeeded, where Alaric and Valia had failed, in crossing to the last Western province not yet ravaged by Germanic tribes. The new king of the Vandals who led this invasion of Africa was Gaiseric, often called Genseric by Greek historians, a man of immense ambition and the ability to match it. The behavior of Boniface in this situation is uncertain, but in any case the invasion was facilitated by his failure to oppose it actively. That it succeeded so quickly and completely, however, was due to the astute, ruthless, and brilliant mind of Gaiseric, by far the cleverest of all the Germanic leaders of this period. The combined forces of Boniface and of the East under Aspar were disastrously defeated in 430, and by 435 Gaiseric was accorded a treaty acknowledging him as the ruler over all the western provinces in Africa. In 432 Boniface returned from Africa and was named by Placidia to the post held by Aëtius. When Aëtius refused to give it up he was defeated in battle by Boniface and fled to his friends the Huns, but when Boniface shortly afterward died he reappeared, beat Boniface's son-in-law Sebastian,[17] and reestablished himself as the military leader of the West, a position he was to maintain till the end of his life. He was also granted the great honor of being made a patrician. Under his over-all command the Burgundians were beaten by the Huns in 435 and their king Guntiarius (Gundahar, later the hero of the *Niebelungenlied*) killed, the Goths fought to a standstill by 437, and a rebellion of the Armoricans in northwest Gaul repressed in 438–39 and again in 442. His final great victory in the West was to be against Attila in 451.

J.A.fr.201(3)   These events were summed up after his death. *He had been the guardian of Placidia, who was the mother of Valentinian, and of her son when he was a youth, through his connection with the barbarians. He had made war on Boniface when he crossed from Libya with a great force, so that he died by disease under the burden of his cares, and Aëtius became master of his wife and property. He had killed by craft Felix, who had held the generalship with him, when he found out that at Placidia's instigation this man was making preparations for his removal. He had warred with the Goths of western Galatia who attacked the territories of the Romans. He had also subdued the Aemorichians (Armoricans) who were hostile to the Romans. To put it briefly, he had wielded the greatest power so that not only kings but even nations dwelling nearby came at his orders.*

Only in Africa did his leadership fail. The treaty of 435 was soon violated by Gaiseric; in 439 Carthage was in his possession and Vandal pirates began to harass the coasts of the whole Mediterranean. In 442 a new treaty was concluded giving the Vandals all the richest lands in Africa while restoring to Roman control the less valuable lands east of what is now Tunisia and in the west, and an attempt was made to pacify Gaiseric permanently by betrothing Valentinian's eldest daughter to the Vandal king's son Huneric. But since Huneric was already married to a daughter of Theodoric, king of the Visigoths, Gaiseric was induced to send this girl back to Gaul repudiated and mutilated. In this way Aëtius' diplomacy divided the two Germanic peoples by bitter hostility, and Gaiseric remained satisfied with his kingdom in Africa until the death of Valentinian III. The story of the war of Aëtius with Attila will be reserved for the next chapter.

J.A.fr.200(1)   Nothing could better illustrate the chaotic and blind degeneration of the Western court than the some-

what confused story of Aëtius' death. Valentinian, having
fallen in love with the wife of Maximus, a senator, used to
play at draughts with him. When Maximus lost and did not
have what he owed, the emperor took his ring. Rising, he
gave it to one of Maximus' friends so that the man showed
it to Maximus' wife and, as though from her husband, thus
ordered her to come to the palace to dine with him there.
She came, thinking this the truth, and when it was announced to the emperor, he arose and without Maximus'
knowledge seduced her. After the lovemaking the wife went
to meet her husband as he came, wailing and reproaching
him as her betrayer. When he learned the whole story he
nursed his anger at the emperor. Knowing that while Aëtius
lived he could not exact vengeance, he laid plans through
the emperor's eunuchs to destroy Aëtius as though he were
a traitor.

J.A.fr.201(1)   The affairs of the Western Romans were in
confusion, and Maximus, a well-born man, powerful and
twice consul in 433 and 443, was hostile to Aëtius, the
general of the forces in Italy. Since he knew that Heraclius,
a eunuch who had the greatest influence with the ruler, was
also hostile to Aëtius, he made an agreement with him
with the same end in view (for both were striving to sub-
stitute their power for his). They persuaded the emperor
that unless he quickly slew Aëtius, he would be slain by him.

P.Uncert.1   They went about their plot to work on the
suspicious emperor in this way. The eunuch suggested that
the intimates of Valentinian [18] (I mean the army of the
women's apartments), who were always the instigators of
despicable actions, should accuse Aëtius of acting against
the emperor, so that he might usurp his wealth. . . . They
strove to persuade the emperor, for the weight of gold put
at their disposal was heavy, consuming their inner hearts
with a slow fire. (Eunuchs are terrible in sewing up their
hurts when the promise of gold lies before them. The race is
insatiable and always open for gain, and there is nothing
wicked accomplished within the palace without their evil
influence.) The emperor was persuaded by the false ac-

cusations, and, being aroused to the need for the death of
Aëtius, quicker than the word he killed him.

J.A.fr.201(2)   Since Valentinian was fated to come to grief
by losing the defense of his office, he approved of the words
of Maximus and Heraclius and contrived the death of
the man when Aëtius was about to consult the emperor
in the palace on his resolutions and was examining proposals
to bring in money. While Aëtius was laying the matter of
the revenues before him and was making a calculation of the
total money collected from the taxes, Valentinian jumped
up with a cry from his seat and said he would no longer
stand being abused by such treacheries. He charged Aëtius
with being to blame for his troubles and indicated that
Aëtius desired the power of the Western as well as of the
Eastern Empire.[19] As Aëtius stood amazed at the unexpectedness of his anger and tried to appease his unreason-
ing ire, the emperor drew his sword from its scabbard. He
attacked with Heraclius, for this fellow was carrying a cleaver
under his cloak (for he was a chamberlain—primicerius
sacri cubiculi). Both of them together directed their blows
against the head of Aëtius and killed him—a man who had
performed many brave deeds against both internal and
foreign enemies.

J.A.fr.200(1)ctd.   When he had been put to death the emperor
said to a person able to surmise the truth, "Was the death
of Aëtius not well accomplished?" He answered, "Whether
well or not I do not know, but I do know that you have
cut off your right hand with your left."

J.A.fr.201(4)   After the murder of Aëtius, Valentinian also
put to death Boethius, a prefect who had been favored by
Aëtius in the highest degree. When he had exposed them
unburied in the Forum, he straightway summoned the
senate and made many fearful charges against the men, lest
because of Aëtius it should in any way support an in-
surrection. After Aëtius' removal Maximus constantly resorted to Valentinian so that he might be advanced to the
consular office. Failing this he wished to attain the rank of
patrician, but Heraclius did not acquiesce in his possession

of this dignity. Acting from the same ambition, he thwarted the ambitions of Maximus and persuaded Valentinian that having freed himself of the oppression of Aëtius he should not transfer that man's power to others. Maximus, failing in both his hopes, was bitterly angry. He summoned Optila and Thraustila, brave Scythians who had campaigned with Aëtius and had been assigned to attend on Valentinian, and talked to them. He gave and received guarantees, put the blame for Aëtius' murder on the emperor, and urged that the better course would be to take revenge on him. Those who avenged the fallen man would, he said, justly have the greatest blessings.

(5)   Not many days later Valentinian rode in the Field of Ares (the Campus Martius) with a few bodyguards and the followers of Optila and Thraustila. When he had dismounted from his horse and proceeded to archery, Optila and his friends attacked him. Optila struck Valentinian on his temple and when he turned around to see the striker he dealt him a second blow on the face and felled him, and Thraustila slew Heraclius. Taking the emperor's diadem and horse, they hastened to Maximus. Whether from its unexpectedness [20] or whether those present feared the reputation of the men in battle, their attack brought them into no danger. A divine sign occurred at the death of Valentinian. A swarm of bees approached the blood which had flowed out on the ground from him, sucked it up, and drank it all. Thus Valentinian died, having lived thirty-seven years.

J.A.fr.200(2)   What happened to Maximus' wife on whose account, in part at least, he had dared kill his emperor we are not told. But finding the emperor bereft of Aëtius, Maximus killed him and married the Empress Eudoxia, who was the daughter of Theodosius the Younger. Thinking to win her good will toward him he said, "I have become the murderer of Valentinian out of love for you." But she, being of free spirit answered, "Alas that I was an accessory to the death of my husband and my emperor." She wrote to Gaiseric, who then held Libya, to come with all speed and take possession of Rome. He came and took the city in 455, and captured Eudoxia and her daughter. Maximus, hated because of his murder of the emperor, was pursued and easily put to death.

During all the years since Alaric left the Eastern Empire in 408 the only barbarian threat there, though a grievous one, was from the Huns. No German tribe was able to settle in these regions permanently against the will of the government, though of course many were always in its employ as mercenaries and allies. Furthermore, with the downfall of Gaïnas the leadership of the armies was in native hands for some years. But soon on the scene appeared several foreign generals destined to wield the chief military power of Constantinople for half a century. Areobindus, a Goth, came to the fore in the brief Persian war of 422, and in 441 he led an eastern expedition against the Vandal pirates who were attacking Sicily. Of considerably more stature was the Alan Ardaburius, who had also played an active role in the Persian war and whom we have already seen as the leader of the Theodosian forces against Joannes in 424–25. For this success he was rewarded with the consulship in 427, but it was his son, Aspar, whom we have also seen opposing Joannes, who of all these foreign generals was destined to play the largest role in Eastern affairs.

Aspar must have been only a young man in 424, since he seems to have still been active at the time of his death in 471; indeed, in 465 at the time of a great fire at Constantinople he is said to have run about the streets with a pail of water on his shoulders urging all to help fight the blaze. In spite of his youth he was put in charge of the Western expedition against the Vandals in Africa which Gaiseric so disastrously defeated in 431. This, however, seems to have hurt his career and popularity with Placidia no more than it hurt Boniface's, and in 434 he was named as the Western consul; Areobindus was the Eastern consul at the same time so that two foreigners held the consulship together. But it was in the East that his future destiny lay, and, though at times in apparent eclipse, he generally was the power behind Theodosius, Marcian, and Leo until

471, and we shall see more of him. Though he seems to have been on reasonably good terms with Attila and his followers, probably because of his German connections, and it is not recorded he ever fought against them, he was still, with Areobindus, a master of soldiers in 449 when Priscus heard his name praised by Attila's lieutenant Berichus.

The death of Theodosius the Great saw the empire still intact; the deaths of his grandsons Theodosius II and Valentinian III half a century later found half the empire on the edge of complete destruction. It is true that the East came through these critical years damaged and devastated in many regions, but it remained in control of the same extent of territory and had no foreign kingdoms within it. In the West on the other hand, the Vandals controlled most of Africa, the Sueves had permanently settled in northwestern Spain, the Visigoths had a virtually independent state in southwestern Gaul, Britain had passed completely and irrecoverably into the hands of the Saxons and their kin, and eastern Gaul was ruled by Burgundians. Franks had crossed the lower Rhine and could not be removed, and the upper Danubian provinces, Rhaetia, Noricum, and Pannonia, though in name still part of the empire, were in practice lost to its control. Italy several times invaded and terribly ravaged by foreign and civil wars alone was still free of permanent foreign settlers, but for only another quarter century.

chapter **3**

The Huns

THE chief threat to the empire in the first half of the century came from the Huns. Whether this oriental people can be identified with the Hiong Nu who attacked the empire of China in the second and first centuries B.C. is a much disputed and still unsettled problem. In any case they first seem to have attracted Roman attention in the last quarter of the fourth century, when the historian Ammianus records that "they are faithless in truces" and that "they burn with an infinite greed for gold." [1]

P.fr.10   The following myth shows the impression they first made on the Romans. *Their cruel tribe, as Priscus the historian relates, settled on the further bank of the swamp of Maeotis. They were skilled in hunting but in no other task except this. After they had grown into a nation they disturbed the peace of the neighboring races by thefts and plundering.*[2]

While the hunters of this tribe were as usual seeking game on the far bank of Lake Maeotis, they saw a deer appear unexpectedly before them and enter the swamp, leading them on as a guide of the way, now advancing and now standing still. The hunters followed it on foot and crossed the Maeotic swamp, which they had thought was as impassable as the sea. When the unknown Scythian land appeared, the deer disappeared. The spirits, I believe, from whom they derive their descent did this through envy of the Scythians. The Huns, who had been completely ignorant that any other world existed beyond the Maeotic swamp, were filled with admiration of the Scythian country, and, since they were quick of mind, believed that the passage, familiar to no previous age, had been shown to them

57

by the gods. They returned to their own people, told them
what had happened, praised Scythia, and persuaded them to
follow along the way which the deer, as their guide, had
shown them. They hastened to Scythia, sacrificing to Victory
the Scythians they fell in with on their entrance; the
remainder they conquered and subdued. Soon they crossed
the huge swamp and like some tempest of nations overwhelmed the Alipzuri, the Alcidzuri, the Itimari, the Tun-
cassi, and the Boisci who bordered on the shore of Scythia.[3]

They subdued the Alans also, wearing out by constant warfare a race which was equal to them in war but unlike
them in civilization, mode of life, and appearance. Those
men, whom they perhaps in no wise surpassed in war, they
put to flight by the terror of their looks, inspiring them
with no little horror by their awful aspect and by their
horribly swarthy appearance. They have a sort of shapeless
lump, if I may say so, not a face, and pinholes rather than
eyes. Their wild appearance gives evidence of the hardihood
of their spirits, for they are cruel even to their children on
the first day they are born. They cut the cheeks of the males
with a sword so that before they receive the nourishment
of milk they are compelled to learn to endure a wound. They
grow old without beards, and the youths are without good
looks, because a face furrowed by a sword spoils by its scars
the natural grace of a beard. Somewhat short in stature,
they are trained to quick bodily movement and are very alert
in horsemanship and ready with bow and arrow; they have
broad shoulders, thickset necks, and are always erect and
proud. These men, in short, live in the form of humans but
with the savagery of beasts.

By 375, we know, they had incorporated into their loose
federation the Alans and a majority of the Ostrogoths and
were in alliance with the Visigoths in an abortive attack on
Constantinople after the battle of Hadrianople in 378. It
was undoubtedly the pressure of the Hunnish expansion
westward which led Valens to admit the Visigoths into the
empire in 375 and which drove the other German tribes
across the Rhine in 405-6. Theodosius the Great seems to

have made some arrangement with the tribe, possibly settling them in Pannonia.⁴ But that they were never really subdued is seen by the behavior of Uldin (or Uldes), one of their kings, in 395.⁵ When proposals of peace were made to him "he replied by pointing to the sun and saying that he could easily, if he so desired, subdue every part of the earth . . . While he was uttering this sort of threat and ordering as large a tribute as he pleased and saying that on this condition peace could be established or the war continued," part of his army was induced to desert and the remainder conquered.⁶ The Huns for some years were alternately enemies or allies of the Roman empires. This same Uldin in 400–401 was an ally of the Eastern Empire against Gaïnas and later was serving with Stilicho against Radagaisus in 406.⁷

O.fr.18   The historian Olympiodorus in the first section of his history *discusses Donatus and the Huns and the excellent archery of their kings and says that he himself, the historian, went on an embassy to them and to Donatus. Tragically, he tells of his journey by sea and its danger, and how Donatus, deceived by an oath, was wickedly strangled, how Charaton the foremost of the kings was inflamed with wrath at the murder, and how he was soothed and pacified again by regal gifts.* Donatus and Charaton were only senior kings, in no way the equals of the great Attila, and the episode here recorded probably took place in 412–13 while Jovinus was still emperor in Gaul.

Aëtius in 423–24 enlisted Huns in support of the usurper Joannes, and a grant of land in Pannonia was made or at least confirmed.⁸ At the same time treaties were made with the Eastern Empire probably involving payments of subsidies to the Huns.

P.fr.1   In 432 or 433 a Hunnish ruler—called by Roman and Greek historians Roas, Rugila, or Roua, king of the Huns—intending to go to war with the Amilzouri, Itimari, Tonosours, Boiskoi, and other races dwelling on the Danube and who had taken refuge in a Roman alliance, sent Eslas, a man accustomed to attend to the differences

between him and the Romans, to threaten to break the
existing truce if they should not surrender all those who had
taken refuge among them. When the Romans were planning
to send an embassy to the Huns, Plinthas and Dionysius
wished to go on it—Plinthas being a Scythian and Dionysius
a Thracian by race—both men being leaders of armies and
having attained the consulship among the Romans. Plinthas
had been consul in 419 and was at this time the most influential man at court. Dionysius had been consul in 429.
Since he thought that Eslas would reach Roua before the
embassy about to be sent out, Plinthas dispatched Sengilach,
probably an Alan or a Hun judging from his name, a fellow
of his personal suite, to persuade Roua to enter into negotiations with him and not with any other Romans.

Roua having died and the kingdom of the Huns having
devolved on Attila (and Bleda) [9] the Roman senate decided
that Plinthas should make his embassy to them. When this
decree had been ratified for him by the emperor, Plinthas
wished to have Epigenes also accompany him on the embassy,
since he was a man with the greatest reputation for wisdom
and had the position of quaestor. Approval being gained
for this both set out on their embassy and reached Margus
in 435.[10] This is a city of the Moesians in Illyria, lying on
the Danube River opposite the fort of Constantia which is
situated on the opposite bank, where the royal tents of the
Scythians are also gathered. They held a meeting outside
the city mounted on their horses, for it does not seem proper
to the barbarians to confer dismounted, and so the Roman
ambassadors, mindful of their own dignity, followed the
same practice as the Scythians in order not to find themselves on foot in discussion with mounted men.[11] . . .
[It was agreed that in the future the Romans should not
receive] those who fled from Scythia and also that those
who had already fled along with the Roman prisoners who
had escaped to their own lands without ransom should be
surrendered unless for each fugitive eight gold pieces (solidi)
should be given to those who had captured him in war. It
was further agreed that the Romans should make an alliance

with no barbarian tribe which was waging war against the Huns, that there should be markets with equal rights and safe for both Romans and Huns, that the treaty should be maintained and continue, and that 700 lbs. of gold be paid over each year by the Romans to the Scythian rulers. (Earlier 350 lbs. had been the payment.)

On these terms the Romans and Huns made a treaty and swore to each other by their own native oaths and returned each to his own country. Those who had fled to the Romans were handed back to the barbarians. Among them were the children Mama and Atakam, scions of the royal house. Those who received them crucified them in Carsum, a Thracian fortress, thus exacting the penalty of their flight. Attila, Bleda, and their court having established peace with the Romans marched through the tribes in Scythia subduing them and undertook a war against the Sorosgi. Who these were is unknown.

Attila, who comes on the stage of history so suddenly in this way, was the son of a man whose name is variously recorded (Mundiuch, Mondzuccus, Mauzuchus, Munsuchus, Mundicius, Beneducus, or Moundiouchus). This man's brothers were Roua, Octar, and Oebarsius; Bleda was Attila's brother, probably his older brother. The two ruled jointly till 444 or 445, when Attila murdered Bleda. "He was a man born to shake the races of the world, a terror to all lands, who in some way or other frightened everyone by the dread report noised abroad about him, for he was haughty in his carriage, casting his eyes about him on all sides so that the proud man's power was to be seen in the very movements of his body. A lover of war, he was personally restrained in action, most impressive in counsel, gracious to suppliants, and generous to those to whom he had once given his trust. He was short of stature with a broad chest, massive head, and small eyes. His beard was thin and sprinkled with grey, his nose flat, and his complexion swarthy, showing thus the signs of his origins." [12]

P.fr.1a　　　　　Sometime in the next few years Valips, who formerly roused the Rubi against the Romans of the East,

*seizing the city of Novidunum which lies on the bank of
the river, laid hands on certain of the citizens and, having
gathered all the money in the city, prepared, with those
who chose to revolt with him, to lay waste the lands of
the Thracians and Illyrians. When the force sent by the
emperor was about to overcome him and he was besieged
he warded off the besiegers from the circuit walls as long
as he and those with him could hold out. When they grew
tired of their labor through constantly fighting the Roman
host, they placed the children of the prisoners on the battlements and so checked the onset of the opposing javelins.
The soldiers, loving their Roman children, neither threw
against them on the walls nor hurled their javelins. And
so after a while the siege was lifted for him on terms.*

These Rubi were probably the Rugi who later under
Odovacar were to play a decisive role in Italy. They were
possibly a complex of tribes of which the Saraguri, Onoguri,
Ulmerguri, and even those tribes mentioned in Priscus'
fragments 1 and 10—the Alipzuri, Alcidzuri, and Amilzouri
and others of similar name [13]—may be branches. There is
no reason to believe that at this time the Rugi were part
of Attila's empire but rather, it has been plausibly suggested,[14] that they had settled inside the empire as allies
under their chieftain Valips. Tacitus [15] says that the Rugi
originally came from northern Germany, and if they can be
identified here they must, like the two branches of the
Goths, have hit the eastern frontiers before moving westward again inside the empire. After Attila's death they were
living in Bizye and Arcadiopolis—modern Vize and Lü-
leburaz in European Turkey.

For eight years after his accession to power Attila was
occupied in building his empire in the northern lands, in
reducing the Ostrogoths and Gepids to positions of sub-
servience or alliance, and in attacking the Persian Empire.
But in 441 a great attack was made on the Eastern Empire.
P.fr.2 *When the Scythians at the time of the as-
sembly at the market, arranged for under the Treaty of
Margus, attacked the Romans and killed many men who*

were probably merchants,[16] the Romans sent to the Scythians, holding them to blame for the seizure of the fortress
and their contempt of the peace treaty. This fortress was
probably Constantia opposite Margus. They answered that
they had not started the trouble but had done these things
in self-defense, for the bishop of Margus coming to their
land and searching thoroughly for the chests of their kings
had despoiled the graves of their buried treasures. And they
said that if the Romans should not give up this man and
also surrender the fugitives according to their pledges (for
there were very many among the Romans) they would
declare war. The Romans averred that this excuse was not
valid, but the barbarians, trusting in their own words, utterly
despised any trial of the disputed matters and turned to
war. They crossed the Danube and laid waste many cities
and forts on the river. Among these they took Viminacium,
which was a city of the Moesians in Illyria. While this was
going on, some were arguing that the bishop of Margus
should be given up so that the danger of war, for the sake
of one man, might not be brought on the Romans as a
whole. But this man, suspecting that he would be surrendered, without the knowledge of those in the city, came to
the enemy and promised that he would hand over the city
to them if the Scythian kings made any reasonable proposal.
They said that they would treat him well in every way if
he should bring his promise to fulfillment. When they had
given their right hands and oaths for the things promised,
he returned to the Roman land with a great host of barbarians, and, having laid this force as an ambush on the
opposite bank, he roused it during the night according to
the agreement and put the city into the hands of its enemies.
Margus having been ravaged in this way, the possessions of
the barbarians were increased to an even greater extent.

P.fr.1b   One episode of this attack has come down
to us. The Scythians were besieging Naissus. This is a city
of the Illyrians lying on the Danuba River.[17] They say that
Constantine was its founder [18] the same man who also built
the city at Byzantium named after himself. The barbarians,

being on the point of capturing a city so populous and fortified besides, were advancing with every attempt. Since
those in the city were not very confident about going out to
battle, the barbarians bridged the river at the southern part
where it flowed past the city so that a crossing would be
easy for a large number of men,[19] and they brought their
engines of war to the circuit wall—first wooden beams
mounted on wheels because their approach was easy. Men
standing on the beams shot arrows against those defending
the city from the battlements, and other men grabbing another projecting beam shoved the wheels ahead on foot.
Thus, they drove the engines ahead wherever it was necessary so that it was possible to shoot successfully through
the windows made in the screens. In order that the fight
might be free of danger for the men on the beams they
were protected by willow twigs interwoven with rawhide and
leather screens, a defense against other missiles and whatever fire weapons might be sent against them.

Many engines were in this way brought close to the city
wall, so that those on the battlements, on account of the
multitude of the missiles, retired, and the so-called rams
advanced. The ram is a huge machine. A beam with a metal
head is suspended by loose chains from timbers inclined
toward each other, and there are screens like those just
mentioned for the sake of the safety of those working it.
With small ropes from a projecting horn at the back, men
forcibly draw it backward from the place which is to receive
the blow and then let it go, so that with a swing it crushes
every part of the wall which comes in its way. From the
walls the defenders hurled down stones by the wagon load
which had been collected when the engines had been
brought up to the circuit wall, and they smashed some along
with the men themselves, but they did not hold out against
the vast number of engines. Then the enemy brought up
scaling ladders. And so in some places the wall was toppled
by the rams, and elsewhere men on the battlements were
overpowered by the multitude of siege engines. The city was
captured when the barbarians entered where the circuit wall

had been broken by the hammering of the ram and also when by means of the ladders they scaled the part of the wall not yet fallen.

P.fr.3 After this attack a one year's truce was arranged, but a further attack was launched in 443. In the reign of Theodosius the Younger, Attila, the king of the Huns, having collected his own army, sent letters to the emperor concerning the fugitives and the tribute, advising that all those who under the excuse of this war had not been surrendered should be sent to him as quickly as possible, and that ambassadors should come to hold discussions concerning the arrangements of the tribute owing him. He added that if they should delay or should proceed to war he would not willingly hold back his Scythian horde. When the emperor had read these messages he and his court answered that they would by no means surrender those who had fled to them, that they would submit to war and would send ambassadors to cut off the tribute. When the sentiments of the Romans were announced to Attila he angrily ravaged the Roman territory—seizing certain fortresses and making an attack on Ratiaria, a very large and populous city.

P.fr.4 In the same year Theodosius sent Senator, a man of consular rank, on an embassy to Attila. Though he had the name of ambassador, he was not confident of reaching the Huns on foot and so sailed to the Black Sea and the city of Odessus, where Theodolus, sent out as general, was stationed.

P.fr.5 Attila seems to have been impressed by Senator,[20] but further fighting apparently occurred, necessitating a second embassy in the same year. After the fight in the Chersonese further treaties were made by the Romans with the Huns through Anatolius as ambassador. This man had been consul in 440 and at this time was master of soldiers in the East. Later, he was recalled to be made master of soldiers praesentalis when Zeno went to the East and as such, as we shall see, made a second embassy to Attila.[21] The Huns made peace on condition that the fugitives should be given back to the Huns and that 6000 lbs. of gold should be paid to them in place of the former contributions; each year a tribute of 2100 lbs. of gold to them was agreed on; for each Roman prisoner of war who escaped and crossed over to his own land without ransom there was to be paid twelve gold pieces or if those who received him back did not pay the fugitive was to be returned; and the Romans were to receive no barbarian who fled to them. The Romans feigned that they voluntarily made these agreements, but actually it was by necessity and by the exceeding great fear which constrained their rulers. In spite of the fact that the whole injunction was harsh, they had to be satisfied to make peace in eager haste. They sent the contribution of the tributes, which was very heavy, although their resources and the imperial treasuries had been exhausted—not for necessities but because of disgusting spectacles, unrestrained ambitions and pleasures, and dissolute feasts such as no one of healthy mind, not even in prosperous times, should indulge in except those taking small thought for arms. The result was that they submitted to payment of tribute not only to the Scythians but also to the other barbarians dwelling near the Roman territory.

For the tributes and moneys which it was necessary to send to the Huns the emperor compelled everyone to join in paying a war tax, both those who paid taxes in kind and those relieved for a time from any very heavy land tax either by the decision of the judges or by the liberalities of the emperors. Those registered in the senate paid, as the war tax, sums of gold specified in proportion to their proper rank, and for many their good fortune brought a change in life. For they paid under torture what those assigned to do this by the emperor assessed them. And men who were formerly well-to-do displayed their wives' ornaments and their furniture in the marketplace. After the war this calamity came on the Romans, and many either starved themselves to death or hanged themselves. Then, after Scottas, a prominent Hunnish noble and brother of Onegesius, arrived on this business the treasuries were drained on the spur of the moment and the gold and fugitives were sent off.

Though it has been estimated that between 443 and 450 the Huns were paid £1,000,000 (1923) or 22,000 pounds of gold, it is certain that this picture of extreme hardship is vastly exaggerated and only the evidence of partisanship of the landed classes.[22] *The Romans killed the majority of those who refused compliance with their surrender. Among them were members of the Scythian royal family who had refused to serve under Attila and had come to the Romans. Adding to these orders of his, Attila commanded the Asimuntians to hand back whatever prisoners they happened to have whether Romans or barbarians. Asemus is a strong fortress not very far from Illyricum and adjacent to the Thracian boundary, whose native inhabitants inflicted many terrible deeds on the enemy, not only warding them from the walls but even undertaking battles outside the ditch. They fought against a boundless multitude and generals who had the greatest reputation among the Scythians. The Huns, being at a loss, retired slowly from the fortress. Then the Asimuntians rushed out and, being further from their homes than usual, since spies had told them that the enemy were going away with the Roman plunder, fell on them by surprise. Though fewer than the Huns opposing them but excelling them in bravery and strength, they made the Hunnish spoils their own. Thus the Asimuntians in this war killed many Scythians, freed many Romans, and received those who had run away from their enemies.*

Attila said that he would not lead back his army or ratify the peace treaty unless the Romans who had escaped to these people should be surrendered, or else ransoms paid for them, and the barbarian prisoners led off by the Asimuntians be given up. It was not possible for Anatolius the ambassador to oppose him nor for Theodolus, the commander of the military forces in Thrace. Even when they put forward reasonable arguments they did not persuade the barbarian since, on the one hand, he was very self-confident and was readily hasting to arms, and, on the other hand, they themselves were cowering on account of past events. They sent letters to the Asimuntians ordering them either to give up the Ro-

man prisoners who had fled to them or for each to pay over twelve pieces of gold, and to dismiss the Hun prisoners. The Asimuntians, acknowledging the letters to them, said that they had set at liberty those Romans who had fled to them, that they had killed all the Scythian prisoners they had, but that they had two under arrest because, after the siege had been going on for a time, the enemy had sprung out of ambush and seized some of the children who were grazing cattle before the fortress. If the Huns did not surrender these boys, they said, neither would they themselves give up their captives according to the laws of war. When those who had gone to the Asimuntians had announced these things, it seemed best to the king of the Scythians and to the Roman commanders to search out the children who the Asimuntians said had been seized. When none was found the barbarian prisoners of the Asimuntians were given up, the Scythians having sworn that they did not have the children. The Asimuntians also swore that the Romans who had fled to them had been sent away free. They swore this even though there were Romans among them; they did not think they had sworn a false oath since it was for the safety of men of their own race.

P.fr.6   Between 443 and 447 there was an unstable peace with the Huns. When the peace was made Attila again sent ambassadors to the Eastern Romans demanding the fugitives. And they, receiving these envoys and flattering them with very many gifts, sent them back again, saying that they had no fugitives. And again he sent other men. When they had transacted their business a third embassy arrived and after it a fourth, for the barbarian, seeing clearly the Romans' liberality, which they exercised through caution lest the peace treaties be broken, wished to benefit his retinue. And so he sent them to the Romans, forming new excuses and finding new pretexts. They gave ear to every order and obeyed the command of their master in whatever he ordered. They were not only wary of undertaking war on him, but they also feared the Parthians who were, it chanced, making preparations for war, the Vandals who were troubling the sea

coasts, the Isaurians who had set out on banditry, the Saracens who were overrunning the eastern part of their empire, and the united Ethiopian races. Being humbled, they
danced attendance on Attila and strove to meet the other
races with military power, mustering their forces and appoint-
ing generals.

Nothing could more clearly show the sad state of Rome's
power under Theodosius than this list of serious dangers.
There had been a brief outbreak of hostilities with Persia
(miscalled Parthia) in 444 followed by a one year's peace,
and though the Persians were in these years themselves engaged with the Huns the danger from the great eastern
empire of Persia was always present, even if war did not actually break out. The Vandals on the sea were only temporarily pacified by a treaty made by the Eastern Empire with
Gaiseric in 442, and the Isaurians of Cilicia—from time
immemorial given to piracy when there was no strong
Mediterranean naval power to stop them—now seem to be
operating also on land and remained a thorn in the empire's
flesh even when, as later under Zeno, they were useful as
military bulwarks of the empire. We know little of the
Saracen or Ethiopian raids except that peace was made with
both these peoples in 451.[23]

P.fr.3a   At about this time the court at Constantinople came under the sinister influence of Chrysaphius
Zstommas. Before this a most attractive man had held great
power at court. He was Cyrus, a pagan, a poet and a friend
of the Empress Eudocia and sole consul in 441. Cyrus was
put forward in Constantinople as praetorian prefect and prefect of the city. He used to go out as praetorian prefect in
the carriage of the prefects and return sitting in the carriage
of the city prefect, for he controlled the two offices as many
as four times, because he was completely incorruptible. He
also contrived to kindle evening lights in the workshops as
well as at night.[24] The factions in the Hippodrome cried
out to him all day, "Constantine founded, Cyrus restored."
The emperor was angry at him because they shouted these
things, and, having confiscated his property, relieved him of

his post, made him a priest, and sent him as bishop to
Smyrna in Asia or according to other authorities, to Kotyaium
in Phrygia, modern Kutahya. Cyrus' downfall occurred in 442
or 443, and he was succeeded by Chrysaphius who soon
"controlled everything, plundering the possessions of all and
being hated by all." [25]

P.fr.7   He brought the empire into considerable
danger when after a new attack in 447 a Roman ambassador,
Anatolius, had conducted negotiations with Attila early in
448 [26] by which fugitives from the Huns were to be restored
and some land ceded to them, and then somewhat later in
the same year when *Edeco came again as ambassador—a*
Scythian who had performed outstanding deeds in the war
—along with Orestes, who though he was of the Roman
race dwelt in the land of Pannonia by the Saus River, a
country subject to the barbarian by the treaty of Aëtius, the
general of the Western Romans. Orestes became the father
of Romulus Augustulus, last emperor of the West; and the
father of Odovacar, the first barbarian king of Italy, was
called Edico. While there is no proof that the Edeco here and
Odovacar's father were the same man, "there is a touch of
dramatic completeness in the working out of the squabble
for precedence between Edeco and Orestes in the persons of
their sons . . . which, until the theory can be actually
proved to be untrue, will always commend it to the artistic
instincts of the historian." [27]

This Edeco, coming to the court, handed over the letters
from Attila in which he held the Romans to blame in the
matter of the fugitives. In retaliation Attila threatened to
resort to arms if the Romans did not surrender them to him
and if they did not refrain from plowing the land captured
in the war. He asserted that the length of this tract was
downstream on the Danube from the land of the Pannonians
as far as Novae in Thrace, a distance of 300 miles, that the
breadth was five days' march, and that the market town was
not to be in Illyria on the bank of the Danube River as
formerly, but at Naissus, which, after it had been laid waste
by him, he set as the frontier of the lands of the Scythians

and Romans, it being five days' journey distant from the
Danube River for an unencumbered man. He gave orders
that envoys should come to him to discuss controversial
points—not just ordinary individuals but the most outstanding of those with consular rank. If they hesitated to send
these men he said he would come down to Sardica to receive
them. When these letters had been read to the emperor,
Edeco left with Bigilas,[28] who had interpreted word for word
whatever resolutions of Attila the barbarian had uttered.

When he had come to other quarters to hold a conference with Chrysaphius, the chamberlain of the emperor and
a man of very great power, he marveled at the splendor of the
royal rooms. When the barbarian's conversation with Chrysaphius began, Bigilas the interpreter said that Edeco was
praising the palace and admiring the wealth among them.
Chrysaphius said that Edeco might also be the lord of a
golden-roofed house and of such wealth if he would disre-
gard Scythian matters and take up Roman ways. The other
answered that it was not right for the servant of another
master to do this without his lord's permission. Then the
eunuch enquired whether admission to Attila's presence was
easy for him and whether he had any authority among the
Scythians. In reply Edeco said that he was an intimate friend
of Attila and that he was entrusted with his bodyguard along
with men chosen for this duty. On specified days, he said,
each of them in turn guarded Attila with arms. The eunuch
then said that if he received oaths he would make him very
important and advantageous proposals, but that leisure was
essential for this. He would attain this by coming to dinner
with him without Orestes and his other fellow envoys.

Edeco undertook to do this and came to a feast at the
eunuch's residence. They gave their right hands and oaths to
each other through the interpreter Bigilas, the eunuch promising that he would speak with a view not to Edeco's harm
but to his very great advantage, and Edeco promising that he
would not tell the proposals to be made to him, even if he
did not aim at their goal. Then the eunuch said to Edeco
that, if, having crossed into Scythia, he should slay Attila

and come back to the Romans, he would have a happy life and great wealth. Edeco promised and said that he needed money for the deed, not a great deal, but fifty pounds of gold to be given to the force under his command so that they might perfectly co-operate with him in the attack. When the eunuch promised to give the gold forthwith, the barbarian said that he should be sent to tell Attila about the embassy and that Bigilas should be dispatched with him to receive the answer from Attila about the fugitives. Through Bigilas, he said, he would disclose in what way his gold might be sent, for Attila would question him closely, like the other ambassadors, as to who had given him gifts and how much money he had received from the Romans, and it would not be possible to hide the money on account of those journeying with him.

It seemed to the eunuch that he spoke with sense, and accepting the advice of the barbarian he sent him away after dinner and took the plan to the emperor. The latter summoned Martialus, the master of offices, and told him of the agreements with the barbarian. Of necessity he had confidence in the opinion of this officer, for the master is privy to all the emperor's plans, since under him the messengers, interpreters, and soldiers of the imperial bodyguard are organized. It seemed best to those who made these plans concerning the proposals to send out not Bigilas alone but also Maximinus as ambassador to Attila.

This man had been the assessor of Ardaburius in settling the Persian treaty of 422, and under Marcian was to be made grand chamberlain and thus one of the four chief ministers of state. Gibbon calls him "the wise and eloquent Maximin," and he certainly seems to have been one of the abler soldiers and diplomats of his day.[29]

P.fr.8   When Chrysaphius, the eunuch, had counseled Edeco to kill Attila, it seemed best to the Emperor Theodosius and the master of offices, Martialus, who were making plans concerning the proposals, to send out not only Bigilas but also Maximinus as ambassador to Attila. They ordered Bigilas to do whatever Edeco thought best under the guise of undertaking the duty of interpreter, and Maximinus, who knew nothing of the things planned by them, to hand over the emperor's letters. It had been written for the sake of the men undertaking the embassy that Bigilas was the interpreter and that Maximinus was of higher position than Bigilas, a man of illustrious lineage and a councilor to the emperor in the most important matters. Further, it was stated that it was not right for a man who was breaking the truce to cross into the territory of the Romans. The emperor added, "I have sent you seventeen fugitives in addition to those already given, since there are no others." These were the words in the letters. He ordered Maximinus to speak to Attila face to face so that the latter need not ask ambassadors of higher rank to cross over to him; [30] for this had not been done in the case of his ancestors or in the case of other rulers of Scythia, but rather any chance soldier had made an embassy as a messenger. And for setting in order the matters in dispute it seemed best that he should send Onegesius to the Romans, for, since Sardica had been destroyed, it was not possible for him (that is, Attila) to proceed to that town with a man of consular rank.

Maximinus, by his entreaties, persuaded me to set out on this embassy with him. So then, along with the barbarians we took to the road and reached Sardica, a thirteen days' journey from Constantinople for a man traveling light. Halting there we thought it well to invite Edeco and the barbarians traveling with him to dinner. Thereupon, the inhabitants gave us sheep and cattle, which we slaughtered and so prepared a meal. During the course of the party as the barbarians praised Attila and we the emperor, Bigilas said that it was not fitting to compare a god and a man, meaning Attila by the man and Theodosius by the god. Then the Huns were irritated, and growing hot, little by little became angry. But we turned the talk to other matters, and with friendly overtures they themselves calmed down their spirit; after dinner, as we separated, Maximinus flattered Edeco and Orestes with gifts of silken garments and Indian gems. [31]

While awaiting the departure of Edeco, Orestes said to Maximinus that he was wise and most noble in that he had not given offense like those at the imperial court. For they, he said, having invited Edeco to a feast without himself, had honored him with gifts. This speech was meaningless to us since he knew nothing of what has been revealed above, and he went away having made no answer to us though we repeatedly asked how and when he had been overlooked and Edeco honored. On the next day as we were advancing we told Bigilas what Orestes had said to us. He said that Orestes ought not to be angry that he had not had the same treatment as Edeco, for he was a servant and secretary of Attila but Edeco was a man foremost in military matters and, since he was of the Hunnish race,³² far superior to Orestes. Saying this and having conversed in private with Edeco, he later on reported to us, either speaking the truth or dissembling, that he had told him what had been said and with difficulty had soothed him as he had become very angry on account of it.

Arriving at Naissus we found the city destitute of men, since it had been razed by the enemy. In the Christian hostels³³ were found people afflicted by disease. Halting in an open place a short distance from the river—for every place on the bank was full of the bones of those slain in war—we came the next day to Agintheus, the commander of the forces in Illyria, not far from Naissus, to announce the commands of the emperor and to receive the fugitives. He had to hand over five of the seventeen about whom it had been written to Attila.³⁴ We conversed with him and arranged that he should hand over to the Huns the five fugitives whom he sent with us, after having treated them kindly.

Having passed the night we made a journey from the frontiers at Naissus toward the Danube River and entered a certain thickly shaded place where the path had many turns and twists and windings. Here, when the day dawned, the rising sun was seen in front of us, though we had been under the impression we had been traveling toward the west, with the result that those ignorant of the topography of the country cried out, supposing that surely the sun was going in the opposite direction and was thus portending strange and unusual events. Owing to the unevenness of the place that part of the road turned toward the east.

After this difficult ground we found ourselves on a wooded plain. Barbarian ferrymen received us, and in single-log boats which they themselves build, cutting and hollowing out the trees, they ferried us across the Danube River. They had not made these preparations for our sake, but had just ferried across a barbarian band which had met us on the road, because Attila was desirous of crossing to Roman territory as if to a hunt. But the royal Scythian really had the intention of doing this as a preparation for war, on the pretext that all the fugitives had not been given up.

Having crossed the Danube and proceeded with the barbarians about seventy stades, roughly eight miles, we were forced to wait in a certain place in order that Edeco and his suite might go to Attila as heralds of our arrival. The barbarians who had acted as our guides remained with us, and in the late afternoon when we were taking our dinner the clatter of horses was heard coming toward us. Then two Scythians appeared and ordered us to set out to Attila. First we asked them to come to dinner and they, dismounting from their horses, were treated well, and then next day they guided us on our way. About the ninth hour of the day, that is, at three P.M., we came to the tents of Attila— it turned out that he had many of them—but when we wished to pitch our tents on a certain hill, the barbarians who met us prevented us, because the tent of Attila was on low ground. We lodged where it seemed best to the Scythians, and Edeco and Orestes and Scottas and other picked men from among the Huns came and asked us what we were seeking to gain by making an embassy.

We were amazed at the unexpected enquiry and looked at one another, but they continued to importune us for an answer. We replied that the emperor had given us orders to talk with Attila and with no others, but Scottas, becoming angry, answered that this was the order of their own leader,

for they would not have come to us with meddling inter-
ference on their own.

We answered that this law had never been laid down for
ambassadors—namely that, neither having met nor come
into the presence of those to whom they had been sent, they
should negotiate through others the things for which they
were making the embassy. Moreover, we said, the Scythians
were not ignorant of this since they made frequent embassies
to the emperor; it was right that we get equal treatment,
and we would not otherwise tell the business of our embassy.

So they broke off and went to Attila and again returned
without Edeco. They told us everything for which we had
come as envoys and ordered us to depart as quickly as possible unless we had anything else to say. We were still
more at a loss at these words, for it was not easy to see how
matters resolved by the emperor in secret had become well
known.

We considered that there was no advantage for our embassy in answering unless we had access to Attila himself.
So we said, "The enquiry of your leader is whether we come
as ambassadors to treat of the matters mentioned by the
Scythians or on other business, but by no means did we
come to discuss this with other men." And they ordered us
to depart forthwith.

As we were making preparations for the journey Bigilas
found fault with us on account of our answer, saying it was
better to be caught in a lie than to return without success.
"If," said he, "I had conversed with Attila I should easily
have persuaded him to put aside his disagreements with the
Romans, since I became his friend on the embassy with
Anatolius." [35] He said this and that Edeco was well disposed
toward him. With this argument of the embassy and of
matters which had to be spoken of in any case, he tried to
gain, either truly or falsely, his chance to make plans for
what they had resolved against Attila and for bringing the
gold which Edeco had said was necessary to distribute among
the appointed men. But without his knowledge he was
betrayed, for Edeco had either given a false promise or had

become afraid that Orestes would tell Attila what he had said to us in Sardica after the banquet. In that case he feared that he would be held at fault for having conversed with the emperor and the eunuch without Orestes, and so he revealed to Attila the plot against him and the amount of gold to be sent out. And he also announced the purpose of our embassy.

Our baggage had already been packed on the beasts of burden, and, having no choice, we were trying to begin our journey during the night when other barbarians came and said that Attila bade us wait on account of the hour. At the very place from which we had just set out some men arrived bringing us an ox and river fish from Attila, and so we dined and then turned to sleep.

When day came we thought the barbarian might make some mild and soothing statement, but he sent the same men again and ordered us to leave unless we had something else to say besides the things they already knew. We made no answer and prepared for the journey, although Bigilas argued obstinately that we should say that there were other things to tell them. When I saw that Maximinus was in great dejection I took Rusticius,[36] who knew the language of the barbarians thoroughly and who had come with us to Scythia not for the sake of the embassy but on business with Constantius.[37] He was an Italian whom Aëtius, the general of the Western Romans, had sent to Attila as his secretary. I took Rusticius to Scottas, for Onegesius was not there at the time. Addressing him through Rusticius as interpreter I said that he would receive many gifts from Maximinus if he should make preparations for him to gain entrance to Attila. Maximinus' embassy would be profitable, I said, not only to the Romans and Huns but also to Onegesius, who the emperor desired should come to him to compose the disputes for the two nations, and who would thus obtain very great gifts. Since Onegesius was not present, I said it was necessary for him to help us—or rather his brother—in this noble enterprise. I said that I had learned that Attila trusted him also, but that the reports about him

*would not seem true if we should not know his power from
personal experience. In answer he said that we should no
longer be in doubt about his either speaking or acting on
equal terms with his brother before Attila. Then he mounted
his horse straightway and rode to the tent of Attila.*

*I returned to Maximinus, who, with Bigilas, was troubled
and at a loss in the present circumstances. I told what I
had said to Scottas and what I had heard from him and
declared that it was necessary to prepare gifts for the barbarian and to consider what we should say to him. Both
men jumped up, for they had been lying on the grass. They
praised the deed and called back those who had already set
out with the beasts of burden. Then they considered how
to address Attila and how to present him with both the
emperor's gifts and the things which Maximinus had brought
for him.*

*While we were thus engaged Attila summoned us through
Scottas, and so we came to his tent, which was guarded by
a band of barbarians around it. When we made our entrance
we found Attila sitting on a wooden seat. As we stood a
little apart from the throne, Maximinus went forward, greeted
the barbarian, and gave him the letters from the emperor,
saying that the emperor prayed that he and his followers were
safe and sound.*

*He answered that for himself the Romans would have
whatever they wished. Straightway, he turned his words
against Bigilas, calling him a shameless beast and asked why
he desired to come to him when he knew the terms made by
him and Anatolius for peace, adding that he had said that
no ambassadors ought to come to him before all the fugitives
had been surrendered to the barbarians.*

*Bigilas said that there was not a single refugee of the
Scythian race among the Romans, for all of them had been
surrendered. Attila became even angrier and, railing at him
violently, said with a shout that he would have impaled
him and given him to the birds for food if he had not
thought it an outrage to the law of embassies to exact this
punishment from him for his effrontery and recklessness of*

speech. He said there were among the Romans many refugees of his race whose names, written down on a piece of paper, he ordered his secretaries to read out. When they had gone through all of them, he ordered Bigilas to depart without more ado. He sent Eslas with him to tell the Romans to send back to him all the barbarians who had fled to them from the time of Carpileon, who as the son of Aëtius, the general of the Romans of the West, had been a hostage at his court.[38] He would not allow his own servants to go to war against him, even though they were unable to help those who turned over to them the protection of their native land, for, said he, what city or what fortress he set out to capture would be saved by these refugees? When Bigilas and Eslas had announced his resolutions concerning the fugitives he ordered them to return and say whether the Romans were willing to surrender them or whether they were going to undertake war on their behalf.

He also ordered, first of all, that Maximinus should remain so that through him he could answer the emperor concerning the things written about, and he accepted the gifts. Having presented them and returned to our tent we discussed privately each of the things that had been said. Bigilas expressed surprise that though Attila had seemed mild and gentle to him when he had made the former embassy now he railed at him harshly. I said I was afraid that certain of the barbarians who had feasted with us at Sardica had made Attila hostile by informing him that he had called the emperor of the Romans a god but Attila a man. Maximinus accepted this explanation as likely, since, indeed, he was not an accomplice in the conspiracy which the eunuch had devised against the barbarian. But Bigilas was in doubt and seemed to me to be at a loss for Attila's motive in assailing him. He did not think, as he told us afterward, that the events at Sardica nor the details of the plot had been told to Attila, since no one else from the throng, on account of the fear prevailing over all, would dare to come into conversation with him, and Edeco would hold his peace on account of his oaths and the uncertainty of the business, lest he, as a participant of such plans, should be considered to have been in favor of them and should suffer the death penalty.

While we were in such great doubt Edeco came and took Bigilas outside our gathering, pretending to be in earnest about the plot. He gave orders for the gold to be brought for those who would be involved with him in this business and left. When I enquired closely what Edeco had told him he tried to deceive me—himself being deceived—and hiding the true reason said that Edeco had reported that Attila was angry with him on account of the fugitives, for it was necessary that he receive all or that ambassadors of the highest rank come to him.

As we were discussing these matters some of Attila's retinue came and told both Bigilas and ourselves not to buy any Roman prisoner or barbarian slave or horses or anything else except things necessary for food until the disputes between the Romans and Huns had been resolved.

The barbarian did this cunningly, so that Bigilas would be easily caught in the business directed against himself— he would be at a loss for a reason for bringing the gold— and also in order that we might wait for Onegesius to receive the emperor's gifts which we wished to give, he used the pretence of an answer to be given to the embassy.

It happened that Onegesius with the elder of Attila's sons had been sent to the nation of Akatiri.[39] This is a Hunnish nation which submitted to Attila for the following reason. The nation had many rulers according to the tribes and clans, and the Emperor Theodosius sent gifts to them so that, with his moral support, they might renounce their alliance with Attila and join an alliance with the Romans. But the man who brought the gifts had not given them out to the various kings according to the rank of each. The result was that Kouridachus, the elder in office, received the gifts second, and so, being overlooked and deprived of his proper honors, he had called Attila in against his fellow kings. Without delay Attila had sent a force and, having destroyed some and subdued others, he summoned Kouridachus to share the prizes of victory. But he, suspecting a plot, said, "It is difficult for a man to come into the presence of a god; for if it is not possible to look directly at the disc of the sun how might anyone look at the greatest of the gods without suffering?" So Kouridachus stayed in his own territories and saved his dominion when all the rest of the nation of the Akatiri submitted to Attila. Wishing to appoint his elder son king of this nation [40] Attila sent Onegesius for this purpose. Wherefore, as has been said, he compelled us to wait while Bigilas and Eslas crossed to Roman territory on the pretext of the fugitives, but in truth so that Bigilas might bring the gold for Edeco.

When Bigilas had set out, we waited one day after his departure for home and on the next proceeded with Attila to the northern parts of the country. We advanced with the barbarian for a time and then turned along a different road, the Scythians who were guiding us having ordered us to do this, while Attila was to proceed to a certain village where he wished to marry the daughter of Escam. [41] He had many wives but he was taking this woman also according to the Scythian custom. From here we proceeded along a level road lying in a plain and crossed navigable rivers, of which the greatest after the Danube, were the Drecon, so called, the Tigas, and the Tiphesas. We were carried across these in boats made of a single piece of wood, such as those dwelling along the rivers use. We crossed the other rivers on rafts which the barbarians carry on wagons for use in the marshy places.

At the villages food was supplied to us generously, millet instead of wheat and mead—as it is called in the native tongue—instead of wine. The attendants following us were also supplied with millet and a drink made of barley was provided; the barbarians call this "kamon." [42] Having completed a long journey, late in the afternoon we camped by a certain lake which had fresh water and whence the inhabitants of the nearby village drew their water. A wind and a storm arose on a sudden, accompanied by thunder and frequent lightning flashes and a heavy downpour of rain,

and not only overturned our tent but also rolled all our
gear into the water of the lake. Terrified by the tumult which
ruled the air and by what had happened, we left the place
and were separated from one another as, in the dark and
the rain, each of us took whatever road he thought would
be easy for himself. When we came to the huts of the village
—for we returned to it, all by different routes—we met in
the same place and searched, shouting for the things we
needed. The Scythians leapt out at the tumult and lit the
reeds which they used for fire, and, having made a light,
they asked why we raised such an outcry. The barbarians
with us answered that we had been thrown into confusion
by the storm, and so they summoned us to their own huts
and, burning a great many reeds, furnished us shelter.

A woman rules in the village—she had been one of Bleda's
wives—and she sent us provisions and good-looking women
to comfort us. This is a Scythian compliment,[43] but we,
when the eatables had been laid out, showed them kindness
but refused intercourse with them. We remained in the
huts until daylight and then turned to search for our baggage. We found it all, some in the place where we had chanced
to halt, some on the bank of the lake, and some in the water
itself. We spent that day in the village drying out all our
things, for the storm had stopped and the sun was shining.
Having taken care of our horses and the other baggage
animals we went to the princess and greeted her and repaid
her with gifts, three silver drinking bowls, red skins, pepper
from India, fruit of the palm, and other sweetmeats, gifts
esteemed by the barbarians because they do not often come
to them. And we thanked her for the kindness of her
hospitality.

Having completed a journey of seven days we waited in a
certain village, our Scythian guides having ordered us to do
so, because Attila was going to follow the same road and it
behooved us to proceed behind him. There we met some
of the Western Romans, themselves also on an embassy to
Attila. Among them was Romulus, a man honored with the
rank of count, and Promotus who governed the province of

Noricum, and Romanus, the commander of a military corps with the rank of duke. With them was Constantius whom Aëtius had sent to Attila as his secretary, and Tatulus, the father of Orestes who was with Edeco, these men making the journey not on account of ambassadorial duties but out of friendship for the others—Constantius on account of his former acquaintance with these men in the Italies and Tatulus on account of his kinship. His son Orestes had married the daughter of Romulus, who was from Patavio—a city in Noricum.

They were making this embassy in order to pacify Attila who desired that Silvanus, the manager of the bank of Armius [44] at Rome, be surrendered to him because he had received some golden bowls from Constantius. This Constantius hailed from the western Galatians or Gauls, and had himself also been sent to Attila and Bleda as a secretary just as the Constantius after him. At the time when Sirmium in Pannonia was being besieged by the Scythians [45] he received the bowls from the bishop of the city on condition that he ransom him if the city should happen to be captured and he survive, or else, if he should be killed, to rescue those of the citizens who were being led off as prisoners. But Constantius, after the enslaving of the city, took small account of his agreements and, coming to Rome on some business, obtained gold from Silvanus, giving him the bowls on condition that within a stated time he either repay the money lent at interest and receive back the sureties or that Silvanus use them for whatever he wished. But then Attila and Bleda, holding Constantius in suspicion of treachery, crucified him.

After a time, when the affair of the bowls was revealed to Attila, he desired that Silvanus be surrendered to him as a thief of his possessions. Therefore, the envoys had been sent from Aëtius and the emperor of the Western Romans to say that Silvanus, since he was the creditor of Constantius, had the bowls as sureties and had not received them as stolen goods and that he had given them in exchange for money to priests and not to ordinary people: [46] for it is not right for men to use for their own purposes drinking cups dedicated to God. If, therefore, Attila would not desist for this just reason or out of reverence for divinity from demanding the bowls, they said that they would send gold in place of them but that they declined to send Silvanus, for they would not give up a man who had done no wrong. This was the reason for their embassy, and they were following Attila closely so that the barbarian might answer them and send them away.

Having come on the same journey, therefore, we waited for him to advance ahead and then with all the crowd followed closely. We crossed certain rivers and came to a very large village in which the dwelling of Attila was said to be more notable than those elsewhere.[47] It had been fitted together with highly polished timbers and boards and encircled with a wooden palisade, conceived not for safety but for beauty. Next to the king's dwelling that of Onegesius was outstanding, and it also had a circuit of timbers but was not embellished with towers in the same way as Attila's. Not far from the enclosure there was a large bath which Onegesius, who had power second only to Attila among the Scythians, had built, fetching the stones from the land of Pannonia. There is neither stone nor tree among the barbarians living in those parts, but they use imported wood. The builder of the bath, taken as a captive from Sirmium, thought that he would receive his freedom as pay for his ingenious work. But he was disappointed and fell into a greater distress of slavery among the Scythians, for Onegesius appointed him bath man, and he had to wait on him and his household when they washed.

Maidens came to meet Attila as he entered this village, advancing before him in rows under fine white linen cloths stretched out to such a length that under each cloth, which was held up by the hands of women along either side, seven or even more girls walked. There were many such formations of women under the linen cloths, and they sang Scythian songs. When he came near the house of Onegesius (for the road to the palace led past it), the wife of Onegesius

came out with a host of servants, some bearing dainties and
others wine, and (this is the greatest honor among the
Scythians) greeted him and asked him to partake of the
food which she brought for him with friendly hospitality.
To gratify the wife of his intimate friend, he ate sitting on
his horse, the barbarians accompanying him having raised
the silver platter up to him. Having also tasted the wine
proffered to him he went on to the palace, which was higher
than the other houses and situated on a high place.

We remained in the house of Onegesius, since he himself bade us, for he had returned with the son of Attila.[48]
We had dinner there, his wife and the outstanding members
of his family receiving us; he himself after his return went
at once into conference with Attila to tell him the results
of the business for which he had been sent and about the
accident which had befallen Attila's son (for the latter had
slipped and broken his right hand), and so he did not have
leisure to dine with us. After dinner we left the house of
Onegesius and pitched our tents near the house of Attila
so that Maximinus, when he had to go to Attila or else
go into conference with other men of his court, might be
separated by no great distance from them.

We spent the night in the place we had taken up
our quarters, and when day dawned Maximinus sent me
to Onegesius to present the gifts which he was giving and
those the emperor had sent and to ascertain where and when
he wished to confer with him. When I arrived with the
servants carrying these gifts, I waited patiently, the doors
being still closed, until someone should come out and
disclose our arrival.

While I was waiting and strolling about in front of the
stockade of the house a man in Scythian dress whom I
thought to be a native approached me. But he greeted me
in the Hellenic language, saying, "Hail" (chaire), and I
marveled that a Scythian was speaking Hellenic. Being a
mixture of peoples, in addition to their own barbaric tongue
those who have dealings with the Romans cultivate the
tongue of the Huns or Goths or even Latins, but it is not

easy for any of them to speak in the Hellenic language,
except those led as captives from Thrace and the seacoast
of Illyricum. When come upon, these are easily recognized
from their ragged clothes and the squalor of their heads as
men who have met with ill fortune. But this man was like
a well-dressed Scythian living in luxury and had his hair
clipped all around.[49]

Having greeted him in turn I asked who he was and from
where he had come into this barbaric land and taken up
a Scythian life. He in turn asked why I was so eager to know
this. I answered that the reason for my curiosity was his
Hellenic speech. Then laughing, he said that he was a
Greek by race and that he had gone for trade to Viminacium,
the city of Moesia on the Danube River, and had lived in it
for a long time and had married a very rich woman. But
when the city came under the barbarians [50] he had been
stripped of his prosperity, and on account of the wealth
belonging to him had been assigned to Onegesius in the
distribution of the spoils—for the elite of the Scythians,
after Attila, took the captives selected from among the
well-to-do because they sold for the most money. He had
fought bravely in the later battles with the Romans and
the nation of the Akatiri, and, having given his barbarian
master, according to the law of the Scythians, what he had
gained for himself in the war, he had obtained his freedom.
He had married a barbarian woman and had children; he
was a partaker of the table of Onegesius and led a better
life at present than he had formerly.

Among the Scythians, said he, men are accustomed to
live at ease after a war, each enjoying what he has, causing
very little or no trouble and not being troubled. Among
the Romans, however, men are easily destroyed in war, in
the first place because they put their hopes of safety in
others, since on account of their tyrants all men are not
allowed to use arms. For those who do use them the
cowardice of their generals, who cannot support the conduct
of war, is more perilous. In peace, moreover, experiences are
more grievous than the evils of the wars, on account of

the very heavy taxes and the wrongs suffered at the hands of wicked men, since the laws are not imposed on all. If the transgressor of the law be of the monied class, it is not likely that he pays the penalty of his wrongdoing; if he should be poor and ignorant of how to handle the business, he endures the penalty according to the law—if he does not depart life before his trial. For the course of these cases is long protracted, and a great deal of money is expended on them. Probably the most grievous suffering of all is to obtain the rights of the law for pay. No one will even grant a court to a wronged man unless he lays aside some money for the judge and his attendants.

In answer to him, as he was putting forward this and many other arguments, I mildly said that he should also hear the arguments on my side. Then I said that the founders of the Roman constitution were wise and noble men, with the result that affairs are not carried on haphazardly. They appointed some to be guardians of the laws and others to pay attention to arms and to practice military exercises; they were set to no other task than to be prepared for battle and to go to war in confidence, as to a familiar exercise, fear having been eradicated beforehand through training. Others engaged in farming and the care of the land were appointed to support both themselves and those fighting on their behalf by collecting the military provisions tax.[51] And others they assigned to take thought for those who had been wronged—men to support the claim of those unable, on account of a deficiency in their nature, to plead their own rights, and judges to uphold the intention of the law. Nor was there any lack of thought for those who came before the judges—among these men were some to see to it that he who obtained the decision of the judges should get his claim and that the one convicted of wrongdoing should not be compelled to pay more than the decision of the judges willed. If those who had these matters under their care did not exist, the reason for another case would arise from the same cause, the winner of the case either proceeding against his enemy too harshly, or the one with the adverse decision persisting in his illegal contention. There was, furthermore, a fixed sum of money for such men, payable by those contesting the case, like that paid by the farmers to the soldiers. Is it not right, I said, to support him who comes to your aid and repay his kindness? Just so is the provisioning of his horse a benefit to the horseman, the care of his cattle to the shepherd, of his dogs to the hunter, and of other creatures to men who have them for their own protection and assistance. When men pay the price of going to justice and lose the case, let them attribute this misfortune to their own injustice and not to anything else.

As for the time spent on cases being too long, should it occur, it is due to the concern for justice, so that the judges might not fail in exactitude by acting in an offhand manner. It is better that by considering they end a case late than that by hurrying they not only wrong mankind but also offend God, the founder of justice. The laws are imposed on everyone—even the emperor obeys them—and it is not true (as was part of his charge) that the well-to-do assault the poor with impunity, unless indeed someone escapes punishment by eluding detection. This escape is not for the rich alone, but any poor man might also discover it. For though they are offenders they would not suffer punishment because of a lack of evidence; and this happens among all peoples, not only among the Romans. For the freedom he had obtained, I told the man he had to acknowledge thanks to fortune and not to the master who had led him out to war. Indeed, through inexperience he might have perished at the hands of the enemy or, fleeing, been punished by his owner. The Romans are wont to treat even their servants better. They show the attitude of fathers or teachers to them, so that restrained from vulgar habits they pursue what has been thought good for them, and their masters chastise them for their sins as they do their own children. It is unlawful to inflict death on them as it is for the Scythians. There are also many ways of conferring freedom, which they give freely, not only when they are still alive but also when they die, having arranged their estates as they wish. And whatever a man plans for his possessions on his death is legally binding.

My interlocutor wept and said that the laws were excellent and the constitution of the Romans fair, but that the rulers were ruining it by not taking thought for it like their predecessors.[52] While we were discussing these things someone from inside arrived and opened the doors of the enclosure. I ran forward and asked what Onegesius was doing, for I desired to announce something to him from the ambassador who had come from the Romans. He answered that I should meet him if I waited a little, for he was about to go out.

Indeed, not much time passed until I saw him coming out. Going up to him I said that the Roman ambassador greeted him and that I had come with gifts from him and that I also had the gold sent from the emperor. I asked when and where he wished to hold a discussion with Maximinus, as the latter was anxious to have a meeting. He ordered his attendants to accept the gold and the gifts and told me to report to Maximinus that he would come to him at once. I returned and announced that Onegesius was at hand. And straightway he came to the tent.

Addressing Maximinus, he gave thanks both to him and to the emperor and asked what Maximinus wished to say that he had summoned him. The Roman answered that the time had come when Onegesius would have greater honor among men if he went to the emperor and, with his intelligence, put the disputes in order and established concord between Romans and Huns. He said there would be advantage not only for both nations, but he would also obtain many benefits for his own household, since he and his children would be forever the friends of the emperor and his race.

Onegesius said, "And what actions would be gratifying to the emperor, or how may the disputes be settled for him?" Maximinus answered that, having crossed into Roman territory, he would earn the emperor's gratitude and would

settle the disputes by thoroughly examining their causes
and removing them according to the terms of the peace.
The other said that he would tell the emperor and his
ministers the things which Attila desired. "Or do the Romans think," he said, "that they will move me by entreaty
to such an extent that I will betray my master, neglect my
upbringing among the Scythians and my wives and my
children, and think slavery under Attila no better than
wealth among the Romans?" He added that it would be more
advantageous for him, by remaining in his own country, to
appease the spirit of his master respecting his causes to be
angry at the Romans than, by going to them, to subject
himself to blame for having done things other than seemed
best to Attila.

Saying this he departed, first commanding that I confer
with him on the matters we wished to ask of him, since
continuous visiting was not fitting for Maximinus—a man
acting in an official capacity.

The next day I approached the enclosure of Attila with
gifts for his wife. Her name was Kreka,[53] and by her Attila
had three sons, the elder being ruler of the Akatiri and of the
other peoples dwelling along the Black Sea in Scythia. Inside the enclosure were many houses, some of carved planks
beautifully fitted together, and others of clean beams
smoothly planed straight; they were laid on timbers which
formed circles. Beginning at the ground level the circles
rose to a moderate height. Here dwelt the wife of Attila.
I gained entrance through the barbarians at the door and
came upon her lying on a soft spread. The floor was covered
with mats of felted wool. A number of servants were waiting on her in a circle, and maidservants, sitting on the floor
in front of her, were embroidering with color fine linens to be
placed as ornament over their barbarian clothes. Approaching, I greeted her and presented our gifts and then went out.
I walked to the other house in which Attila happened to be
staying and waited for Onegesius to come out, as he had left
his own house and was within. Standing among the throng,
for I was hindered by no one—being known to the guards

of Attila and those who accompanied him—I saw a crowd advancing and a tumult and a stir arising around the place, since Attila was about to come out. He came from his house walking with a haughty strut, looking around here and there. When he had come out he stood in front of his house with Onegesius, and many who had disputes with one another came and received his judgment. Then he returned into the house and received barbarian ambassadors who had come to him.

Romulus, Promotus, and Romanus, who had come from Italy to Attila as ambassadors on the matter of the golden cups, approached while I was waiting for Onegesius. With them were Rusticius, who was in Constantius' retinue, and Constantiolus, a man of the Pannonian territory governed by Attila. They came to talk and asked whether we had been dismissed or whether we were being forced to remain. I said that I was still waiting before the enclosures in order to learn this from Onegesius. When I asked, in turn, whether Attila had made a mild and gentle reply concerning their embassy, they said that he had not changed his mind, but was going to declare war unless Silvanus or the drinking cups were sent to him.

We were amazed at the barbarian for his unreasonableness, and Romulus, an ambassador experienced in many affairs, took up the discourse and said that his very great fortune and the power derived from good luck exalted him so that he could not endure just proposals unless he thought they came from himself. By no one who had ever yet ruled over Scythia, or indeed any other land, had such great things been achieved in such a short time, since he ruled even the islands of the Ocean and, in addition to all Scythia, held the Romans also to the payment of tribute. He is aiming, he said, at greater achievements beyond his present ones and desires to go against the Persians to expand his territory to even greater size.

When one of us asked what route he could take against the Persians, Romulus said that the land of the Medes was separated by no great distance from Scythia and that the

Huns were not ignorant of this route. Long ago [54] they had come upon it when famine was overwhelming their country, and the Romans had not opposed them on account of the war they were engaged in at that time. Basich and Kursich, men who later had come to Rome to make an alliance, being of the Scythian royal family and rulers of a vast horde, had advanced into the territory of the Medes. Those who went across say that they traversed a desert country, crossed a certain swamp which Romulus thought was the Maeotis, spent fifteen days crossing over some mountains, and so descended into Media. A Persian host came on them as they were plundering and overrunning the land, and, being on higher ground than they, filled the air with missiles so that, encompassed by danger, the Huns had to beat a retreat and retire across the mountains. They took little plunder, for the greatest part was seized by the Medes. Being watchful for the pursuit of the enemy they took another road, and, having marched . . . days [55] from the flame which rises from the stone under the sea they arrived home. Thus, they know the land of the Medes is not far from Scythia. Attila, if he wished to go there, would not have much trouble, nor would he have a long journey, and so would subdue the Medes, Parthians, and Persians and force them to submit to the payment of tribute, for he had a military force which no nation could resist.

When we prayed that he would go against the Persians and turn the war against them instead of us, Constantiolus said that he feared that once having subdued the Persians with ease Attila would return as a tyrant instead of a friend to us. At present we brought him gold for the sake of his rank, but if he overwhelmed the Parthians, Medes, and Persians, he would no longer endure the rule of Romans independent of himself, but considering them his servants would openly impose harsh and intolerable injunctions on them. The rank which Constantiolus mentioned was general of the Romans, master of soldiers, the favor of which title Attila received from the emperor as a pretext for concealing the tribute. Thus, the contributions were sent to him under the pretence of military provisions supplied to generals. Therefore, he said, after the Medes, Parthians, and Persians were conquered he would shake off the name by which the Romans wished to call him and the rank with which they thought they had honored him and would force them to address him as emperor instead of general. Even now, when angry he was used to say that his servants were the generals of that ruler (the emperor) and that he himself had leaders of worth equal to the emperors of the Romans. There would be, in short, an increase in his present power, and God had revealed this in bringing to light the sword of Ares. This was a sacred object honored among the Scythian kings, since it was dedicated to the overseer of wars. It had been hidden in ancient times and then discovered through the agency of an ox.

P.fr.10   When a herdsman noticed one of his herd limping and found no reason for such a wound, being disturbed, he followed the tracks of blood. At length he came upon a sword which the heifer had heedlessly trodden on while grazing the grass. He dug it up and bore it directly to Attila. He rejoiced at this gift and thought—since he was a man of high spirit—that he had been appointed chieftain of the whole world and that through the sword of Mars supremacy in war had been granted to him.

P.fr.8 ctd.   Just as each of us desired to say something about the present situation, Onegesius came out and we went to him to learn about the affairs we were engaged in. Having spoken first to some barbarians he ordered me to ask Maximinus what man of consular rank the Romans were sending as ambassador to Attila. When I came to the tent I told what had been said to me and deliberated with Maximinus as to what I ought to say regarding the matters about which the barbarian sought information from us. I returned to Onegesius and said that the Romans wished him to come to them to talk about the disputes, and, if they should fail to obtain this, the emperor would send out whomever he wished as ambassador. Immediately, he ordered me to fetch Maximinus, and when he came he led him

into Attila's presence. When Maximinus came out a little
later he said that the barbarian wished either Nomus the
consul of 445 or Anatolius or Senator [56] to be sent as ambassador and would not receive any other except the men
named. When Maximinus had answered that by naming
men for an embassy he must needs render them suspect
to the emperor, Attila had said that if they did not choose
to do what he wished the disputes would be settled by arms.

When we returned to our tent the father of Orestes,
Tatulus, came and said, "Attila invites you both to a banquet
and this will start about the ninth hour of the day." We
waited for the right time and when those of us who had
been invited to the feast and the ambassadors of the Western Romans had arrived, we stood on the threshold before
Attila. The cupbearers gave us a cup, according to local
custom, so that we might pray before sitting down. When
this was done and we had tasted the cup we went to the
seats in which we were to sit while dining.

All the chairs were ranged along the walls of the house
on either side. In the middle sat Attila on a couch, another
couch being set behind him, and back of this steps led up
to his bed, which was covered with white linens and colored
embroideries for ornament, just as the Hellenes and Romans
prepare for those who marry. The position of those dining
on the right of Attila is considered most honorable, and
second the position on the left, where we happened to be
and where Berichus, a Goth but still a noble among the
Scythians, sat above us. Onegesius sat on a chair at the right
of the king's couch, and opposite Onegesius two of Attila's
sons sat on a chair. The eldest son sat on his couch, not
near him but at the end, looking at the ground out of
respect for his father.

When all were arranged in order a cupbearer approached
and offered Attila an ivy-wood cup of wine. He took it and
saluted the first in rank, and the one honored by the greeting stood up. It was not right for him to sit down until
the king had either tasted the wine or drunk it up and had
given the cup back to the cupbearer. All those present

honored him in the same way as he remained seated, taking the cups and, after a salutation, tasting them. Each guest had his own cupbearer who had to come forward in order when Attila's cupbearer retired. After the second man had been honored and the others in order, Attila greeted us also with the same ritual according to the order of the seats. When everyone had been honored by this salutation the cupbearers went out, and tables for three or four or more men were set up next to that of Attila. From these each was able to partake of the things placed on his plate without leaving the original arrangement of chairs. Attila's servant was the first to enter, bearing a platter full of meat, and then the servants who waited on the rest placed bread and viands on the tables. While sumptuous food had been prepared—served on silver plates—for the other barbarians and for us, for Attila there was nothing but meat on a wooden trencher. He showed himself temperate in all other ways too, for gold and silver goblets were offered to the men at the feast, but his mug was of wood. His dress too was plain, having care for nothing other than to be clean, nor was the sword by his side, nor the clasps of his barbarian boots, nor the bridle of his horse, like those of other Scythians, adorned with gold or gems or anything of high price.

When the food placed on the first platters had been consumed we all stood up and no one went back to his seat until each, in the previous order, had drunk the goblet of wine which was presented to him, with a prayer that Attila should be healthy. When he had been honored in this way we sat down, and a second plate with edibles was placed on each table. After all had partaken of this and had stood up in the same way and again drunk wine we sat down.

As evening came on pine torches were lit up, and two barbarians, advancing in front of Attila, sang songs which they had composed, chanting his victories and his virtues in war. Those at the feast looked at the men; some took delight in the verses, some, reminded of wars, were excited in their souls, and others, whose bodies were weakened by time and whose spirits were compelled to rest, gave way

to tears. After the songs a certain crazed Scythian came forward, who forced everyone to burst out laughing by uttering
monstrous and unintelligible words and nothing at all sane.
After him Zercon the Moor entered.

P.fr.11   This man, a Scythian so called, was a Moor
by race. On account of the deformity of his body, the lisp
of his voice, and his appearance he was an object of laughter.
He was somewhat short, hump-shouldered, with distorted
feet, and a nose indicated only by the nostrils, because of
its exceeding flatness. He was presented to Aspar, son of
Ardaburius,[57] during the time he spent in Libya and was
captured when the barbarians invaded Thrace and was
brought to the Scythian kings. Attila could not endure the
sight of him, but Bleda was exceedingly pleased with him,
not only when he uttered comical words but also when he
walked about in silence and moved his body clumsily. He
was with him when he feasted and when he was on a campaign, wearing, on these expeditions, armor aimed at causing
merriment. Bleda held him in high esteem and, when he
ran away along with other Roman captives, he neglected
the others completely but ordered him to be sought for
with all diligence. When he saw him caught and brought
back to him in chains, he laughed and, having slackened
his anger, asked the reason for his flight and why he considered the life of the Romans better than that among them.
Zercon answered that his flight was a crime, but that he
had reason for his crime, namely that no wife had been
given to him. Bleda, being reduced to further laughter,
gave him from among the well-born women a wife who had
been one of the attendants on the queen but who, on account of some misdemeanor, was no longer in her service.
So he passed all his time in Bleda's company. After the
latter's death Attila gave Zercon as a gift to Aëtius, the
general of the Western Romans, who sent him back to Aspar.

P.fr.8 ctd.   Edeco had persuaded him to come to Attila
to recover through his influence the wife he had received
in marriage in the country of the barbarians, since he was
favored by Bleda. He had left her in Scythia when he was

sent as a gift from Attila to Aëtius. But he was disappointed in his hope, for Attila was angry because he had returned to his country. At the time of the banquet, he came forward, and by his appearance, his dress, his voice, and the words he confusedly uttered (for he mixed the tongue of the Huns and the Goths with that of the Latins), he softened everyone except Attila and caused unquenchable laughter to arise.

But Attila remained unmoved and his expression unaltered, nor in speech nor action did he reveal that he had any laughter in him, except when his youngest son (Ernach was the boy's name) came in and stood before him. He pinched the lad's cheeks and looked on him with serene eyes. I was surprised that he should take small account of his other sons but give his attention to this one, until a barbarian sitting beside me who knew the Latin language, warning me to repeat nothing of what he was about to tell me, said that the seers had prophesied to Attila that his race would fail but would be restored by this son. Since they were dragging out the night in the feast, we retired, not wishing to continue with the drinking any longer.

When the day came we went to Onegesius and said that we ought to be dismissed, so as not to waste time to no purpose. He said that Attila also desired to send us away. After a short time he took council with the picked men on Attila's resolutions and drew up the letters to be handed to the emperor—his secretaries and Rusticius being present. This man, sprung from the land of Upper Moesia, had been captured in war and, on account of his skill in speech, was employed in drawing up letters for the barbarian.

When he came out of the meeting we pleaded with him for the liberation of the wife of Syllus and her children, who had been sold into slavery in the capture of Ratiaria. He did not oppose their liberation, but wished to sell them for a great deal of money. We entreated him to pity them for their misfortune and consider their former happiness, and he went to Attila and dismissed the woman for 500 pieces of gold and sent the boys as a gift to the emperor.

In the meantime, Kreka, the wife of Attila, invited us to
dine at the house of Adamis, who had charge of her affairs.
We went with certain of the picked men of the nation
and met with a friendly welcome. They greeted us with
gracious words and food. With Scythian liberality each of
those present stood up and gave us a full cup and then,
having embraced and kissed the one who was drinking,
received it back. After the dinner we went to our tent and
turned in to sleep.

On the next day Attila again summoned us to a banquet,
and, as previously, we came before him and feasted. It turned
out that sitting beside him on the couch was not the eldest
of his sons, but Oebarsius, who was his uncle on his father's
side. Throughout the banquet he showed us kindness in his
speech and ordered us to tell the emperor to give Constantius, who had been sent to him from Aëtius as secretary, the wife he had promised him. Constantius had
come to the Emperor Theodosius with the ambassadors
from Attila and had said that he would arrange for a long
peace between the Romans and Huns if the emperor would
give him a wealthy wife. The emperor had agreed and had
said he would give him the daughter of Saturninus,[58] a man
honored for his wealth and family. But Athenaïs or Eudocia
(for she was called by both names) had destroyed Saturninus, and Zeno did not agree that his promise should be
fulfilled. He was a man of consular rank and had a great
force of Isaurians under his command with which he had
been appointed to guard Constantinople at the time of the
war. Then, when he was in command of the military forces
in the East, he carried the girl off from her castle and
betrothed her to a certain Rufus, one of his attendants.[59]
When this girl was taken from him, Constantius besought
the barbarian not to overlook the insult to him, but asked
that either this girl or another be given him as wife, bringing her dowry with her. On the occasion of the feast,
therefore, the barbarian ordered Maximinus to say to the
emperor that Constantius ought not to be cheated of the
expectations raised by the emperor, for it did not befit an

emperor to lie.[60] Attila gave these commands since Constantius promised to give him money if a woman of wealth
among the Romans was betrothed to him.

We retired from the banquet after nightfall, and three
days passed before we were dismissed, honored with suitable
gifts. Attila sent Berichus, a man of the elite and the ruler
of many villages in Scythia who had sat above us at the
banquet, on an embassy to the emperor for various reasons,
but especially that as an ambassador he might receive gifts
from the Romans.[61]

As we were on our journey and encamped at a certain
village, a Scythian was caught who had crossed from Roman
territory into the land of the barbarians in order to spy.
Attila ordered him to be impaled. On the next day, as we
were proceeding through other villages, two men who were
slaves of the Scythians were brought in, their hands bound
behind them, because they had destroyed their masters during the war. They crucified them, putting the heads of
both on two beams with horns.

As long as we were traversing Scythia Berichus accompanied us on the journey and seemed mild and friendly,
but when we crossed the Danube he adopted the attitude
of an enemy toward us, for some previous reason or other
learned from his servants. He took back the horse which he
had earlier presented to Maximinus—Attila had ordered all
the elite of his court to show friendship to Maximinus with
gifts, and each, including Berichus, had sent a horse to him.
Taking a few of these Maximinus sent back the rest, being
eager to show discretion in his moderation. Berichus took
back his horse, and did not continue to travel or eat with
us. It came to this pass though there was a pact of friendship for us in the land of the barbarians.

Thence we held our way through Philippopolis to Adrianopolis. Stopping there, we came into conversation with
Berichus and blamed him for his silence toward us, because
he was angry at people who had done him no wrong. When
we had paid court to him and had invited him to dinner
we set out again. We met Bigilas on the road, packing up

for his return to Scythia; we related Attila's answer to our
embassy and continued our return journey.

When we came to Constantinople we thought Berichus
had been turned from his anger, but he had not shed his
savage nature. He again withdrew in disagreement, charg-
ing Maximinus with having said—when he had crossed
into Scythia—that the generals Areobindus and Aspar [62]
had no influence with the emperor and that he held their
powers in contempt, since he had proof of their barbaric
inconstancy.[63]

When Bigilas had marched to where Attila happened to
be staying, the barbarians surrounded and held him, having
been prepared for this, and took the money which he was
bringing to Edeco. When they led him before Attila he
asked him why he was bringing so much gold. He answered
that it was for provisioning himself and those accompanying him, so that through lack of supplies or scarcity of horses
or baggage animals expended on the long journey he might
not stray from his zeal for the embassy. It was also supplied
to purchase fugitives, for many in Roman territory had
begged him to liberate their kinsmen.

Then Attila spoke: "No longer, you worthless beast (so
he named Bigilas), will you escape justice by deception. Nor
will there be any excuse sufficient for you to avoid punishment. Your supply of ready money is greater than necessary
for your provisioning, or for the horses and baggage animals
to be bought by you, or for the freeing of prisoners, a
thing, furthermore, which I forbade Maximinus to do when
he came to me." Saying this, he ordered the Roman's son
(for he had followed Bigilas for the first time into the land
of the barbarians) to be struck down with a sword unless
Bigilas should first say why and for what purpose he was
bringing the money.

When he beheld his son under threat of death he took
to tears and lamentations and called aloud on justice to turn
the sword against himself and not against a youth who had
done no wrong. With no hesitation he told of the plans
made by himself, Edeco, the eunuch, and the emperor, and

begged unceasingly to be put to death and his son set free.
When Attila knew from the things told by Edeco that he
was telling no lies, he ordered him to be put in chains and
vowed not to free him until having sent his son back he
should bring another fifty pounds of gold to him as his
ransom. The one was bound and the other departed for
Roman territory, and Attila sent Orestes and Eslas to Constantinople.

P.fr.9   It is worth including here a later summary
of this famous journey, since it adds one or two new details.
Having crossed rivers mighty indeed—namely the Tisia,
Tibisia, and Dricca—we came to the place where long ago
Vidigoia, the bravest of the Goths, perished by the treachery
of the Sarmatians. (This man, also called Vidicula and
Indigoia, was one of the subjects of early Gothic lays, and
judging by the mention of the Sarmatian-Gothic war he
probably died in 331–32 or 334, when the two tribes were
fighting during Constantine's reign. The term Sarmatians
here indicates a Teutonic people who later included the
Vandals, dwelling to the north of the Goths and usually
allied to Rome.[64]) Not far from there we reached the village
where King Attila was staying, a village, I say, like a very
large city, in which we found wooden walls made with
smooth planks, their jointure imitating solidity to such an
extent that the union of the boards could scarcely be seen
by close scrutiny. You might see there dining rooms extended to a liberal circumference and porticoes laid out in
all splendor. The area of the courtyard was bounded by a
huge circuit wall so that its very size might show it to be
the royal palace. This was the house of Attila, the king
who held the whole barbarian world, and he preferred this
dwelling to the cities captured by him.

P.fr.12   When Bigilas was caught plotting against
Attila, Attila seized him and the hundred pounds of gold [65]
sent from the eunuch Chrysaphius, and forthwith dispatched
Orestes and Eslas to Constantinople. He ordered Orestes
to hang around his neck the bag in which Bigilas had put
the gold to be given to Edeco, and so to come before the

emperor. Having shown it to him and to the eunuch he
was to ask whether they recognized it. Then Eslas was to
speak from memory saying, "Theodosius is the son of a
nobly born father; Attila also is of noble birth, having succeeded his father Mundiuch,[66] and he has preserved his
high descent. Theodosius, since he has undertaken the payment of tribute to him, has cast out his own nobility and
is his slave. Therefore, he does not act with justice toward
his superior—one whom fortune has shown to be his master
—because he has secretly made an attack like a miserable
houseslave. And Attila will not free of blame those who
have sinned against him unless Theodosius should hand over
the eunuch for punishment."

So the men came to Constantinople with these instruc-
tions. It happened that Chrysaphius was also sought by Zeno,
possibly because he was angry at the confiscation of Rufus'
wife's property, in which move he saw the hand of the
powerful chamberlain. Maximinus had, indeed, announced
that Attila had said the emperor ought to fulfill his promise
and give Constantius his wife, who should not have been
betrothed to another man contrary to the emperor's wish.
Attila argued that either the man who had dared to give
her away ought to be punished, or else the emperor's affairs
were in such a state that he did not even control his own
house servants. Against these, if he wished, Attila said he
was ready to make an alliance. Theodosius was vexed at
heart and confiscated the property of the girl.

P.fr.13   Being sought by both Attila and Zeno,
Chrysaphius was in sore distress. Since all men united in
bearing him good will and holding him in high regard,[67]
it seemed best to send Anatolius and Nomus on an embassy to Attila. Anatolius was the commander of the troops
about the emperor (master of soldiers praesentalis) [68] and
was the one who had fixed the terms of the peace with
him in early 448; Nomus had held the position of master
of offices [69] and was reckoned, with Anatolius, among the
patricians who surpass all others in rank. Nomus was sent
with Anatolius not only because of the greatness of his

fortune, but also because he was well disposed to Chrysaphius and would prevail over the barbarian by his liberality,
for when he was anxious to settle the matter at hand there
was no sparing of money on his part. These men were sent
to divert Attila from his anger, to persuade him to keep
the peace according to the contract, and to say that a wife
would be betrothed to Constantius in no way inferior to
the daughter of Saturninus either in birth or wealth. She
had not wished this marriage but had married another man
according to the law, since among the Romans it was not
right to betroth a woman to a man against her will. The
eunuch also sent gold to the barbarian so that he was
mollified and diverted from his wrath.

P.fr.14   Anatolius and Nomus and their train having
crossed the Danube advanced into Scythia as far as the
River Drecon, so-called. Attila, through respect for these
men, held a meeting with them there so that they might
not be afflicted by the journey. At first he argued arrogantly,
but overcome by the magnitude of the gifts and appeased
by soft words, he swore to keep the peace according to the
agreements, to retire from the land of the Romans bordering on the Danube, and even to refrain from pressing the
business of the fugitives before the emperor, if the Romans
would not again receive any others who escaped from him.
He dismissed Bigilas after receiving fifty pounds of gold,
which his son had brought to him when he came to Scythia
with the ambassadors. He also dismissed very many prisoners
without ransom since he was well-disposed toward Anatolius
and Nomus. He presented them with horses and skins of
wild animals, with which the Scythian kings adorn themselves, and sent them away with Constantius so that the
emperor might fulfill his promise to him. When the ambassadors had returned and had related everything said and
done, a woman was betrothed to Constantius. She had
been the wife of Armatius, the son of Plinthas,[70] who had
been a Roman general and had held consular rank. Armatius
had gone to Libya at the time of the fight against the
Ausorians,[71] and had attained success, but had become sick

and ended his life. The emperor persuaded the wife of
this man, distinguished for her birth and wealth, to marry
Constantius. When the differences with Attila were thus
resolved, Theodosius began to fear lest Zeno, who had not
been appeased in his demands for Chrysaphius, should seize
the sovereignty for himself.[72]

J.A.fr.199(1)   Theodosius the Younger was angry at Zeno,
for he was afraid that sometime he also might engage in a
revolution, and he thought that he was in danger of a
cowardly attack. This man profoundly disturbed him.
Though he readily forgave all other sins, he was bitter and
unalterable not only against those who plotted revolution
but even against those thought worthy of the imperial
power, and he proceeded to put them out of the way. In
addition to the persons mentioned he also overthrew Baudon
and Daniel for having engaged in a revolution. With the
same purpose, therefore, in his eagerness to punish Zeno he
held to his earlier plan of opposing him, and so Maximinus
crossed to Isauropolis and seized the districts there beforehand, and he sent a force by sea to the east to subdue Zeno.
He did not hesitate to do what seemed best to him, but
when a greater object of fear agitated him he delayed his
preparations.

(2)   In June 450 a messenger arrived at Constantinople from the West announcing that Attila was involved with the royal family at Rome, since Honoria, the
daughter of Placidia and sister of Valentinian III, the ruler
of the West, had summoned him to her help. Honoria,
though of the royal line and herself possessing the symbols
of authority, was caught going secretly to bed with a certain
Eugenius, who had the management of her affairs. He was
put to death for this crime, and she was deprived of her
royal position and betrothed to Herculanus, a man of consular rank[73] and of such good character that it was not
expected that he would aspire to royalty or revolution. She
brought her affairs to disastrous and terrible trouble by
sending Hyacinthus, a eunuch, to Attila so that for money
he might avenge her marriage. In addition to this she also

sent a ring pledging herself to the barbarian, who made ready
to go against the Western Empire. He wanted to capture
Aëtius first, for he thought he would not otherwise attain
his ends unless he put him out of the way. When Theodosius learned of these things, he sent to Valentinian to
surrender Honoria to Attila. Valentinian arrested Hyacinthus and examined the whole matter thoroughly; after in-
flicting many bodily tortures on him, he ordered that he be
beheaded. Valentinian granted his sister Honoria to his
mother as a boon, since she persistently asked for her. And
so Honoria was freed from her danger at this time.

Only a few weeks after this last craven surrender to the
Hun, on July 28, 450, Theodosius died [74] and was succeeded by the stronger Marcian. One of his first acts was
the execution of Chrysaphius, and almost at once Attila
was made aware that a stronger policy toward him would
be taken by Constantinople, a policy made practicable by
Attila's turning his attention toward the West.

P.fr.15   When it was announced to Attila that
Marcian had come to the Roman throne in the East after
the death of Theodosius, the Hun told him what had happened in the matter of Honoria. And he sent men to the
ruler of the Western Romans to argue that Honoria, whom
he had pledged to himself in marriage, should in no way be
ill-treated, for he would avenge her if she did not receive the
scepter of sovereignty. He sent also to the Eastern Romans
concerning the appointed tribute, but his ambassadors returned from both missions with nothing accomplished. The
Romans of the West answered that Honoria could not
come to him in marriage having been given to another
man and that the royal power did not belong to her, since
the control of the Roman Empire belonged to males not
to females. And the Romans of the East said that they
would not submit to paying the tribute which Theodosius
had arranged: to one who was peaceful they would give
gifts, but against one threatening war they would let loose
arms and men inferior in no way to his power.

Attila was of two minds and at a loss which he should

attack first, but finally it seemed better to him to enter on
the greater war and to march against the West, since his
fight there would be not only against the Italians but also
against the Goths and Franks—against the Italians so as
to seize Honoria along with her money, and against the
Goths in order to earn the gratitude of Gaiseric, the Vandal
king.

P.fr.16   Attila's excuse for his war against the Franks
was the death of their king [75] and the disagreement of his
children over the rule, the elder, who decided to bring
Attila in as his ally, and the younger, Aëtius. I saw this
boy when he was at Rome [76] on an embassy, a lad without
down on his cheeks as yet and with fair hair so long that it
poured down around his shoulders. Aëtius had made him his
adopted son, along with the emperor given him very many
gifts, and sent him away in friendship and alliance. For
these reasons Attila was making his expedition, and again
he sent certain men of his court to Italy that the Romans
might surrender Honoria. He said, she had been joined to
him in marriage, and as proof he dispatched the ring sent
by her in order that it might be shown. He also said that
Valentinian should withdraw from half of the empire in
his favor, since Honoria had received its control from her
father and had been deprived of it by the greed of her
brother. When the Western Romans held their former
opinion and paid no attention to his proposal, he devoted
himself eagerly to preparation for war and collected the
whole force of his fighting men.

Not without reason the ensuing campaign has been called
one of the decisive events of European history,[77] even
though its details and the exact location of the culminating
battle, like the defeat of Varus in the Teutoberg Forest,
cannot be surely determined. It must be borne in mind that
Attila posed a threat to much more than the Roman government; he was a danger to Roman civilization and to the
Christian religion. However independent politically the
various Germanic tribes who had settled in Gaul might
consider themselves at this time, most of them were not only

Christian but fully conscious of the merits of Roman material, spiritual, and cultural civilization. It is not surprising,
therefore, that quite apart from more personal reasons for
hostility to the Hun the various Germanic chieftains of
the West readily allied themselves with Rome and placed
themselves under the command of the great Roman general
Aëtius. Though this remarkable man had in the preceding
few years been leader of the Roman forces against the
Franks, Burgundians, and Visigoths he now found most of
these tribes and others too his eager if temporary allies.

Attila with his vast host of Mongols and subject Germans
invaded central Gaul, where his cavalry could operate
better and the chances for plunder were enormous. Some
towns fell to him, but his army was not trained or eager for
siege warfare and many withstood the passing storm, though
compelled to see their countryside ravaged. For weeks, while
mutual suspicions delayed the formation of the great Christian alliance, nothing could withstand these attacks, but in
the end Theodoric with his Visigoths joined Aëtius and
the other allies, and Attila could be opposed. The two
armies met, probably near Troyes, in the Mauriac or Ca-
talaunian Plain, whence Attila had retired from the siege
of Orleans. As Gibbon says, "The nations from the Volga
to the Atlantic were assembled."

In the engagement which followed, our sources [78] say
that 162,000 or 300,000 lives were lost—numbers which,
however exaggerated, indicate a very heavy slaughter on
both sides. At first the Roman center was pierced and the
full weight of the Huns directed against the Visigoths on
the right wing. Their king, the noble Theodoric, was fatally
wounded and his troops disorganized, when the battle was
restored by a flank charge of Visigothic cavalry under Thorismund. The Huns, forced to retire in disorder to the circle
of their wagons, were expecting annihilation as night fell,
but their enemies had also suffered severely. Furthermore,
Thorismund, the new Visigothic king, fearing for his throne,
retired and the great alliance broke up. Nevertheless, Attila
had been so severely mauled in the battle that after several

days delay in camp he retreated beyond the Rhine, cautiously followed by the remaining allies, and so "confessed the last victory which was achieved in the name of the Western empire." [79]

This defeat in Gaul seems in no way to have seriously weakened Attila's formidable power or his violent spirit. In the next year, 452, he attacked Italy itself and laid siege to the rich and strong city of Aquileia on the northern Adriatic coast. After three months of arduous siege, during which his army suffered severely from shortages of provisions, the town was finally captured and so completely sacked and destroyed that even its ruins could scarcely be discovered a hundred years later.[80] Other towns were treated similarly or surrendered, most notable among the latter being the great city of Milan. The court fled from Ravenna to Rome and Aëtius, without his allies, did not dare to join battle.

P.fr.17   Though Attila's mind had been bent on going to Rome his attendants, as the historian Priscus relates, deterred him, not because they were kindly disposed to the city—to which they were hostile—but holding up the example of Alaric, at one time king of the Visigoths. They were afraid for the good fortune of their own king, because Alaric had not long survived the capture of Rome, but had at once departed from humanity. While Attila's mind wavered in doubt between going or not and he was hesitating, turning the matter over in his mind, an embassy came from Rome seeking peace. Even Pope Leo himself came to him in the Ambuleian district of the Veneti where the Mincius River is crossed at the well-traveled ford. Attila soon laid aside his violent temper and returned whence he had come from beyond the Danube with the promise of peace. But he proclaimed above all, and with threats, that he would inflict heavier penalties on Italy unless Honoria, the sister of the Emperor Valentinian and daughter of Placidia Augusta, should be sent to him along with the share of the royal wealth due her. In his decision to retire, however, he was motivated much more by famine in Italy than by the entreaties or bribes of the embassy.[81]

P.fr.19   After his return to the north he engaged in
another abortive attack on Gaul and was again repulsed by
Thorismund, the Visigothic king, but at the same time he
was again threatening the Eastern Empire. *After Attila had
reduced Italy to slavery and had returned to his own territories, he notified those ruling the Eastern Romans that
he would wage war and enslave their land because the tribute
fixed by Theodosius had not been sent.*

P.fr.18   When Attila demanded the tribute arranged
by Theodosius and threatened war, the Romans answered
that they were sending ambassadors to him, and Apollonius
was dispatched. His brother had married the sister of Satur-
inus,[82] the girl whom Theodosius desired to marry to Constantius but whom Zeno had given in marriage to Rufus.
But the emperor had departed from among mankind, and
so Apollonius, who had been among the friends of Zeno
and had attained the rank of general, was sent on the
embassy to Attila.

He crossed the Danube, but did not gain admittance to
the barbarian, who was angry that the tribute had not been
brought, which he said had been arranged for him by nobler
and more kingly men. He did not receive the man sent as
ambassador and scorned the one who had sent him. Apollonius on this occasion is revealed to have performed the
deed of a brave man. When Attila did not suffer his embassy to approach nor wish to converse with him and when
he ordered him to send him whatever gifts he had brought
from the emperor and threatened his death if he did not
give them, he said, "It is not meet for the Scythians to
demand anything, either gifts or spoils, which they cannot
take." Thus, he made it clear that the gifts would be given
if they received him as an ambassador and would be as
spoils only if they killed him and carried them off. And
so he retired having accomplished nothing.

P.fr.23   But the great Hun had not long to live. In
*453, a few weeks or months later, at the time of his death,
as the historian Priscus reports, Attila took in marriage a
very beautiful girl, Ildico by name—after numerous other

wives according to the custom of his race. Worn out by excessive merriment at his wedding and sodden with sleep and wine he lay on his back. In this position a hemorrhage which ordinarily would have flowed from his nose, since it was hindered from its accustomed channels, poured down his throat in deadly passage and killed him. So drunkenness put a shameful end to a king famed in war.

(According to more romantic rumors current in Roman circles he was stabbed with a knife by a woman.[83]) But late on the following day the royal attendants, suspecting some misfortune, after loud shouts broke down the doors. They found Attila dead from a flow of blood, unwounded, and the girl with downcast look weeping beneath her veil. Then, as is the custom of that race, they cut off part of their hair and disfigured their faces horribly with deep wounds so that the distinguished warrior might be bewailed, not with feminine lamentations and tears, but with manly blood. Concerning this event, it happened miraculously to Marcian, emperor of the East, who was disturbed about his fierce enemy, that a divinity standing near him in his dreams showed the bow of Attila broken that very night, as if the Huns owed much to this weapon. Priscus, the historian, says he accepts this on true evidence. Attila was considered fearsome to such a degree by the empires that supernatural signs showed his death to rulers by way of a boon. We shall not omit to say a little about the many ways in which his corpse was honored by his race.[84]

In the middle of a plain in a silk tent his body was laid out and solemnly displayed to inspire awe. The most select horsemen of the whole Hunnish race rode around him where he had been placed, in the fashion of the circus races, uttering his funeral song as follows: "Chief of the Huns, King Attila, born of Mundiuch his father, lord of the mightiest races, who alone, with power unknown before his time, held the Scythian and German realms and even terrified both empires of the Roman world, captured their cities, and, placated by their prayers, took yearly tribute from them to save the rest from being plundered. When he had done all these things through the kindness of fortune, neither by an enemy's wound nor a friend's treachery but with his nation secure, amid his pleasures, and in happiness and without sense of pain he fell. Who then would consider this a death which no one thinks should be avenged?" After he had been mourned with such lamentations they celebrated a "Strava," as they call it, over his tomb with great revelry, coupling opposite extremes of feeling in turn among themselves. They expressed funereal grief mixed with joy and then secretly by night they buried the body in the ground. They bound his coffins the first with gold, the second with silver, and the third with the strength of iron, showing by such a device that these suited a most mighty king—iron, because with it he subdued nations, gold and silver because he received the honors of both empires. They added arms of enemies gained in battles, fittings costly in the gleam of their various precious stones and ornaments of every kind and sort whereby royal state is upheld. In order that human curiosity might be kept away from such great riches, they slaughtered those appointed to the task —a grim payment for their work—and so sudden death covered the buriers and the buried.

Thus, Attila became a legend to terrify the fancy and haunt the folklore of succeeding ages. In the *Niebelungenlied* Ildico became Kiemhilde and Attila Etzel. His genius alone had held the loose fabric of his empire together, and at his death dissensions almost at once tore it apart. The subject allies, especially the Gepids and Ostrogoths, broke free, and in the battle of Nedao in 454 the quarreling sons of Attila were decisively defeated, and Ellac, the elder, killed. This battle ended for all time the monolithic Hunnish empire, and though various Hunnish tribes are heard of periodically they no longer offered any serious threats to the Romans.

chapter **4**

The Vandals and the Collapse
of the West

VALENTINIAN III had reigned as boy and man for thirty
years before he was murdered in 455; in the succeeding
twenty-one years before the rule of Italy passed to a barbarian king no less than nine emperors were proclaimed in
Italy, though only four of them were officially recognized
in Constantinople. It was a period of almost incessant troubles fomented by barbarians within the government or outside it; and the tribe most threatening was the Vandal kingdom in Africa under its great leader Gaiseric. The annexa-
tion of Africa by a foreign tribe was more serious to Rome
and Italy than the loss of Gaul or Spain or Britain, since
from that area the city had for centuries drawn an important
part of its food supply. Furthermore, alone of the Germans
at this time in Western lands, the Vandals had taken to
the sea on wide-ranging and very damaging piratical raids.
After six centuries Rome again felt danger from Carthage
and this time Carthage was to be victorious.

J.A.fr.201(6)   After the murder of Valentinian by Maximus, Rome was in a state of confusion and disturbance, and
the military forces were divided among themselves, some
wishing Maximus to assume the royal power and some eager
for Maximian to seize the throne. The son of Domninus,
an Egyptian merchant who had made his fortune in Italy,
he had held the position of attendant on Aëtius. In addition,
Eudoxia, the wife of Valentinian, strongly favored Majorian.
But Maximus gained control of the palace by distributing
money and forced Eudoxia to marry him by threatening
her with death, thinking that his position would be more

secure. So Maximus came to the leadership of the Roman Empire.

When Gaiseric, the ruler of the Vandals, learned of the deaths of Aëtius and Valentinian he believed the time was ripe for attacking the Italian lands, since the peace had been dissolved by the death of those who had concluded it and since the man who had attained the throne did not have any considerable power. They say also that Eudoxia, Valentinian's wife, in distress at the destruction of her husband and the compulsion of her marriage, secretly summoned him. This is the more likely because Maximus had also married his son to Eudoxia's daughter Eudocia, a girl who was already betrothed to Gaiseric's son Huneric. It was natural that the empress should appeal to Gaiseric and that he should come. With a great fleet and with the nation under his command he crossed from Africa to Rome. When Maximus learnt that Gaiseric had taken up a position in Azestus (a place near Rome), he was terrified and fled on his horse. When the royal bodyguards and the especially trusted freemen of his company deserted him, those who saw him hurrying away reviled and abused him terribly. As he was leaving the city someone threw a stone and hit him on the temple, killing him. A mob tore his body apart and, carrying his limbs on a pole, raised a shout of praise. Thus did he come to the end of his life after three months of supreme power. Gaiseric entered Rome three days later on June 2, 455.

The sack was far more complete than that of Alaric forty-five years before, and when the Vandals at length returned to their ships they took with them all the movable public and private wealth of the city as well as Eudoxia, Eudocia (who soon married Huneric), Placidia, her other daughter who was the wife of Olybrius, and Gaudentius, the son of Aëtius.

The new emperor was Avitus, first proclaimed by his old friends the Visigoths, and soon officially accepted by the East. He was never popular in Rome because of his failure to deal adequately with the Vandals, who even extended their authority in Africa over areas left to Rome by the treaty of 442 and raided Sicily again.

P.fr.24   When Gaiseric had laid Rome waste, while Avitus was emperor, Marcian, the emperor of the Romans of the East, sent ambassadors to Gaiseric, the ruler of the Vandals, to order him to keep away from the land of the Italians and to send back the royal women whom he had led off as prisoners—the wife of Valentinian and her daughters. The ambassadors returned to the East having accomplished nothing, for Gaiseric paid no heed to those dispatched from Marcian nor did he set the women free. Marcian sent further letters to him and dispatched Bleda on an embassy. This man was a bishop of the Arian heresy of Gaiseric, for the Vandals were also of the Christian religion. When Bleda saw that he was not paying attention to his embassy, he adopted stronger words and said that it would not profit him, exalted by his present honor and glory, to stir up war against the emperor of the Romans of the East by not freeing the royal women. But neither the reasonableness of the preceding statements of the embassy nor fear of the threats forced Gaiseric to take moderate counsel. He sent Bleda away unsuccessful and again sent his forces over to Sicily and to the part of Italy near it and ravaged the whole land. Avitus, the emperor of the Western Romans, also sent an embassy to Gaiseric and reminded him of his former agreements, saying that if he did not keep them, he would make preparations, relying both on his own host and the aid of his allies. He also sent Ricimer to Sicily with an army. Of mixed Visigothic and Suevian blood, he had been appointed master of soldiers by Avitus and was for the next sixteen years the strong man in the West, making and unmaking emperors at will. He won a naval victory over the Vandals in 456 in Corsican waters and kept them from Sicily. At the same time Theodoric II of the Visigoths in the name of the emperor attacked and defeated the Sueves in Spain, and henceforth they were of little importance in the affairs of western Europe.

J.A.fr.202   Neither victory was enough to make Avitus
popular. When Avitus was emperor of Rome there was famine at the same time because of the Vandal control of the
sea. The mob put the blame on Avitus and compelled him
to dismiss from the city of the Romans his allies who had
entered with him from Gaul. He also sent away the Goths,
whom he had brought in for his own guard, after distributing
money to them derived from public works whose bronze
fittings he sold to the merchants, for there was no gold in
the royal treasuries. This removal of adornments from their
city roused the Romans to revolt.[1]

Majorian and Ricimer openly rebelled, for they no longer
feared the Goths, and Avitus, fearing internal disturbances
and the hostilities of the Vandals, left Rome on the road to
Gaul. Attacking him on the road, Majorian and Ricimer
compelled him to flee to a holy precinct at Placentia, renounce his office, and remove his royal raiment. Majorian
and his company did not withdraw from the blockade until
Avitus died of starvation. He had held the imperial office
for eight months. Some say he was strangled and others that
having been made a bishop he soon died.[2] This was the end
of Avitus' life and reign.

For five months the Eastern emperor was sole ruler of the
empire, but in April 457 Majorian was recognized as the Western ruler, and he in turn recognized the powerful Ricimer
by making him a patrician. His first task was to re-establish
his authority in Gaul, since the Visigoths had broken off
relations and the Burgundians had rebelled when Avitus,
their own candidate for the throne, had been removed.

P.fr.27   This was successfully accomplished in 458–
59. Majorian, the emperor of the Western Romans, when
the Goths in Gaul were his allies again, overcame the tribes
living in his dominion, some by arms and some by diplomacy.
His second task was to remove from Italy the continuing
danger from the Vandals. Some raiders were beaten in Cam-
pania, but Gaiseric obviously had to be beaten in Africa
really to solve the problem. Majorian even attempted to
cross over to Libya with a great force, after about three

*hundred ships had been collected by him in Spain. The
ruler of the Vandals first sent envoys to him to resolve the
disagreements by diplomacy.* When the emperor was not
persuaded, he laid waste all the land of the Moors to which
Majorian and his troops had to cross from Spain and
harassed the surrounding waters. Probably, Majorian had
chosen the route through Spain because he had heard of
some defection among the Moors subject to Gaiseric,[3] but,
in any case, this fleet like all other expeditions against the
Vandals accomplished nothing. It was destroyed by Gaiseric
while still in port, and the expedition was abandoned in
460.

J.A.fr.203   *Majorian broke off the war on disgraceful
terms and departed.* By this treaty Mauretania and Tripolitania, areas which Gaiseric had already seized, were formally
ceded to the Vandal kingdom.[4] This spelled the doom of
Majorian. *While he was still on the way to Italy, Ricimer
plotted his death. When Majorian had dismissed the allies
after their return and was going home to Rome with his
attendants, Ricimer and his party arrested him, stripped
him of his purple robe and diadem, beat him, and beheaded him.* Thus ended Majorian's life in August, 461.

Ricimer's next choice for emperor fell on Severus, who
remained his puppet and was not recognized in Constantinople. The Vandal raids and the increasingly independent
attitude of the Germans in Gaul remained Ricimer's chief
problems, complicated at times by other troubles. For instance, in 461 trouble arose with a general called Marcellinus. He had been a pupil of Aëtius and an adviser of
Majorian, but apparently continued for a while to serve
Ricimer as the commander of Scythian (Hunnish) forces
stationed in Sicily to oppose the Vandal raids. He was "a
reasonable and noble man, learned, courageous, and states-
manlike" and an adherent of the old pagan religion. After
leaving Sicily and setting up a virtually independent duke-
dom in Dalmatia with the backing of Leo, the Eastern
emperor, he was again called to Rome's help in 464,[5] and
in the great expedition of 468. In this last effort he re-

conquered Sardinia for Rome, but was shortly afterward
killed. His removal from the Sicilian command in 461
opened the way for renewed Vandal raids on that island
and on Italy in the ensuing years.[6]

P.fr.29   *Since Gaiseric no longer abided by the treaty
with Majorian, he sent a host of Vandals and Moors to
sack Italy and Sicily. Marcellinus had retired from the island
beforehand because Ricimer, to win over to himself his
force, prevailed by money on the Scythians—these were in
the majority—to leave Marcellinus and come over to him.
This caused Marcellinus to retire from Sicily, for he feared
the plot since he could not contend with the wealth of
Ricimer.*

*Then an embassy was sent to Gaiseric, first from Ricimer
to say that he ought not utterly to neglect the treaty, and
second from the ruler of the Romans in the East to induce
him to retire from Sicily and Italy and send back the royal
women. Gaiseric, though many embassies had been sent
to him at different times, did not dismiss the women until
he had betrothed the elder daughter of Valentinian (Eudocia
was her name) to his son Huneric. Then he sent back
Eudoxia, the daughter of Theodosius II, with Placidia, her
other daughter, whom Olybrius had married. Gaiseric did
not cease from ravaging the Italies and Sicily, but pillaged
them the more, desiring that, after Majorian, Olybrius
should be emperor of the Romans of the West by reason of
his kinship by marriage.*

*This year saw, therefore, a treaty made with the Eastern
Empire but not with the Western,[7] hence the raids on
Western lands continued in the next few years.*

P.fr.30   *The Western Romans came to fear Marcellinus, the "ruler of Dalmatia and the Epirote Illyrians"[8]
lest, he should bring war against them when his forces were
increased, since their affairs were variously disturbed by the
Vandals and by Aegidius. This man, sprung from the Gauls
of the West, had campaigned with Majorian, had very great
forces under his command, and was angry on account of the
killing of that emperor. He refused to recognize Severus*

and nominally as master of soldiers in Gaul led the Franks in their struggle to stop the expanding power of the Visigoths, but in fact he was an independent ruler with his capital at Soissons. He died in 464. Meanwhile, in 462–63 the disagreement with the Goths in Gaul deterred him from war against the Italians. Being at odds with them about the land bordering on theirs he fought valiantly and displayed in that war the noblest actions of a brave man.

For these reasons the Western Romans sent ambassadors to the Eastern ones to reconcile Marcellinus and the Vandals to them. Phylarchus was sent to Marcellinus and persuaded him not to take up arms against the Romans. But after he had crossed to the Vandals he returned having accomplished nothing, since Gaiseric would not refrain from going to war unless the wealth of Valentinian and Aëtius was given to him. He had, indeed, obtained a share in the wealth of Valentinian from the Eastern Romans under the pretext of Eudocia, who had married his son Huneric. Wherefore, each year he held this as an excuse for war, and straightway at the beginning of spring he made an expedition with his army to Sicily and the Italies. He did not lightly attack the cities in which there chanced to be a military force of Italians, but seized the places in which there did not happen to be a rival force and ravaged and enslaved them. The Italians could not bring assistance to all parts accessible to the Vandals, being overpowered by the number of the enemy and by not having a naval force. They asked for, but did not get this, from the Eastern rulers, on account of their treaty with Gaiseric. This indeed worked great harm on the Romans in the West because of the division of the empire. So with little opposition Gaiseric annexed Sardinia, Corsica, and the Balearic Islands.

J.A.fr.204   Furthermore, we again hear that Gaiseric ravaged the lands of Italy wanting Olybrius to be emperor of the West because of his relationship by marriage. He did not make the obvious pretext for the war the fact that Olybrius had not become the ruler of the West, but rather that he had not been given the property of Valentinian

and Aëtius. He demanded this partly in the name of
Eudocia, whom his son had married, and partly since Gaudentius, Aëtius' son, was living with him, after being captured at Rome in 455.

P.fr.31   At about this time a group of Alans attacked
the West and also disturbed the Danube frontier in the
East.[9] While the fugitive races were contending with the
Romans of the East an embassy came from the Italians
and said that they could not resist unless they reconciled
the Vandals to themselves. . . . Tatian, a man enrolled
in the order of patricians, was sent on an embassy to the
Vandals for the sake of the Italians.

P.fr.32   Tatian, having accomplished nothing, at
once returned from the Vandals, since his arguments were
not accepted by Gaiseric.[10]

In 465 Severus died, and a year and a half elapsed before his successor was chosen. In the meantime Gaiseric
raided the Peloponnesus and roused Leo to unite the whole
forces of both empires to meet the common threat. Anthemius was chosen in the East to be the Western Augustus,
and Ricimer's agreement to this was secured by having him
marry Anthemius' daughter. This arrangement, of course,
did not suit Gaiseric's plans for Olybrius.

P.fr.40   The Emperor Leo sent Phylarchus to Gaiseric to inform him about the sovereignty of Anthemius
and to threaten war unless he left Italy and Sicily. He returned and announced that Gaiseric was unwilling to submit to the commands of the emperor but was preparing
for war because the treaty of 462 had been broken by the
Eastern Romans.

P.fr.42   The next move was to organize the most
ambitious expedition yet assembled against the Vandals in
Africa. Therefore, in 468 the Emperor Leo equipped and
sent a great expedition against Gaiseric, the ruler of the
Africans, who, after the death of Marcian, had committed
many terrible depredations against the lands under the
sovereignty of the Romans, pillaging and enslaving many
men and demolishing their cities. Wherefore the emperor,

aroused to anger, collected from all the eastern sea eleven hundred ships,[11] filled them with soldiers and arms and sent them against Gaiseric. They say that he spent 1300 centenaria of gold on this expedition. As general and commander of the expedition he appointed Basiliscus, the brother of the Augusta Verina, a man who had already enjoyed the honor of a consulship and had often conquered the Scythians in Thrace. When no small force from the East had been collected, he engaged frequently in sea fights with Gaiseric and sent 340 of his ships to the bottom. Then he could have conquered Carthage itself. Later on, being enticed by Gaiseric with gifts and much money, he gave way and was willingly overcome, as Priscus the Thracian writes in his history.

C.fr.2   Regarding the expenditures on this expedition we have other conflicting reports. Joannes Lydas, a treasury official himself under Justinian, says that 65,000 pounds of gold and 700,000 pounds of silver were collected. And Candidus, the historian, says that Leo the Butcher, who ruled after Marcian, lavished limitless money on the expedition against the Vandals. For, as those who administered these things reveal, 47,000 pounds of gold were raised through the prefects, 17,000 pounds of gold through the count of the treasury, and 700,000 pounds of silver, apart from adequate amounts raised from the public funds and from the Emperor Anthemius.[12]

The incompetent Basiliscus, deliberately chosen by Aspar in the expectation that he would fail, be disgraced, and so removed as a rival to Aspar's own position at court was balanced by the very competent Marcellinus, the chief western general. The real defeat, after successes in Tripolitania, Sardinia, and on the sea around Sicily, came when Gaiseric sent fire ships among the Roman armada. It retreated to Sicily and there Marcellinus was murdered. The whole expedition, leaderless and ineffective, was disbanded; Basiliscus was disgraced, and the defeat of such a grandiose scheme caused a terrible shock to morale and near bankruptcy in the East.

In the meantime in Gaul, Euric, the ablest man since
Alaric, had seized the Visigothic crown and was bent on
acquiring all Gaul as his kingdom. Anthemius in spite of
the help of the Burgundians was unsuccessful in aiding the
Gallo-Romans, a fact which contributed to his unpopularity
in Italy as an easterner. But even so he was preferred to
Ricimer, and soon hostility grew between the Greek Augustus and the German general.

J.A.fr.207   About 470 Anthemius, the emperor of the
West, fell into a serious sickness by sorcery and punished
many men involved in this crime, especially Romanus,[13]
who had held the post of master and was enrolled among
the patricians, being a very close friend of Ricimer. Whereupon, Ricimer left Rome in anger and summoned 6000
men who were drawn up under his command for the war
against the Vandals. This war was forgotten, and while
Anthemius ruled in Rome Ricimer maintained himself in
armed opposition at Milan.

J.A.fr.209(1)   Ricimer was aroused to hostility against
Anthemius, the emperor of the West, and though married
to Alypia, his daughter, he waged a civil war inside the city
for five[14] months. Both those in authority and the mob
sided with Anthemius, but the host of his fellow barbarians
were with Ricimer. Odovacar was also with him, a man of the
race of those called Sciri, the son of Edeco and the brother
of Onoulph who was both the bodyguard and butcher of
Harmatius. Anthemius was living in the palace. Ricimer cut
off the districts by the Tiber and afflicted those inside with
hunger. Bilimer, a Gallic general, had come to Anthemius'
aid and been beaten. Hence, when there was an engagement
with them, a great part of Anthemius' faction fell. Ricimer
overwhelmed the rest by treachery and appointed Olybrius
emperor. Civil war had then afflicted Rome for five whole
months, until those around Anthemius gave in to the barbarians and left their ruler defenseless. He mingled with
those begging alms and went among the suppliants of the
martyr Chrysogonus. The church—now known as Santa
Maria in Trastavere—is still standing. There he was be-

headed in 472 by Gundobad, Ricimer's brother, after reigning five years, three months, and eighteen days.

(2)   Ricimer did not deem him worthy of royal burial and appointed Olybrius to the imperial authority, and thus Gaiseric's nominee at last came into power. When Olybrius became ruler over the Romans in this way, Ricimer departed life within thirty days, after vomiting much blood. Olybrius survived only thirteen days after this, and then, attacked by dropsy, he died, having been reckoned among the emperors for six months. Gundobad, his nephew, succeeded to Ricimer's position [15] and raised Glycerius, who had the office of count of domestics (comes domesticorum), to the throne. When Leo, the emperor of the East, learned of the election of Glycerius, he appointed Nepos as general of an expedition against him. He took Rome, captured Glycerius without a fight, and, having stripped him of royalty, appointed him bishop of Salona. He had enjoyed his rule for eight months. Nepos was immediately appointed emperor and ruled Rome.

While most of the information contained in this account is not found elsewhere the chronology is much at fault. The facts are as follows: Anthemius was killed on July 11, not July 29 according to Joannes, reckoning from the known date of his coronation on April 12, 467; Ricimer died forty days later on August 18; Olybrius died more than two months later on November 2, in the seventh month of his reign. He had been set up by Ricimer in Milan before the attack on Rome began. Glycerius was proclaimed on March 5, 473, and Nepos on June 24, 474, so that the former reigned much longer than eight months.[16]

With Ricimer's death, however willing he may have been to sacrifice the best interests of the empire in internal good government to his own ambitions, the last strong figure of the Western Roman Empire leaves the scene. The Visigoths under Euric were now fully independent of the empire and had conquered a large part of Gaul, and the Burgundians too, for so long Rome's staunchest allies, had grown in power and independence. In the north the Franks main-

tained their nominal allegiance to the empire, but Roman
civilization was declining and when Clovis became their
king in 481 he annexed the remaining parts of Gaul that
still owed allegiance to Constantinople, and within twenty
years his people had overthrown Euric's huge Visigothic
kingdom in Gaul and Spain. The Franks were converted
to the Catholic faith, and this fact spelling the end of
Arian dominance in the West removed what was at this
period the most important distinction felt between Roman
and barbarian.

M.fr.3   In Constantinople early in 474 Zeno became emperor and early in his reign because he was too
unwarlike a man and because great confusion reigned on
all sides, he resolved to send an embassy to the Vandal at
Carthage. He chose Severus, a senator, as ambassador, a
man considered to excel in moderation and in desire for
justice. He sent him out after he had made him a patrician
in order that, in keeping with the importance of his embassy, he might make a more majestic impression. So he
set sail, but the Vandal, learning that an embassy would
be coming, anticipated it by making a sea raid and capturing
Nicopolis. The ambassador Severus crossed from Sicily and
reached Carthage. He blamed the Vandal severely for sail-
ing away, but the latter said he had acted as an enemy.
Now, however, he said, since Severus had come as an ambassador, he would accept favorably his representations concerning peace. He marveled at Severus' moderation and his
way of life and, in admiration of his words, was prepared to
do everything he proposed, continually putting his upright-
ness to the test. Severus appeared particularly honorable
to him in that when the barbarian gave him money and
bestowed gifts on him suited to an ambassador he refused
everything, saying that in place of these things the reward
most worth while for a man who was an ambassador was
the redemption of prisoners. Commending the man for
this sentiment the king said, "Whatever prisoners I, along
with my sons, have obtained in the distribution of them,
I hand over freely to you. As for the rest who have been

portioned out, you are at liberty to buy them back from each owner if you so desire, but even I would be unable to compel their captors to do this against their will." Thereupon, Severus freed without payment those whom the Vandal personally owned, and, selling his clothing and all his equipment by public herald, with whatever money he had he bought back such prisoners as he could. This truce made by Severus also induced a temporary cessation of persecution of the orthodox Christians in Africa by the Arian Vandals.[17] It lasted for two generations until the final and successful attack on Africa made by Justinian, but its long life was very largely due not so much to Severus' character as to the death of Gaiseric in 477 and a succession of far inferior rulers to his throne.

M.fr.13   For instance in 478 ambassadors came to Byzantium from Carthage, under the leadership of Alexander, the guardian of Olybrius' wife. He formerly had been sent there by Zeno with the agreement of Placidia herself. The ambassadors said that Honoric (or Huneric) had honestly set himself up as a friend of the emperor, and so loved all things Roman that he was renouncing everything which he had formerly claimed for public revenues and also the other moneys which Leo had earlier seized from his wife, and he was also returning whatever had been seized from the merchants in Carthage during the war just finished [18] and whatsoever else his father had formerly had litigation about with the Romans. He asked for a secure peace and to be in no way suspected by the Romans of not honestly concluding the treaty and whatever else he agreed to. He gave thanks that the emperor had honored the wife of Olybrius, and said he was ready to do for the emperor anything he wished. This was the plausible pretext for his words, when, in truth, the Vandals feared the very suspicion of war, since after the death of Gaiseric they had fallen into complete softness, having neither the same strength for action nor the same military forces which he had kept ready for every action so as always to act more quickly than any opponent could expect. Zeno received

*the envoys in friendly fashion and extended the respect
due them. When he had honored them with fitting gifts
and had made Alexander a comes rerum privatarum, he
dismissed them.* Either this was an honorary title here or
Alexander stayed on in Constantinople to exercise his new
office.[19]

In the West after Ricimer's death, as we have seen,
Glycerius was nominated. His only important act was to
divert the Ostrogoths under Vidimir from Italy against
Gaul. Since he was not recognized in the East, Leo in
473 selected as emperor Julius Nepos, a nephew of Marcellinus and related to Leo's family. Glycerius was deposed
without trouble, and the post of master of soldiers, occupied for a few years by Gundobad, was conferred on
Orestes, the man already seen as Attila's secretary. Orestes
determined to set his own son on the Western throne, and
in August 475 drove Nepos out of the peninsula to Dalmatia,
where he continued to live as the only constitutional
Western emperor until his death in 480. Since Orestes had
married the daughter of Count Romulus, his son was given
the name of Romulus Augustulus and though a mere youth
ruled, under his father's authority and control, for twelve
months. He was the last Roman emperor of the West.
"These names, Julius, Augustulus, Romulus, in the pages
of the chroniclers, meet us like ghosts re-arisen from past
days of Roman history." [20]

The Western armies commanded by Ricimer and his
successors were composed almost wholly of Heruls, Rugi,
and Sciri—East German tribes. These men now began to
demand permanent land in Italy, such as the Visigoths had
been granted in Gaul, and when Orestes refused to allow
the soil of Italy to be thus violated they found a leader
in Odovacar and mutinied. This man whose name is variously spelled Odoachus and Odoacer by the Greeks was,
as already seen, a Scirian, though Jordanes and others call
him a Goth, a Rugian, a king of the Turcilingi, and a king
of the Heruls. His father was Edeco, quite probably the
same man we have noticed at Attila's court, though there

he is described as a "Hun by birth." This may only mean that as a German in the service of Attila he was accepted as a Hun.[21]

Odovacar had been born in 433. In 476 the German soldiers in Italy chose him as their leader against Orestes, who was easily captured and put to death. The young Augustulus was deposed but spared. Though he became king of his mixed host he wanted to legitimize his position in Italy by receiving official recognition from the Eastern Empire as a successor to Ricimer but without Ricimer's puppet emperors. When Zeno, who had temporarily been displaced by the usurper Basiliscus, recovered his throne Odovacar induced Augustulus to write to him to arrange this new scheme of things. Thus was the color, if not the reality, of legitimacy preserved for a time, even though, of course, Augustulus was himself considered a usurper in the East. Nepos was the only legitimate ruler of the West in 477.

M.fr.10   When Augustus (Augustulus), the son of Orestes, heard that Zeno had again gained the kingship of the East, having driven Basiliscus out, he caused the senate to send an embassy to tell Zeno that they had no need of a separate empire but that a single common emperor would be sufficient for both territories, and, moreover, that Odovacar had been chosen by them as a suitable man to safeguard their affairs, since he had political understanding along with military skill; they asked Zeno to award Odovacar the patrician honor and grant him the government of the Italies. The men from the senate in Rome reached Byzantium carrying these messages. They also brought the decorations and insignia of imperial authority as proof of their sincerity in proposing a single authority at Constantinople over all the empire. On the same day messengers from Nepos also came to congratulate Zeno on the recent events concerning his restoration, and at the same time to ask him zealously to help Nepos, a man who had suffered equal misfortunes, in the recovery of his empire. They asked that he grant money and an army for this purpose and that he co-operate in his restoration in any other ways that might be necessary. Nepos had sent the men to say these things. Zeno gave the following answer to these arrivals and to the men from the senate: the Western Romans had received two men from the Eastern Empire and had driven out one, Nepos, and killed the other, Anthemius. Now, he said, they knew what ought to be done. While their emperor was still alive, they should hold no other thought than to receive him back on his return. To the barbarians he replied that it would be well if Odovacar were to receive the patrician rank from the Emperor Nepos and that he himself would grant it unless Nepos granted it first. He commended him in that he had displayed this initial instance of guarding good order, suitable to the Romans, and trusted for this reason that he would quickly receive back the emperor who had given him his position of honor, if he truly wished to act with justice. He sent a royal epistle about what he desired to Odovacar and in this letter named him a patrician, thus showing typical vacillation or duplicity. Zeno gave this help to Nepos, pitying his sufferings because of his own, and holding to the principle that the common lot of fortune is to grieve with the unfortunate. At the same time Verina also joined in urging this, giving a helping hand to the wife of Nepos, her relation. Odovacar naturally refused the claims of Nepos, as Zeno obviously knew he would.

C.fr.1   Zeno also favored Odovacar in another case. After the overthrow of Nepos, emperor of Rome, and the expulsion of Augustulus, Odovacar became master of Italy and of Rome itself. When the western Galatians rebelled against him, they and Odovacar both sent embassies to Zeno, but Zeno inclined rather toward Odovacar.

The change in the form of government in the West of 476 was only the application to Italy for the first time of principles which had obtained elsewhere throughout most of this century. Land in Italy was formally granted to barbarian tribesmen exactly as land had been granted to the Visigoths in Gaul and to the Vandals in Africa. Italy did not cease to be Roman simply because there was no resident

Roman emperor, but just as the Visigoths and Vandals had bit by bit established complete independence for themselves so also in time the German rulers in Italy would do likewise. Even before, though the old offices like the consulship and prefectures continued for local affairs, the central authority was weak, and, for example, very little revenue can have been sent to Constantinople from the West. The continuance of the single Roman Empire was more a figment of pious hope, of conservative legalism and of tradition, than a constitutional and governmental reality.

With Julius Nepos' death in 480 the ambiguous relationship of the independent viceroy in Italy with the emperor at Constantinople was resolved, and for six years there was a shaky peace. When Odovacar corresponded with the rebel Illus in Asia, however, even though he sent no help, Zeno became suspicious and openly hostile. Odovacar was diverted from an attack on Illyria by the Rugi whom Zeno stirred up to invade Italy. Then, two years later in 488 he rid himself at once of his Italian viceroy and the troublesome Theodoric, king of the Ostrogoths, by dispatching the latter to supersede the former. But this is part of the story of the Ostrogoths.

chapter 5

The East, 450–91

THEODOSIUS II left no male heir, but the succession was quietly accomplished by the marriage of Pulcheria, his sister, to Marcian, a distinguished general, who thereupon assumed the purple. Since Attila was by this time engaged in his western ventures it was safe for Marcian to discontinue the annual subsidies to the Huns, for which he has probably been overpraised. The saving of money, however, enabled him to reduce taxes and deal easily with such slight disorders as came up on the Syrian and Egyptian frontiers. On his death in 457 no obvious successor was in sight and, as in other such crises, the real choice lay with the army. Aspar was the undisputed commander of the army by now and, like Ricimer in the West at the same period, he determined to set up his own candidate and so perpetuate his power. He chose Leo, one of his subordinate officers.[1]

M.fr.2a   We have several nearly contemporary characterizations of this man. *Leo, the emperor of the Romans, the Butcher, seemed to be the luckiest of all emperors up to his time—awesome to all who lived under his authority as well as to such of the barbarians as his reputation reached. Yet he left this opinion about himself among many men.* "I," says Malchus, "*do not consider it happiness if anyone seizes the goods of his subjects and continually pays informers to this end, acts as accuser when he can find no other man, and collects gold from every part of the land for himself alone. Leo rendered cities empty of the wealth which they formerly had, so that he could no longer easily collect the tribute which they had been accustomed to pay.*" In a word, Malchus strongly affirms that he was the repository of every evil. He also once exiled the grammarian, Hyper-

echius. And yet there was another side to his nature perhaps seen by another observer. *When he said that a sum of money should be given to the philosopher Eulogius, and when one of the eunuchs said that this money ought to be paid to the soldiers, he replied, "May it happen in my time that the pay of the soldiers is handed over to teachers."*

C.fr.1   The historian Candidus begins his history from the proclamation of Leo, who was from Dacia in Illyria. *He had commanded a military force and was commander of the troops in Selymbria.* These Selymbrian cohorts guarded the city gate of that name and the district just west of Constantinople with headquarters in Selymbria on the Propontus east of Heraclea. *He was appointed to the imperial office by the efforts of Aspar, an Alan by race, who had engaged in military affairs from young manhood and who, from three marriages, had begotten Ardaburius, Patricius, Ermenaric, and two daughters.* . . .

In his first book Candidus tells of the primacy of Aspar and his sons, the proclamation of Leo by Aspar, the fire which swept the city in 465, and what was done by Aspar at this time for the common advantage, also about Tatian and Vivianus, the one a trusted councilor of Leo, prefect of Constantinople under him, and consul in 466, who had earlier presided at the council of Calchedon, and the other a rival of Tatian and consul in 463, and how Aspar and the emperor differed concerning them, and what they declared plainly to one another. Aspar at one time is said to have grabbed the emperor's cloak and to have declared, "Emperor, it is not right that the man wearing this cloak should lie." Leo answered, "Nor is it right that he should be restrained and driven like a slave." [1a] Candidus also tells how the emperor for this reason befriended the Isaurian people in the person of Tarasicodissa, the son of Rusumbladeotus,[2] whom he made his son-in-law (having changed his name to Zeno) when he lost his former wife by a natural death; how Ardaburius prepared to oppose the emperor and make the Isaurians his partisans, but Martin, an attendant of Ardaburius, told Tarasicodissa what was being brewed by Ardaburius against the emperor; and how, for this reason, their mutual suspicion having grown stronger, the Emperor Leo in 471 destroyed Aspar and his children, Ardaburius, and the Caesar Patricius. For this act he was nicknamed "Butcher," but the Caesar, though wounded, was unexpectedly saved and lived,[3] and Ermenaric, the other son, not being present with his father,[4] escaped murder at this time. The Emperor Leo made Tarasicodissa the husband of his daughter Ariadne about 466, changed his name to Zeno, and appointed him general of the East in 469. Candidus relates the fortunes and misfortunes of Basiliscus in Africa in 468, how Leo desired and plotted to name Zeno, his son-in-law, emperor but was unable to do so since his subjects would not have him, and how, before his death, he crowned his grandson emperor—the son of Zeno and Ariadne.

This is a good summary of the reign and points to the one internal problem that persisted all through these years of Leo and Zeno—whether the German supremacy at the Western court was to be duplicated in the East or not. The choice was not easy, since the alternative to Germanic domination by men like Aspar, was domination by the almost equally uncivilized natives of Isauria in wild south-central Asia Minor; but at any rate the East, unlike the West, did have a feasible alternative and Leo finally availed himself of it.

For many years Aspar and his family remained supreme at the court and the German faction with them. His son married the emperor's daughter and was created Caesar, and his other sons had almost equally high honors and titles, but Zeno moved slowly, first, to balance their power by that of the Isaurians and, finally in 471, to overthrow it altogether. That story will be told in detail later. In the meantime, the empire after the respite under Marcian and after Attila's death was again being threatened from the north.

P.fr.30   In 462–63 a group of Hunnish tribes—fragments no doubt of Attila's great empire—the Saraguri,

Orogi, and Onoguri [5] sent ambassadors to the Eastern Romans. These were races who had been expelled from their own abodes when the Sabiri came against them in battle. The latter, in turn, had been driven out by the Avars, men who had been made nomads by the races inhabiting the Ocean coast. (The latter left this country on account of the mist which came from the inroads of the sea and on account of the great number of griffins which appeared. The story was that they would not depart before they had made the race of men their food. Wherefore, driven out by these terrible creatures, the Avars fell on their neighbors, and, since the attackers were more powerful, those who could not resist them migrated.[6]) The Saraguri, driven to search for land, came against the Akatirian Huns and, after many battles, prevailed over them and approached the Romans to obtain their friendship. The emperor and his councilors indulged them, gave them gifts, and dismissed them.

P.fr.36   Again, in the year 467 an embassy came to the Emperor Leo from the sons of Attila to remove the causes of the past disagreements, to conclude a formal peace treaty, and, by going to the same place on the Danube as the Romans, according to the ancient custom, to establish a market place [7] and there exchange whatever they happened to need. Their embassy retired without any success whatever in these matters, for it did not seem right to share the Roman commerce with the ruler of the Huns, since he had done great harm to the empire. The sons of Attila, when they received the answer to their embassy disputed among themselves. Dengizich (or Dintzic), when the embassy returned unsuccessful, wished to go to war with the Romans, but Ernach was opposed to this plan because wars in his country were engaging his attention.

P.fr.38   Dengizich had his way, threatened war against the Romans, and stayed close to the bank of the Danube. When Anagastes the son of Ornigiscles (also called Arnegisclus and Anegisclus) learned this—he had the guardianship of the part of the river in Thrace—he sent out men from his retinue and asked why they were preparing for a fight. Dengizich, scorning Anagastes utterly, dismissed the men without their having accomplished anything and sent men to the emperor to announce that if he did not give land and money to him and the army following him he would begin war. When these ambassadors reached the palace and reported the commands given them, the emperor answered that he would readily do all those things if they would be obedient to him, for he rejoiced in men who came into alliance with him from his enemies. Constantinople's willingness to come to terms, contradicting her earlier attitude, may be accounted for by the necessity of protecting her northern frontiers in preparation for the approaching African expedition.

P.fr.39   In connection with this trouble with the Hunnish tribes, the Ostrogoths also seem to have staged one of their periodic revolts and joined the Huns. Anagastes, Basiliscus, the emperor's brother-in-law, Ostryes, the master of soldiers praesentalis,[8] and other Roman generals penned up and blockaded the Goths in a hollow place. The Scythians, hard pressed by starvation and lack of necessities, made an embassy to the Romans. They said they were surrendering themselves and that as long as they inhabited the land they would obey the Romans in every way. When the Romans answered that they would take their embassy to the emperor, the barbarians said that they wished to arrange a treaty on account of the famine and could not possibly make a long armistice. The commanders of the Roman formations took counsel and promised to supply food until the decision of the emperor came, if, in turn, they would split themselves into just as many groups as the Roman force was divided into. Caring for them would thus be easy, since the generals would attend to them in separate groups and not altogether, and, as a matter of honor, would be responsible for their provisioning.

The Scythians accepted the terms brought by their ambassadors and drew themselves up in as many sections as the Romans were in. Chelchal, a man of Hunnish race and lieutenant general of those in charge of Aspar's forces, came to the barbarian section allotted to them. He summoned the pick of the Goths, who were more numerous than the others, and began the following speech. The emperor would give land, he said, not for their own enjoyment but to the Huns among them. For these men are heedless of cultivation, and, like wolves, attack and plunder the provisions of the Goths, so that they, continuing in the position of servants, suffer hardships in order to provision the Huns, although the Gothic race has remained for all time without a treaty with them and has been pledged by its ancestors to escape from the alliance with the Huns. Thus, the Goths think lightly of their ancestral oaths as well as of the loss of their own property. But he, Chelchal, although he took pride in his Hunnish race, by saying these things to them from a desire for justice, gave them advice about what must be done.

The Goths were greatly disturbed at this and, thinking that Chelchal had said these things with good-will toward them, they attacked the Huns in their midst and slew them. Then, as if at a signal, a mighty battle rose between the races. When Aspar learned this, he and the commanders of the other camps drew up their troops and killed the barbarians they came upon.

When the Scythians perceived the intent of the trick and the treachery, they gathered together and came to blows with the Romans. Aspar's men anticipated them and killed the section allotted to them; but the fight was not without danger for the other generals, since the barbarians fought stoutly. Those who survived broke through the Roman formations and escaped the siege.

J.A.fr.205   About the same time, in the time of the emperors Anthemius and Leo, Oulibus was slain by Anagastes in Thrace, both being men of Scythian race and ready for revolt. The name Oulibus is almost certainly a corruption and quite likely indicates Dengizich. "Both" refers to Oulibus and someone else (not Anagastes and Oulibus), possibly Ernach, Dengizich's brother.

The year 467 ended any serious threat from the Huns
for a long time, but the next year and its disastrously ex-
pensive and futile expedition against Gaiseric raised new
troubles for the emperor. His brother-in-law was in disgrace and Aspar, consequently, at the height of his power.
It was time for Leo to bring the Isaurians and his son-in-law
Zeno, their leader, more to the fore.

J.A.fr.206(1)   He appointed Zeno consul in 469, and about
*the same time the Isaurians made their presence felt in
another region. The Isaurians engaged in plunder and committed murders on the island of Rhodes, but the soldiers
there overwhelmed them. They escaped to their ships and
came to Constantinople, to Zeno, the son-in-law of the
emperor. By disturbing those who were holding a market
they roused the mob to throwing stones. There was a risk
of civil war, but night fell and broke up the fighting.*

(2)   *At this time Anagastes, the commander of
the Thracian forces, rebelled and overwhelmed the fortresses
of the Romans. The reasons for his defection were reported
to be that, while Jordanes, the son of Joannes the Vandal
whom Anegisclus, the father of Anagastes, had killed, was
raised to the consular honor in 470, Anagastes had not
received the election due him, and also that because he
suffered from epilepsy, he feared that sometime he would be
disgraced in the senate by his affliction, if it should attack
him there. Others say that he engaged in the revolt for
money. There being great suspicion about him, men were
finally sent from the royal palace who persuaded him to
cease from his attempt. He revealed that Ardaburius, the
son of Aspar, was the cause of his revolt and sent this man's
letters to the emperor.*

Before this Zeno, the son-in-law of the emperor, having
*the consular office in 469 and also being master of soldiers
for the East—an office he held till 471 when Jordanes replaced him—sent men to remove Indacus from the so-called
hill of Papirius or Cherris. First Leo made this hill his lair,
and then Papirius and his son Indacus, harassing all those
dwelling nearby and murdering the passers-by. Indacus re-*

appears later during Illus' rebellion in 484. "He flourished
in the time of Leo, the emperor after Marcian. He was
outstanding for daring and was very skilled in the use of
his feet, better than the best in bravery, and distinguished
for swiftness of foot. He was speedier than Euchidus, As-
sapus, Chrysomuzus, and Echion, and any other who contended with him in foot racing. He appeared and vanished
like a flash of lightning, coming from his mountain fast-
nessess not like a runner, but like a flyer. A journey a man
with a change of horses was unable to accomplish in one
day, he was able to run without trouble on his own feet.
In one day he went from the fort of Cherris to Antioch
and on the next he reached the above-mentioned fortress
again. From here with no need of rest he came to Neapolis
in Isauria in one day." [9]

Besides attacking this man help was sent against the
Zani (or Tzani) of northeastern Asia Minor, who were
ravaging the districts around Trapezus. Then also raising
war were the Goths, dwelling in western Galatia and of old
named after Alaric (under Euric they were expanding their
empire), and likewise the barbaric horde in Pannonia, the
Ostrogoths, formerly under Valamir and after his death
under Theudomir, his brother.

J.A.fr.208   An interesting report of about this date
dramatically reveals the mysterious seclusion in which
Byzantine emperors lived, modern parallels to which can
only be found in Soviet Russia and, till recently, Japan.
Under the Emperor Leo, Jordanes, the general of the East
and consul, came into the greatest danger, as also did
Miscael (or Michael) and Cosmas, who were chamberlains
of the palace, because they had neglected to guard the
palace while the emperor was living outside, and had shown
the interior to Jordanes who wished to investigate it. These
chamberlains, simply "bedchamber attendants" in the Greek
as usual, might have occupied any of several high posts
or have been mere guards of the silentiarii under the over-
all command of the praepositus. They are otherwise unknown.

When the emperor discovered Ardaburius plotting against him—to return to the struggle of Germans and Isaurians— he recalled Zeno from his eastern command, and without warning Aspar and his family were treacherously attacked and murdered. The German danger was thus abruptly removed from the court, but the inauguration of Isaurian domination was to bring its own long-drawn-out troubles. Of course, German troops were still used in the armies, and in 473 Ostryes was even made master of soldiers in praesenti though he had been a close associate of Aspar and had briefly rebelled after his death. Then too, as we shall see later, the two Ostrogothic leaders called Theodoric were frequently not only in Roman service but called to high military offices. At court, however, the German influence was in eclipse. Leo died in 474 leaving his grandson, Leo II, a boy of six, to succeed him. The boy's father, Zeno, was not long in promoting himself from regent to Augustus. When his son died in the same year his father was sole emperor of the East.

M.fr.9   Zeno, the Roman emperor, was not by nature as cruel as Leo had been, nor was there inherent in him the inexorable passion such as was constant with Leo. But in many matters he showed ambition for honor, and what he did, he did for the sake of glory and to be marveled at, for show rather than truth. Indeed, neither was he skilled in government nor did he have the brains by which it is possible for empires to be ruled firmly. He was not given to such love of money and profit as was Leo, nor to forge false charges against wealthy men, but, on the other hand, he was not wholly above that business. The Romans would have had a happy reign if Sebastian, who then held almost equal power, had not controlled him in any way he wanted to, buying and selling all government business as if in a market place, and allowing nothing to be done in the emperor's palace without payment. Moreover, he sold all public offices, taking the payments partly for his private purse and partly for the emperor's. If another came and gave some additional trifle he was preferred. Of all the business in the palace there was nothing which he did not buy and sell. If Zeno freely

offered an office to someone of his retinue, Sebastian, like a
huckster, often took this office from him for a small price
and gave it to another for a greater price, keeping the theft
hidden from Zeno.

Sebastian was praetorian prefect in 477, 480, and 484
and probably most of the intervening years, but not in
478 when a certain Epinicus was in that office. "Placing no
limits to his money-grubbing, and making a trade of all the
cities and races, he filled the provinces with his outrageous
commands. The ranks of the rulers and the town councils
outside did not stand for this and fled, abandoning the
collection of taxes. Being hard pressed by this man's greed
they sat as suppliants in the common churches, witnesses
to the thefts of the fellow. He was everyone's enemy, giving
no one his due honor. They deprived him of his office
dishonorably and chose instead Laurentius (an error for
Sebastian), a man from the ranks of the rhetors in the
great forum and pre-eminent in this position. Epinicus
did not allow anyone he associated with to ravage or plunder,
in order that he might make more profit." [10]

M.fr.12   One example of official corruption has come
down to us. The governor of Egypt used to pay out scarcely
fifty pounds of gold for his commission, but Zeno, as though
the country had become richer than formerly, called for
almost five hundred pounds.

M.fr.9   Zeno's son by a former wife, also called
Zeno, is given an equally bad reputation. Zeno, the Roman
emperor, wishing to leave his own son Zeno as his successor, caused him to progress through the offices of state,
though he was still a mere youngster, and ordered him to
exercise in order to increase his stature. But the royal servants, who were in charge of lavishing the public funds,
caused the youth to debauch himself in luxurious fashion,
and, as panders, they procured young friends for him and
taught him in foreign ways to rage with a lust for males.
Becoming used to a way of life which found nobility in
voluptuousness and pride and displaying in his face the
smouldering arrogance due to his eager expectation of the

kingship, he began to strut, to raise his neck high, and, in short, to treat everyone as his mere servants. But the Ruler of all men, observing that his wickedness was derived from his nature as well as from his training, ordained that he suffer a discharge from his stomach and, having lain unconscious and befouled in his bed for many days, he departed life while still a youth. Since Zeno in exile promised the succession to the son of Harmatius, the boy Zeno must have died before 475.

M.fr.6   A rather more attractive official is singled out as unique in this reign, although he left his position early. Erythrius was a commander under Zeno, being praetorian prefect in 473-74. When he perceived that the treasury was not full and could bring himself neither to impose a greater burden on the taxpayers than that decreed, nor—because he was a humane man—to render anyone impoverished because of his debts, he left this office with Zeno's permission. It caused grief in the city when he laid down his office; for, alone of those in office in the state at that time, he had acted for the good of all, giving prompt help to those who requested it, and not continually holding to the intention of punishing a person who had formerly offended. The treasury, then, had been reduced to utter penury, so that there was nothing left in it. What Leo had left in the public treasury at his death had all quickly been exhausted by Zeno. He gave freely and carelessly to his friends and was not careful to learn whether, by chance, anyone was stealing the money.

C.fr.1   The historian Candidus summarizes Zeno's reign and tells how, after the death of Leo, his son, Leo, crowned his father, Zeno, with the senate's approval. He narrates in detail the genealogy of the Isaurians, with much effort and argument to prove that they are the descendants of Esau. He tells how Zeno, outwitted by Verina, fled with his wife and mother from the city and from the imperial office in 475, and how Verina, in the hope of marrying Patricius, the master of offices, and of his becoming emperor, put her son-in-law to flight by guile, and how she was dis-

appointed in her hopes since the men in power named
Basiliscus, her brother, emperor. He also tells of the terrible
slaughter of the Isaurians in Constantinople, and how—
after Nepos, the emperor of Rome—Augustulus was made
emperor of Rome by his father, Orestes. This is the first
book.

The second book tells how the master of offices, Patricius,
the lover of Verina, perished when Basiliscus grew angry
at him, and how Verina, hating her brother for this reason,
by supplying money worked with Zeno to restore his imperial office. She suffered extremely at the hands of her
brother, and if Harmatius [11] had not spirited her away from
the church of Hagia Sophia she would speedily have been
put to death. He tells how Harmatius, becoming the seducer
of the wife of Basiliscus, was raised to the greatest heights
of power, how later, entrusted with the war against Zeno,
he deserted to him under certain conditions and at Illus'
instigation, and how he became so well esteemed by Zeno
that he saw his son Basiliscus named Caesar, but, later, he
was butchered, and how from Caesar, his son was enrolled
among the minor church officials (lectors) in Blachernae.
Basiliscus had before this named his own son, Marcus,
Caesar and then emperor. Illus became friendly with Zeno
and strove to restore his imperial authority. Basiliscus,
beaten in the civil war, fled with his wife, Zenonis, and
his children to the church of Hagia Sophia, but by a trick
of Harmatius he was brought out from there and banished
to Cappadocia, where he perished with his whole family
in 476.

When Peter the heretic disturbed the churches of the
East, the Emperor Zeno sent Callandion to be bishop of
Antioch. This Peter, called the Fuller, was a Monophysite
in opposition to the orthodox Zeno. He occupied the
patriarchal throne twice, once in 476–77 and again in 485–
89, and was both times deposed.[12] Since Callandion held
the position in 481–85 he did not immediately succeed
Peter. When he needed money he got it by denunciations,
and many who rebelled against him and were caught paid

their penalty. *Illus contributed greatly to the Roman Empire, both by his manly virtues in war and by his liberalities and just actions in the city. . . . A certain Alan tried to slay Illus and, when he struck the man, he said that Epinicus,*[13] *a servant of Verina, had put him up to the murder. Epinicus was handed over to Illus in 478 and under a promise of forgiveness and rewards told everything—how Verina was plotting against Illus. For this reason Zeno handed Verina over to Illus, who banished her to a fortress in Cilicia and remained safe. Illus became friendly with Pamprepius, a wicked man, through Marsus, and little by little all his affairs were brought into confusion. Then a civil war faced Zeno—the leaders of the rebels being Marcian and Procopius, the sons of Anthemius who had ruled Rome. Through Illus, Zeno triumphed, and Marcian, the elder, was captured, but Procopius fled to Theodoric [Strabo] in Thrace in 484. Marcian was banished to Cappadocia, but escaped and disturbed Galatia around Ankyra. Being captured again, he was sent safely to Isauria. Hatred for Illus rose increasingly in the emperor. Thus is the second book.*

The third book is concerned, among other things, with how Illus openly opposed Zeno in the years 484–88 and named Leontius emperor, with Verina's help; being unsuccessful, they were besieged, captured, and beheaded. The book also deals with other matters up to the death of Zeno in 491.

Only a few of the details of this succession of civil wars and palace revolutions can be supplied with the flesh and blood of living history. As the representative of the Isaurian bandits Zeno was vastly unpopular in Constantinople, and if the pictures we have of him are biased they probably represent accurately the feelings of the day. On his accession he was faced with troubles from the Vandals who captured Nicopolis, from the Ostrogoths under their new young leader Theodoric, and from Huns and Arabs and the Gothic general Strabo. Amid these dangers the Isaurian commanders Illus and his brother Trocundes came to great power, thus intensifying the anti-Isaurian emotions of the capital.

These discontents found a champion in Verina, the wife of Leo and mother-in-law of Zeno, who, to raise her lover Patricius to the throne, obtained the help of her brother Basiliscus. This man had been in retirement since the disgrace of the Vandal expedition of 468, in which he had proved incompetent if not treacherous. He was of the faction of Aspar and the Germans and of necessity, therefore, opposed to the new Isaurian ascendency. He had also had high hopes of succeeding Leo, and in this ambition looked on Zeno as an interloper.

J.A.fr.210   With such a background of hostility it is not surprising that in January 475 a conspiracy was formed against Zeno. *Under the Emperor Zeno, Theodoric, the son of Triarius and the general of Thrace, killed Heracleius, the son of Florus, near the wall of the Chersonese. Scorning obedience to the Romans he proceeded to open war. Illus was sent by Zeno to aid those there and gave great help. As he had associated with Basiliscus and spent time in his company, he was made a party to the plot against the emperor. When Basiliscus undertook to make Harmatius their associate, Illus took the letters to Harmatius and returned to Constantinople. He immediately suggested to Verina that her lover Patricius, a man in the office of master, should seize the supreme power and not hand it over to another. As she desired this on her own account, she readily inclined to the suggestion. While Zeno was attending the first spectacle of the hippodrome, she sent to him, bidding him to come quickly. He came, leaving everything behind, and she told him they must flee quickly if they were to escape the hands of assassins and that all opinions agreed on this. When he heard this Zeno delayed for nothing, but, with Ariadne his wife and Lallis his mother, took all the valuables in the palace and in his royal robes and other insignia on the ninth day of his consulship crossed by night to Calchedon and fled with mules and horses and many Isaurians.*

After Zeno's flight the Isaurians in the city were massacred. But Basiliscus not Patricius was proclaimed emperor, which, of course, led to a breach between Verina and her brother.

M.fr.7   *Basiliscus, the brother of the Empress Verina, in the reign of the Emperor Leo was chosen prefect of the camp in place of Rusticius, being lucky in battle but slow of understanding and rashly hesitant against deceivers.* He was also made consul for 465 as part of Leo's deliberate policy to make him a counterpoise to Aspar. Rusticius had been consul in 464 and master of soldiers in the East before Basiliscus and was presumably a German.

Perhaps the factor that worked most decisively against Basiliscus was his being a Monophysite and working strongly for this heresy against the orthodox Monachians.[14] *As emperor of the Eastern Romans, he exacted taxes from the bishops of the churches and almost banished Acacius, the bishop of Constantinople, but was stopped by the multitude of the so-called Monachians. He was so greedy for money that he did not even keep his hands off those pursuing mean and mechanical arts. Indeed, the whole world was full of tears because of his tax exactions.*

M.fr.8   Basiliscus also raised the powerful hostility of Strabo, who had helped him seize the throne, by bestowing the office of master of soldiers of Thrace and the consulship on his nephew Harmatius, a fop quite unfitted for the job. *Since the Emperor Basiliscus confidently allowed Harmatius to meet the Empress Zenonis like a relative, and as their conversation lasted a long time and their beauty was not negligible, they began to love one another with extraordinary fervor. They continually turned their faces and glanced at one another, exchanging smiles and, later, the burden of a love kept hidden from view. They made Daniel, the eunuch, and Maria, the midwife, privy to their suffering, which was finally cured by the medicine of copulation. Then Zenonis through flattery induced Basiliscus to give her lover the foremost place in the state.*

Theodoric Strabo, seeing that Harmatius was honored by all, took it hard that he was surpassed in reputation by a youth whose only care was for his hair and other such bodily adornment. Puffed up by the mass of his treasure and his extraordinary honors Harmatius thought that no one could surpass him in manliness. This madness so ruled his mind that he adopted the costume of Achilles and went about on horseback vaunting his ancestry before the circus crowds. When the vulgar mob called him Pyrrhus (the son of Achilles) in loud acclamations, it all the more excited his mad desire for glory. If the mob called him this because of his ruddy complexion (for Pyrrhus means "red") it spoke the truth, but if it did this to praise his manliness, it flattered him like a boy. He did not smite heroes as Pyrrhus did, but, like Paris, was mad after women.

M.fr.8b   When he left Constantinople, Zeno retired to his native mountains of Isauria, where in despair he is reported as mourning, "I am a fugitive and wander abroad, unable to rest from my evil fate even with men among whom I hoped to find some consolation for my misfortune."

M.fr.9   The Emperor Zeno, learning of the defeat of his friends, fled to a fortress situated on a hill, which its neighbors called Constantinople. When he learned this he wept and said to those with him, "Mankind is indeed a plaything of God, if the divinity delights in toying with even me in this way. For the seers foretold, maintaining it stoutly, that I would of necessity spend the month of July in Constantinople. I certainly thought that I would return to Constantinople, but now, a fugitive bereft of my possessions, I have come, wretch that I am, to a hill that has the same name."

But he was not quite as friendless as he made believe. Basiliscus had won Illus to his cause and sent him and his brother to hunt down the ex-emperor. But even in the capital Basiliscus' unpopularity had outstripped that of Zeno, and Illus went over to Zeno's side. Perhaps his decision was in part motivated by the fact that he had Zeno's brother Longinus shut up in a fortress as a hostage. Ba-

siliscus then sent Harmatius to oppose the Isaurians, but
he too was won over by promises of high office and the rank
of Caesar for his son. Zeno easily re-entered Constantinople
in August 476, and Basiliscus and his family were exiled
and executed.

M.fr.8a   While Zeno honored his promises to Harmatius, he very soon saw that the fellow got his just deserts.
He had had great power in the court of the Empress
Zenonis and Basiliscus. The Emperor Zeno had him killed,
and the citizens rejoiced exceedingly at his death, for he
sent away, with their hands cut off, the Thracians who had
rebelled under Leo and whom he had caught. He was slain
by Onoulph, a man whom Harmatius had received kindly
when he was in poverty and but newly come from the bar-
barians. He had made him a count of the first rank and
then general of Illyricum, and had furnished him with a
great fortune for high living. The man repaid Harmatius
with barbarian perfidy and bloodstained hand.

M.fr.8c   Onoulph was the son of Edeco and brother
of Odovacar, then establishing his position in Italy, and
he sprang from the race of Thuringi on his father's side
and from the Sciri on his mother's. The Sciri or Scyri were
a Slavic tribe and the Thuringi or Toringi were Germans
from Bavaria, both tribes having been parts of the Hunnish
empire.[15]

With his restoration the troubles of the unfortunate Zeno
were only temporarily finished. Illus was all-powerful at
court and became consul in 478, but he had dangerous
enemies, in particular the Empress Verina, who constantly
plotted against him and threatened the stability of the
government.

J.A.fr.211(1)   There were three attacks on Illus, one by
Paulus, one by an Alan at Epinicus' instigation in 478,
and one hatched by the Empress Ariadne in which Illus'
ear was cut off—which most of our sources confuse.[16]
After Zeno's return some men were detected and arrested
on the charge of rebellion. A year had not elapsed since
Zeno's return, when he and Illus almost quarreled because

Paulus, a friend of the emperor, was caught with his sword drawn in a plot against Illus. Zeno averted the danger then by surrendering the youth to Illus' vengeance. In the following year Illus, having received the consulship and shown zeal in the restoration of the royal palace, was plotted against for the following reason. A certain barbarian, an Alan by race, attacked Illus, sword in hand, in the schola of the master and was arrested. Being put to torture he admitted that the deed was done at the instigation of Epinicus, a Phrygian enrolled among those who manage the contracts. By a change of fortune he came to the notice of the chamberlain Urbicius, the praepositus sacri cubiculi, and had managed the whole of his wealth. Then, becoming a friend of Verina he had risen to the control of the private funds, from there to the control of the imperial treasury, and finally had been elevated to the praetorian prefect's throne. When the business had been thoroughly examined, Illus dismissed the matter, since he was not inclined to store up his anger; he did not even arrest the fellow who had been caught.

(2)   Zeno removed Epinicus from his throne and stripped him of his property and office, for he was eager to soothe Illus. He then overcame Theodoric, called Strabo, and made him an ally and friend with many gifts. Illus sent Epinicus to the land of the Isaurians to be guarded, and seizing on the death of his brother Aspalius as a pretext, he asked permission from the emperor to leave. When he came to the town where Epinicus was held and met him, he learned from him that the plot against him had been concocted by Verina. He pretended not to know this until Zeno recalled him after the disasters caused by the earthquake in September 479, and he came to Calchedon.[17] Illus brought Pamprepius,[18] a man born in Panopolis in Egypt, who had studied literature and lived for long among the Hellenes (that is, pagans). First, Zeno welcomed him with all the men of importance, about fifty stades (six miles) in front of Calchedon. Then, having reported the statements of Epinicus and argued that it was unsafe for him to cross

to Constantinople, Illus demanded Verina. Zeno, having surrendered her, entrusted her to his wife's brother, Matronianus, who took her to Isauria with a large troop, consecrated her in the church at Tarsus, and then shut her up, first at Dalisandus and later at Cherris.

(3)   Illus, coming with Zeno and the queen to Constantinople, immediately brought about the return of Epinicus in gratitude for his revelations. Pamprepius, henceforth, had complete prosperity in his affairs, being appointed to the office of quaestor. A civil war arose at the end of Zeno's consulship in 479 on the part of the brothers Marcian and Procopius at the instigation of Verina.[19] They gathered a horde of barbarians, with many of the citizens besides, and pitched their camp at the so-called house of Caesarius. From there the one marched against Zeno in the palace and the other against Illus in the district of Varanus, so-called. Just at midday, while the palace was quiet, an attack was made on the Stoa of the Delphax in the palace, where the Delphic pillars of variegated color stand. Falling together on the guards, they overwhelmed many of those inside and would have captured the emperor himself; he barely escaped and got safely away. Busalbus fought on their side, a leader of a military force, and Niketas and Theodoric, the son of Triarius. The city mob hurled every kind of object down from the houses on those fighting on the emperor's behalf. While it was light, Marcian and his party triumphed, but when night came on, Illus, with foresight, brought across the Isaurians from Calchedon in pony boats, since the ferrymen there had been seized earlier by Marcian, who was in control of the harbor. On the next day the emperor gathered together those in authority and waited in the royal palace. Then he sent out his military force and overthrew Marcian's faction. He fled, but many on either side were killed. A few of the fugitives also burned down the house of Illus.

(4)   When the civil disturbance ended, Zeno enrolled Marcian among the so-called presbyters and banished him to Caesarea in Cappadocia; he left his wife,

*Leontia, as a fugitive among the so-called Akoimeti ("sleep-
less monks") because she was his wife's sister, and he confiscated the property of the others, who had escaped to
Strabo. At the same period the other Theodoric, the son
of Valamir, had attacked New Epirus and made himself
master of the city of Dyrrhachium (this happened before
Marcian's revolt), and the Isaurians had seized Corycus
and Sebasta in Cilicia. Marcian, escaping from his guards,
attacked Ankyra in Galatia with a great troop of rustics,
but was defeated when Trocundes occupied the place first.
He threw Marcian, who had been overcome with the help
of his own bodyguard, into one of the fortresses in Isauria,
along with his wife* [20]. . . . *At this time Epinicus, Dionysius, who was commander of the palace, and Thraustila,* [21] *who had a reputation as a general, formed a conspiracy; they were caught by the emperor and punished.*

The third attack on Illus was made at the instigation
of Ariadne because Illus would not allow her mother, Verina,
to return from exile. Zeno ordered Urbicius, the chamberlain, to have Illus assassinated, and Urbicius hired a certain
Spanicius or Sporacius for the job. The attempt was made
during a celebration in the hippodrome but failed. The as-
sassin cut off Illus' ear, but was himself killed on the spot.
Illus, as a few years before, again retired to the East, giving
up his office of master of offices and becoming instead master
of soldiers of the East. In Antioch during the next two years,
481–82, he gathered friends and adherents including his old
friend Marsus, one of the commanders against the Vandals
in 468, and the quaestor Pamprepius.

M.fr.20   This man, who was very powerful in the
reign of Zeno and who was born in Egyptian Thebes, displayed shrewdness in every endeavor. Having come to
Athens he was appointed a grammarian by the state and
taught for many years. At the same time he was trained in
the more erudite studies by the great Proclus, the last and
perhaps the greatest of the Neo-Platonists. But a slander was
raised against him by a certain Theagenes, who charged him
with a greater cunning than behooved a school teacher,

and he came to Byzantium. Henceforth, he appeared noble and upright, though in a city made up wholly of Christians he made no disguise of his religion (he was an Hellene, as they called a pagan then), but openly avowed it with free utterances and so gave the impression of knowing bits of secret wisdom. Illus received him kindly when they met, honored him magnificently when he read a poem in public, and gave him a regular stipend, partly from his own pocket and partly, as to a teacher, from the public funds. When Illus went to Isauria the slanderers contrived a calumny against Pamprepius both on account of his religion and because he practiced witchcraft and prophesied for Illus against the emperor. They persuaded Zeno and Verina, then at the height of their power, to expel him from the city in 478. He went to Pergamum in Mysia.

When Illus learned that the man had been driven away on account of his prophecy, he brought him to Isauria and made him his adviser and companion. And since he was a politician full of intelligence, he allowed him to administer the affairs of his office for which he himself did not have leisure. When he returned to Byzantium he took him along and he was made quaestor. When the revolt of Marcian occurred, he encouraged Illus in his hesitation, saying to him, "Providence is with us," and so Illus backed Zeno in this revolt. He aroused suspicion in those who then heard him that he divined these things from some unknown premonition. The event having turned out as it did, when they compared the outcome with his speech, they considered him to be the sole cause of everything that seemed to happen contrary to their expectations, as a mob is wont to do. Thus, the wise men conjectured about him. Whether there is some other explanation, I am able neither strongly to deny nor to believe. Nevertheless, Illus consulted with him first on all matters great and small. He took him to winter at Nicea in 479 or 480, either to avert injury from the populace, or to avoid the fate which was involving the city in butchery.[22]

J.A.fr.214(1)   Though rid of the immediate presence of Illus, Zeno could make no overt move at once because of troubles with the Ostrogoths. In 484 he was ready to act and made a beginning of hostility toward Illus by demanding, first, to receive back his brother Longinus, and then by announcing that Joannes the Scythian was the successor to Illus' office of master of soldiers in the East. He also harangued the people, telling them how hostile he was toward Illus, ordered his closest friends to be driven from the city, and donated their goods to the Isaurian cities.

(2)   Illus, openly rebelling, decked out Marcian for the second time in the royal robes. He sent word to Odovacar, the usurper of the West, and to the rulers of Persia and Armenia and prepared ships. Odovacar answered that he could not make an alliance, but the others promised an alliance when anyone should come to them. The embassy to the Persians left before the proclamation of Marcian, since in January 484 the Ephthalite Huns severely defeated the Persians, killed their king Perozes, and stopped any help being sent to Illus. Zeno ordered Conon, the son of Phuscianus, a man numbered among the priests and bishop of Apamea, to take up arms again against Illus, and he appointed Linges,[23] his bastard brother, general. With these things in view Illus brought Verina to Tarsus and made preparations for her to don the royal robes so that she, being mistress of the empire and standing on the speaker's platform, proclaimed Leontius emperor. (Marcian was set aside.) This man of unknown parentage was from the town of Dalisandus in Lycaonia.[24] When he came to the supreme power, he immediately carried out his duties as he deemed best. He distributed money and went to Antioch.

(5)   The expedition of Conon and Linges was incapable of dealing with the spreading rebellion and Theodoric and the Germans were sent to help.[25] Meanwhile Artemidorus, Trocundes' assistant,[26] and Papimus, who was Illus' cavalry commander, were present having been sent out from Illus' army. When the forces of both emperors came together, Illus' army was found inadequate,

and in exceedingly great fear it turned to the fortress of Cherris. Illus had earlier sent to it supplies sufficient for defending the fortress and his wife, Asteria. He sent to the Empress Verina among others and to Leontius, who left Antioch, to come quickly to him. But when their generals learned these things each fled to a neighboring fortress. Illus himself passed the night with Leontius and then went up to the fortress of Cherris. His Isaurians abandoned them little by little, seizing the lands of the Emperor Zeno for themselves. Leontius spent only sixty-some days in the semblance of imperial power—from July to September 484. Not more than 2000 men followed Illus, and, having chosen the especially loyal ones, the leaders dispersed the rest among the caves which are everywhere formed in this countryside.

(6)   When the flight of Illus and Leontius was announced, Zeno made Kottomenes master of soldiers in praesenti and Longinus of Kardala the master of offices. He recalled the army of Theodoric and ordered the Rugians to remain in the country. During the siege of the fortress engagements were often fought. Verina became exhausted and died nine days after her flight to the fortress and was embalmed in a leaden coffin—later brought to Constantinople by Ariadne. Marsus died after thirty days and was put in the same tomb. Illus turned over the defense of the fortress to Indacus Kottounes and henceforth took his leisure reading books. Leontius spent his time in fasting and laments. Illus and his affairs grew weak on this account, and the counter-fort was betrayed to the Romans by those inside. The counter-fort was some kind of outerwork or fortress on an opposite hill defending the main fortress; its fall, though it did not lead to the surrender of Cherris, nevertheless resulted in Illus and his men being brought to despair.

(7)   The struggle lasted for four years. Those engaged in the siege of Illus and Leontius used many siege engines after their good luck in the matter of the counterfort. The armies being encamped opposite each other, Illus

and Joannes the Scythian came into friendly conversation
and sent a note to Zeno reminding him of Illus' former
good will, but this accomplished nothing and they again
took to arms.

(9)   In 487–88 Zeno was preoccupied with serious
rebellions on the part of Theodoric and his Ostrogoths—
even the capital itself was threatened. After the raising of
the siege of Constantinople by Theodoric in 488, Anthousa,
Illus' daughter, perished in the fortress, and for this reason
Illus utterly neglected the defense of those inside, while
Zeno was free to prosecute the Isaurian war more vigorously.

(10)   According to one story [27] Trocundes was
slain in a skirmish around Cherris and his widow's new
husband came to the fort and betrayed it to the besiegers.
Pamprepius, because of his false prophecies of success, was
executed before the fortress fell. But according to another
story the capture of the fortress of Cherris was accomplished
in this way. Indacus Kottounes for a long time had given
thought to its betrayal, and during this time had been entrusted with the defense of the stronghold. He persuaded
Illus to post his men outside of the fortress, so that should
the enemy attack during the night he and his associate
Leontius might sleep in their usual way. When night came
he lowered a rope in a quiet part of the fort and brought
up the enemy. First the guards of the gates were killed,
then a shout was raised, saying in the Roman fashion,
"Zeno Augustus, may you conquer!" [28] Straightway Indacus
and his fellow traitors were slain, but Illus and Leontius
fled to the shrine of the martyr Conon. When Leontius
wished to kill himself Illus restrained him. The enemy
came, and they were dragged out by force and led away
bound in fetters. Illus, lamenting, asked Paulus and Illus,
who had been his slaves, and their friends to commit the
body of his sister to burial in Tarsus, to guard his wife
without insults, and to be merciful to a certain Conon
since he had been a kindly man. This Conon was neither
Zeno's fighting bishop nor the betrayer of Illus mentioned
below nor, of course, the saint to whose shrine Illus had

fled. Possibly, he was Illus' son-in-law. Still a fifth Conon was Zeno's brother.

(11)   They hastily performed these requests, and safely took both the body and Illus' wife and his daughter Thekle to the chapel of his three children in Tarsus. The victor took the men a little outside the fortress and, when they had with tears, raising their hands to Heaven, addressed many prayers to God, he cut off their heads. Lightning flashes and thunder, hail and wind were suffered by those present, and the executioner went mad and was taken speechless to Tarsus. When Zeno received the heads of the men he impaled them opposite the city, but, admiring Conon, gave orders that he be brought before him. But Conon had already learned of the deaths of Illus and Leontius and wounded himself and died.

(12)   The emperor cruelly persecuted those who had been captured, putting some to death thoughtlessly and depriving others of their property. In royal fashion he buried the body of Verina in Constantinople, placing her in her husband's funeral monument and ordering that she be named Augusta. He destroyed most of the fortresses in Isauria. Those who took part in the betrayal of Illus perished with miserable deaths—the terrible Kottounes, the rustic Conon, Longinus the son of Longinus, and Artemidorus, the attendant of Trocundes.[29]

Thus, in 488 Zeno was at last free of the Isaurian rebellion, and in the same year he rid himself of the Ostrogoths by sending Theodoric against Odovacar in Italy. He maintained Isaurians in prominent positions—Kottomenes and Longinus of Kardala for instance—and after his own brother Longinus was rescued in 485, after being imprisoned ten years by Illus, he too became undeservedly prominent. He was consul in 486 and again in 490.

M.fr.21   Longinus and Conon, brothers of the Emperor Zeno, ruled so lawlessly together that in every city they placed limits to the possessions of others and gave help, for pay, to those who had sinned most flagrantly. Longinus was, furthermore, completely incontinent, always associating with drunkards and always having in his house pliable brothel keepers who were told to bring him the wives of the foremost officials. They brought harlots of marvelous dress and luxurious couches, and tricked him, pretending they were supplying the women demanded. Longinus disbanded a convent of nuns in the following way. While dwelling in the suburb, Pegai, so-called, he was told by the procurers at dinner that the women of this group were exceedingly beautiful. He sent them vegetables and dried fruits, then cloaks and other things, as though they were coy, to avert their fears, for the terrible hawkers after women used fair-seeming means in pursuit of females. Then, going up to the convent he forcibly brought many of these women down. He was so lustful that he fell on free-born women, the wives of officials, and maidens at any unseemly time and acted without any restraint. On his progresses he used to toss silver balls and nut shells. Longinus was the cause of many other sufferings also.

This was the man who, after the death of Zeno's disreputable son of the same name, was destined for the succession. (These two must have contributed very largely to the emperor's unpopularity!) After Zeno's death in 491, however, by the wishes of his widow, Ariadne, the chief ministers, and the army the choice fell on Anastasius, a relatively unimportant but popular figure in the capital. The coronation was further legitimized by his marriage to Ariadne. Under him the Isaurian faction was overthrown, Longinus was forced to enter the priesthood where he died in 499, and the Isaurians were expelled from the capital. It was not till 498 that the last dissident rebels in Isauria were finally crushed.

In this chapter we have only considered half of the problems faced in these years; equal in contemporary eyes to Isaurian dominance was the Ostrogothic power in the East. This is the subject of the next chapter.

chapter 6

The Ostrogoths

THE GOTHS who appeared on the Roman frontiers in the third century were probably Visigoths, the Ostrogoths being a later migration from the north. By the middle of the fourth century, however, the latter were established north of the Danube and Black Sea, where their great King Ermanaric founded a sizable empire. There they were among the first to feel the westward push of the Huns and, though beaten by them, for long acted as a barrier between these savages and the empire in the East. In 380 they attacked the empire unsuccessfully, but some of them were settled as allies (foederati) in Asia Minor in 383–95. They soon rebelled under their King Tribigild and were joined by Gaïnas, a Goth high in the Roman service at the time. Under his leadership they achieved some successes, but, having recrossed into Europe, they were almost annihilated by loyal troops and by the Huns under Uldin in 401. By the time Attila became king of the Huns we find the Ostrogoths his subject allies and their King Valamir (also spelled Walamer or, in Greek, Balamer) an honored councilor to the great Hun. They had already, however, been converted to Arian Christianity by the great Bishop Ulfilas.

At Nedao the Ostrogoths under three brothers of the royal Amal line, Valamir, Theudomir and Widemir—of whom Valamir seems to have been the eldest and most important—joined their cousins the Gepids under Ardaric in destroying their Hunnish masters. After this victory they settled in Pannonia under some sort of treaty with the Romans,[1] and in the same year, 454, Theodoric, destined to become the greatest king in their history, was born to Theudomir. Because Theodoric (Thiuda-reiks[2] in Gothic) was,

it seems, the only heir of the Amal line and as such spent
some time in Constantinople as a hostage for Valamir's good
conduct he was mistakenly thought to be Valamir's son and
is referred to as such rather consistently by Byzantine historians. For seven years there was peace between the Eastern
Empire and the Ostrogoths, but in 461 trouble broke out.

P.fr.28   *When Valamir, the Scythian, broke his
treaty and laid waste many Roman cities and lands, the Romans sent ambassadors to him who censured him for his rebellion. So that he might not again overrun the country,
they arranged to supply him with 300 pounds of gold each
year, for he said he roused his native horde to war through
want of necessities.* As part of this treaty the young Theodoric was sent to the capital, where he spent the next ten
years of his life at court.

In the next few years the Goths in Pannonia came into
more or less constant conflict with their neighbors, especially
the Sciri. This was an Alan race which had settled in
Lower Moesia on the Danube after Nedao, but had been
stirred to war by a certain Suevic King Hunimund, who had
been taken captive by the Ostrogoths. The remnants of this
tribe formed an important part of Odovacar's army in his
final conquest of Italy a few years later.[3]

P.fr.35   *About 471 the Sciri and Goths met in war
and, being separated, both made preparations to call in
allies. Among others, they came to the Eastern Romans.
Aspar thought that an alliance should be made with neither,
but the Emperor Leo wished to help the Sciri. He sent letters
to the general in Illyria ordering him to send them the necessary help against the Goths.* In the fight Valamir was killed,
and, when Widemir left with his followers for Italy and perished there, Theudomir was left as sole ruler of the Goths in
Pannonia.[4]

In the same year Aspar, the great leader of the German
faction at Constantinople, fell, causing severe discontent
among the Goths in Roman service. Possibly as a gesture
to appease the followers of the Amal king his son, now a
lad of seventeen, was sent back to him. To prove his mettle

to his people he almost at once led a successful attack on the Sarmatians who lived at Singidunum, modern Belgrade, farther down the Danube. Two years later in 473 famine drove the Goths southward, where they attacked the important city of Naissus and were only pacified by the grant of lands in Macedonia. Shortly thereafter, Theudomir died and was succeeded by Theodoric as king. He seems to have moved his people almost at once, with or without the sanction of the Roman emperor, to Lower Moesia.

In the meantime in Constantinople another group of Ostrogoths who had taken service with the Romans after Nedao—and were now forming a very important element in the regular Roman army—had come under the domination of a leader also called Theodoric. He was not of the royal Amal line but was distantly connected with it. It has been suggested that this man, the son of Triarius and nicknamed Strabo ("squinter"), had a brother married to Theudomir's sister.[5] He was also the nephew of Aspar's wife and so had come to great prominence in Constantinople under his uncle's favor and correspondingly into temporary eclipse when Aspar and his family were killed. However, the Gothic and other German troops rallied around him in opposition to the Isaurians and proclaimed him king about 474.

M.fr.2   In this dangerous situation the Emperor *Leo sent Telogius the silentiary to the barbarians in Thrace.*[6] *The barbarians received him readily enough and, in turn, sent ambassadors to the emperor, desiring to be friends of the Romans. They asked for three things: first, that Theodoric Strabo, their ruler, receive the inheritance which Aspar had left to him, second, that he be allowed to live in Thrace, and, third, that he be commander of the troops which Aspar had led as master of soldiers in praesenti. The emperor absolutely refused the first two requests and agreed concerning the generalship only on condition that Theodoric be an honest friend to him, and so he dismissed the ambassadors.*

When Theodoric Strabo, the leader of the barbarians, received his ambassadors back from the emperor and found they had accomplished nothing, he sent part of his forces to Philippi and with the rest encamped before Arcadiopolis, besieging it by every means. He did not capture the town by arms but by hunger, which assailed those within. Indeed, they even seized horses and beasts of burden and dead bodies, enduring manfully until help should come from somewhere. When this failed to arrive they gave up hope and surrendered. Those who had been sent against Philippi merely set fire to the suburbs of the city and did no other serious damage. Though these forces were ravaging Thrace, nevertheless the barbarians themselves suffered from famine and sent an embassy for peace to the emperor. The agreement, made under oath, was on these terms: each year 2000 pounds of gold were to be given to the Goths, Theodoric was to be appointed general of the two commands in the emperor's bodyguard,[7] which were highly important posts, and be sole commander of the Goths themselves, the emperor would admit into his own land none who wished to withdraw from the Goths, and Theodoric Strabo would fight with the emperor against everyone that the latter might order except the Vandals.

This treaty was obviously designed to bolster Strabo against Theodoric, the true Gothic king of the Amal line, by giving him a patent of royalty from the empire. That there may have been some misgivings among the Goths themselves is obvious from the reference to deserters. The exception made in favor of the Vandals was not so much because of their common Germanic origin as because of the distances and dangers involved in any attack on them, as shown by the disasters of the expedition of 468, and their common Arian beliefs which had caused Aspar to favor them too.

Strabo naturally came into almost immediate conflict with Zeno, the Isaurian, when he came to the throne, and rebelling advanced as far as the long wall defending the Thracian Chersonese. Heracleius, the master of soldiers for Thrace, was sent against him only to be beaten and captured.[8]

M.fr.5   Of this man we know that he was a general under Zeno, daring and eager to join battle, but, on the other hand, without forethought in dangers and a man who took no counsel before he recklessly went ahead with what he set out to do. He considered rash impetuosity suited to a brave man and this, later, was the cause of his downfall.

M.fr.4   The Emperor Zeno sent an embassy to the commander of the Goths concerning Heracleius, the general who had been captured by the Goths. He promised to redeem him with a ransom of 100 talents, which was agreed on. Zeno ordered the relatives of Heracleius to collect this sum so that he himself might not seem to have been in a position of servitude, since the man would have been freed by others. He sent the money to the Goths in Thrace who took it and dismissed Heracleius from their custody. As he was proceeding to Arcadiopolis, some Goths attacked him. As he was walking along, one of them struck him violently on the shoulder. One of Heracleius' escort rebuked the Goth and said, "How now, fellow, don't you know your place? Don't you know whom you've struck?" The other answered that he knew him well and was going to kill him. Drawing their swords, one cut off Heracleius' head and another his hands. They say that Heracleius suffered according to his just deserts, for he is reported to have ordered soldiers serving under him who were judged to have committed a crime, but not one worthy of the death penalty, to be thrown into a pit and stoned by the whole army. Thereafter the anger of God was visited on him.

Strabo backed Basiliscus in his rebellion, and it was natural that Zeno should favor Theodoric, in spite of the treaty of 474 with Strabo. After Zeno's restoration Strabo was stripped of his generalship, which the Amal received with the title of patrician. Here we see the age-old Roman policy of divide and rule once again in the playing off of the Gothic factions against one another. In the next few years we find first Zeno and Theodoric aligned against Strabo, then the two Goths against Zeno, and finally Strabo and Zeno against Theodoric.

M.fr.11   In 477 or 478 an embassy came to Zeno
from the treaty-Goths of Thrace whom the Romans call
foederati. These allies were soldiers led by Strabo, with
whom the treaty of 474 had not been formally renounced.
They asked Zeno to make peace with Theodoric, the son
of Triarius, who desired to lead a quiet life and not to
undertake war against the state. They asked Zeno to consider how, as an enemy, the son of Triarius had harmed
the Romans, and how Theodoric, the son of Valamir,
though a general and friend, had destroyed their cities;
Zeno should not now look at ancient enmities rather than
at how he might help the common good.

The emperor convened the senate at once and laid the
problem of what he ought to do before it. The senators
said that the public revenue was not sufficient to supply the
subsidies and pay readily to both, since "we are not able
to fulfill our proper obligations even to the soldiers alone."
They concluded that the emperor himself had the right to
make this decision as to which of the barbarians ought to
be chosen as a friend.

Thereupon he summoned to the palace the soldiers stationed in the city and all the scholae, and, mounting the
speaker's platform, he accused Strabo of many things. Among
these were that he had been hostile to the Romans from
the first, that he had despoiled the inhabitants of Thrace,
that along with Harmatius he had cut off their hands,
that he had brought about the expulsion of all the farmers
there, and that he had stirred up the tyranny of Basiliscus
against the state and then had seduced him into putting his
own soldiers out of the way, as though the Goths alone were
sufficient. Finally, now, he was sending an embassy not to
demand peace but the command of the army. "Now then,"
Zeno said, "whatever opinon you yourselves hold about these
matters, I want to hear from you. I have summoned you here
for this purpose, for I know well that those emperors act
safely who share their councils with the soldiers." When
they heard the charges which he had made and saw the

answer wanted, they all shouted that Strabo was an enemy
of the Romans, as were all those who had sided with him.

Zeno did not immediately give this answer to the envoys,
but waited until he should hear more of the events outside the city. Meanwhile, certain men who wrote to Strabo
of the happenings within the city were made prisoners,
among them Anthimus, a physician, Marcellinus, and
Stephanus. Not only had they sent letters of their own, but
they had forged documents of those in authority and dispatched them to him, since they wanted to encourage him
to think that he had sufficient sympathizers in the city.
Three senators, with the master present, investigated these
matters and inflicted many strokes of the lash on these
persons, and imposed perpetual exile on them. Zeno, I
suppose, wished to seem to abstain from the death penalty
and bloodshed.

M.fr.14   Only a few months after this decision, however, when Zeno saw that the situation of Theodoric, the
son of Valamir, was becoming weaker and more precarious,
and that Theodoric, the son of Triarius, was assembling his
tribes and collecting his forces, he considered it better
to dispel the latter's enmity on reasonable terms, if he
was willing to make an agreement. Sending ambassadors,
Zeno demanded that the son of Triarius hand over his
son as hostage, according to his previous request, that he
remain as a private individual among his own people as
at present, causing no trouble, that, just as he had once
demanded, he take whatever property he had seized but
in other respects remain peaceful, and that, receiving no
harm, he cause harm to no one.

The Goth answered that he would not surrender his
son as hostage and that he could not live on his own private
property alone. While he had been by himself without
so many tribes in his retinue, his private property might
have sufficed for a man who lived a very modest life, but
now, since they had imposed on him the necessity of
gathering his tribes, he was compelled either to feed those

who came to him or to fight with them until, either defeated or successful, he should bring a final and indisputable
end to the whole business.

When these messages had been delivered it seemed
best to prepare for war with all care. The emperor quickly
summoned all the legions and units near the Black Sea and
in Asia and those stationed in the eastern districts. There
came, from all sides, no small number. Baggage wagons
were prepared, cattle were bought, and grain and all other
necessities for an army were made ready, since Illus himself was going to march out.

M.fr.15   Apparently Zeno changed his mind about
his choice of generals, and when he had appointed Martinian, a brother-in-law of Illus, as general, and his army had
fallen into utter lack of discipline, he at once sent men
to the son of Valamir, as this seemed a good idea. They
said that he ought to delay battle no longer, but ought to
devote himself to action at once and fulfill the hopes in
accord with which he had been deemed worthy of a Roman
generalship. Hearing this, the Goth sent envoys to Byzantium
in his turn, saying that he would undertake no action until
the emperor and the senate had sworn to him that they
would never again make a compact with the son of Triarius. The senators and the military leaders thereupon swore
not to make such a treaty unless the emperor desired it,
and the emperor promised not to break the agreements already made unless he perceived that the son of Valamir was
first transgressing them.

When these things had been sworn to, it seemed best
for Theodoric to move his force, which was encamped at
Marcianopolis, and to march closer in. When he was at
the gates of the Haemus Range, the master of soldiers of
Thrace would join him with 2000 cavalry and 10,000 heavy
infantry, and when he had crossed the Haemus Range,
another force of 20,000 foot and 6000 horse would meet him
near the Ebro River at Adrianople. Besides, they said another force would come from Heraclea and other towns and
forts near Byzantium if he needed it, so that nothing

might be lacking that would contribute to bringing their
highest hopes to fruition. When Zeno had promised these
arrangements to the ambassadors he sent them quickly
away. Theodoric set out with his army and went to the
pass, as agreed, but when he arrived neither the commander
of Thrace nor those said to have been stationed at the
Ebro River met him. But he passed through the central
deserts and reached the districts around Sondis. This is a
great high mountain, difficult to climb if anyone on top
tries to prevent it. The son of Triarius was by chance encamped on it, and, attacking one another on its approaches,
both sides carried off herds, horses, and other booty.

The son of Triarius, however, continually rode up to the
camp of the other, upbraiding and reproaching him bitterly, calling him a perjurer and a child, a madman, an
enemy of his own race and a traitor who did not know the
reputation of the Romans nor comprehend their intentions.
"They wish," he said, "while resting in peace, that the
Goths wear each other out. They have the victory without the combat whichever of us falls, and whichever destroys
the other will bring them a Cadmean victory, as they say,
leaving fewer of us to oppose their treachery. And now,
having summoned you and promised to come themselves
and to make a common campaign, they are not present, nor
have they arrived at the cities as they said they would; they
have left you to be most vilely destroyed alone and to pay
the just penalty of your audacity at the hands of the race
you have betrayed." When they heard this many of the
son of Valamir's host agreed with the arguments, and,
coming to their general, of their own accord they said
that the other's reproaches were just, and that their leader
ought to cause no more destruction nor adhere to those who
betrayed him, neglecting the ties of a common ancestry.

On the following day Strabo again came to the hill which
overlooked their camp and called out, "Why do you
destroy my kin, you villain? Why have you widowed so many
women? Where are their husbands? How has the wealth,
which everyone had when they set out with you from home

on this campaign, been wasted? Each of them had a pair
or three horses, but now they advance horseless and on foot,
following you through Thrace like slaves, though they are
free men of no mean race. Since coming, have they shared
a single medimnus of gold?" [9]

When they heard this the whole camp, men and women
together, went to their leader Theodoric and with shouting and uproar demanded an alliance. They all said that
if he did not comply, they would desert him and adopt the
expedient course. Thereupon he sent envoys to Theodoric,
the son of Triarius, and both men met by a river, one on
either bank. Keeping the river between them they held a
parley and agreed not to war on each other and arranged
what they thought expedient. When the agreements had
been sworn to, they both sent ambassadors to Byzantium.

M.fr.16   When the two Goths—the son of Valamir
and the son of Triarius—had made a treaty not to war on
each other and had sent envoys to Byzantium, the son of
Valamir accused the emperor of having betrayed him. He
said that finding none of the promised troops he had made
a true compact with Theodoric, the son of Triarius. He
demanded that land be given him on which he could stay
and grain sufficient to keep his army until the harvest and
that the emperor send the collectors of the imperial
revenues (whom the Romans call domestici) as quickly
as possible, to render an account of what the Goths had
received. This was necessary in order to legalize the requisi-
tions made by the Goths. If the Romans did not do these
things for him he said he would be unable to restrain his
great throng from alleviating their needs by pillaging where-
ever they could.

The other Theodoric, the son of Triarius, spoke as follows:
"The son of Triarius demands that the agreements made by
Leo be completely fulfilled for him, that the stipends of
previous years be paid, and that his relatives be handed
back to him alive. If, however, these have died, Illus and
other Isaurians to whom these men had been entrusted
should swear an oath concerning them." If this was an

oath required to furnish legal proof of the deaths of Aspar and his family in order that Strabo might secure his inheritance [10] it seems rather belated considering Strabo's earlier demands for this inheritance.

What answer Zeno made to Strabo, if any, is not recorded but when Zeno heard these demands he answered the son of Valamir that he was a traitor and had done everything contrary to what he had promised. He had promised to wage war unaided and then had called for additional help, and, further, having called for the force of Romans, he had secretly made friendly overtures to Strabo. When the commander of Thrace and others well disposed toward the Roman cause perceived this, they had not dared to meet him nor to unite their forces with his for fear of an ambush. "But now," he said, "if he is willing to make war on the son of Triarius, I will give him the following when he is victorious: 1000 pounds of gold, 40,000 pounds of silver, and, besides, an income of 10,000 nomismata, and I will grant him to marry Juliana, the daughter of Olybrius, the Western emperor, or some other noble woman in the state."

As soon as he said this he decorated most of those who had been sent from the Goth with honors, and he sent ambassadors—first Philoxenus, then Julianus—to see if they could persuade him to break with the son of Triarius. When they could not do so, the emperor sent for the soldiers and entered on the war, calling on them to be of good cheer since he himself was marching out and would suffer whatever was necessary in common with them. When they heard that the emperor himself was willing to lead them out, a most unusual procedure at this period, each of them so spurred himself on to show the emperor that he was a deserving man that even those who formerly gave money to the generals to avoid having to take up arms paid it again for a share in the expedition. Everyone took part in the war with great excitement.

They captured the scouts sent out by Theodoric, and the division of the son of Valamir's bodyguard which had

advanced to the Long Wall, about 40 miles from Constantinople,[11] was nobly beaten off by those on guard. When
Zeno took on his own nature again—and was overcome by
his innate cowardice—they were angry and irritated and
gathered in meetings. They accused each other of utter
cowardice, if, having hands and wielding arms, they endured hearing of such softness, by which all the cities and
might of the Romans would perish and because of which
anyone might hack at Roman possessions as he pleased.
When Martinian perceived this tumult he advised Zeno
to disband the army as quickly as possible, so that they
would not join together and raise a rebellion. The emperor
ordered each unit to depart to its winter quarters, since
there would be peace with Theodoric, the son of Triarius.
So they broke camp—the majority disgusted with the dis-
banding—especially since it turned out that they were split
up before they could, considering the common good, set
up a man able in some way or other to retrieve the empire
from its present disgrace.

M.fr.17   When Zeno had disbanded his army he
sent to arrange peace with Theodoric, the son of Triarius,
on whatever terms he could. Meanwhile, the son of Valamir,
gathering his forces, arrived near Rhodope. He attacked
all the fairest lands of the Thracian country and carried
off the cattle. He wiped out all farming and killed and
despoiled what he could not carry away. When Strabo heard
what was happening, he said he rejoiced that one called
their friend and son was doing the Romans such harm, but
said he was sorry, all the same, because the penalty for
the Romans' folly was being visited on farmers about whom
Zeno or Verina would not care in any way, even if they
perished.

When the ambassadors arrived, they made a peace treaty
on condition that the emperor supply pay and food for
13,000 men whom Strabo chose, that he be appointed commander of the scholae of the imperial guard, that he receive
back whatever property he had formerly had, that he receive

one of the two armies around the emperor, as master of
soldiers praesentalis, and that he have the honors to which
he had been named by Basiliscus. Concerning his relatives
by marriage, if they were dead as Zeno said, there was to be
no more discussion, but if they were alive, they would live
in whatever city Zeno thought best, taking the property
which they had had. When these things were agreed on,
the emperor removed the son of Valamir from office, made
Strabo general in his place, and sent such money as it was
necessary to distribute immediately among the Goths.

M.fr.18   Theodoric now facing the combined forces
of Strabo and the emperor was forced to retreat westward
into Macedonia. The son of Valamir, having lost many
soldiers at the hands of the Roman generals, withdrew
with no little anger because of his sufferings, and burned
and murdered whatever he came on. He destroyed Stobi,
the first city of Macedonia, and slew the soldiers on guard
there who resisted him.

When it was reported that the barbarian was lying in
wait near Thessalonika, the citizens immediately conspired
together and overthrew all the statues of Zeno, suspecting
that the letters of the previous day had been proclaimed
with deceit, and that Zeno and Joannes the praetorian
prefect himself were intending to hand the city over to
the enemy. They attacked the prefect and were ready to
tear him to pieces. They brought fire and would have set
the prefect's palace (praetorium) ablaze, if the clergy and
those in authority had not been beforehand in snatching
the prefect from the anger of the mob and in checking
the disorderly conduct with soothing words. He had not
been the cause of this trouble, they said, nor had the emperor intended hardship or suffering for the city. It was
necessary to defend it and to entrust the job to whomever
they considered trustworthy. They took the keys of the
gates from the prefect and gave them to the archbishop,
planned a watch as strong as possible, and were content with
their general. Since Thessalonika, besides being the seat of

the praetorian prefect of Illyricum, was also the seat of the bishop of that diocese it was natural to choose him as a man bound to oppose the Arian Goths.

Meanwhile Zeno heard of the prevailing danger and saw that it would be best, since no one wished to fight, to turn the barbarian from the destruction of the cities by fair terms of peace, considering the dire straits the latter were in. He sent Artemidorus his relative [12] and Phocas, who had been the secretary of his office when he was a general. They said, "The emperor has made you his friend and has solemnly decorated you with the most glorious honors among the Romans, and he has caused you to command the greatest forces, and though you are a barbarian has distrusted you not at all. But you, seduced we know not how by the guiles of our common enemies, have wiped out the good falling to your lot and have made another man the master of your fate, when you ought not. It would not be right to accuse the emperor of crimes which you have committed against yourself and him. Now, since you have brought yourself to this state, it remains for you to turn from your present misfortune and from damaging cities and people, insofar as you can, and to send an embassy to try to moderate the emperor, who is good."

He was persuaded and sent men with them to Byzantium, himself restraining his army from burning and from murdering men, though, since they were in need of everything, he could not prevent them from providing themselves with necessities. Advancing, he came to Heraclea in Macedonia, and, since the archbishop in this town sent many gifts to his army and himself, he kept all the country unharmed, causing no additional trouble for the inhabitants there, and tried to support his force moderately from the revenues of the district.

When his envoys came to Byzantium, they said that the emperor ought to send an ambassador to him with full powers to deal quickly with all matters, since it was impossible for him to restrain for long such a large force from damage which might benefit them. The emperor sent

Adamantius, the son of Vivianus, a patrician and once prefect of the city, on whom he also conferred consular rank (though not the consulship) and ordered that a district in Pautalia be given to the barbarian. This province is a part of Illyricum not far from the entrance to Thrace. He did this so that, if Theodoric, the son of Triarius, should revolt, he would have the son of Valamir posted in reserve nearby to oppose him, and, if he intended to break the terms of peace, he would be between the forces of Illyricum and Thrace, and would more easily be surrounded. And if Theodoric should say that his army would lack food for the present year, since they had done no sowing and had no hope of fruit in Pautalia, two hundred pounds of gold given to the envoy as he was setting out, were ordered to be handed over to the prefect there to spend on bringing sufficient supplies to the Goths in Pautalia.

While the envoy was still in Byzantium, the soldiers stationed in Thessalonika attacked the prefect Joannes, sword in hand, ambushing him as he was going out. Adamantius was assigned by the orders of Zeno to settle this trouble. While these things were going on in Thessalonika, the son of Valamir was waiting near Heraclea. He had heard of the plans for the Pautalian settlement before the emperor's ambassador arrived, delayed as he was by the events in Thessalonika, and, divining the emperor's motives, decided to seek his fortune farther West. He sent to Sidimundus, who was living in the country around Epidamnus in Epirus, a man descended from the same tribe and at this time appearing to be an ally of the Romans. This countryside was virtually untouched by impoverishment caused by the plundering of contending armies for a century or more.[13] Sidimundus had a rich inheritance and regular pay from the emperor and was a nephew of Aedoingus, or Edwin, who was on very close terms with Verina and had command of the so-called domestici, an office of great importance in the royal palace. Theodoric sent to this man, reminding him of his relationship and asking him to interest himself in finding a way by which he might rule

Epidamnus and the rest of Epirus and cease from his long wandering, so that settling in a walled city he could receive whatever fortune granted.

When Sidimundus received his request, being a barbarian, he thought it better to live with a barbarian than with Romans and went to Epidamnus. He went around to each of its citizens privately, as if out of kindness to them, and advised them to get quickly away to safety to the islands or some other city with whatever they owned. He said that a barbarian was attacking the country and that the emperor, who had sent Adamantius for this purpose, approved. It would be better for them, he said, to remove their belongings at greater leisure while the barbarian was not yet there. He said the same things to the soldiers of the local garrison, 2000 in number, who could easily have warded off anyone who made a sudden attack, and, troubling their minds and always striving to start some new rumor, he persuaded nearly all of them to leave Epidamnus. He argued that by resisting they would incur the anger of the emperor.

Then, he straightway sent to the son of Valamir to hasten there as quickly as possible. The latter was waiting for the message from Sidimundus and also because his sister had been overcome by a disease from which she died, but he pretended that he was waiting for the arrival of the embassy from Zeno and to learn if the messages from the emperor were favorable to him. When he had buried his sister, the summons from Sidimundus arrived. To the citizens of Heraclea, who had abandoned their city and fortified a strong fortress, he sent a demand for a large supply of grain and wine in order to have traveling supplies for his army on his departure. They answered that they could do nothing, as what they had had in the very small fortress had been consumed in their long stay there. In anger he burned as much of the city as he could, since it was empty of men, and straightway set out.

On his journey he marched by a difficult and narrow road leading to New Epirus, so-called. He sent the cavalry

in advance to occupy the heights of the Scardus range for
the army, to advance through those places while they were
still not expected, and to drive back by a sudden attack
any garrison there. When they approached, the soldiers
standing guard on the wall, seeing the multitude of the
enemy and astounded at their sudden appearance, did not
wait to join battle. They did not even have the foresight
to close the fortress, but quickly fled, reckless, in their panic,
of everything which could have helped them at that crisis.

The Goths proceeded on their way through a great
empty land, with Theodoric himself at their head and with
Soas, the greatest of the generals under him, holding the
center and Theodimundus, another son of Valamir, in
charge of the rearguard. Theodoric, in the lead and full
of confidence that no one was following them, ordered
those on the wagons and with the other baggage animals
to advance. He himself hurried on to surprise and capture
whatever town he could. Coming to Lychidnus, he was
repulsed, for it lies in a strong position and is full of springs
inside its walls, and grain had been stored in advance
inside. Descending from there he took Scampia, whose inhabitants had abandoned it some time before. From this
town he proceeded to Epidamnus and seized it.

When Adamantius learned this news he sent forward
one of the royal cavalrymen (whom they call magistriani)
to charge Theodoric with acting contrary to the promise of
his embassy and to order him to keep the peace and not to
seize ships or further disturb the present situation in any
way until he himself should arrive. Lastly, he asked the
Goth to send a man to give pledges for his return after the
embassy and for his complete safety. He sent this message
to the fellow and setting out from Thessalonika came to
Edessa, where Sabinianus and Philoxenus were. Sabinianus
was appointed master of soldiers of Thrace in 479 and proved
himself an able general and disciplinarian.[14]

They handed letters to Sabinianus and, making him a
general, took careful counsel about the situation. Attacking the barbarians as they advanced did not seem safe, for

only a few mercenaries of his own retinue were with
Sabinianus himself—part of the state army and public forces
was scattered in various cities and part was serving with
the general Onoulph. It seemed best to send orders out
to summon the soldiers and also to send the ambassador
to announce the appointment of the general. The horseman, who had been sent on in advance by Adamantius to
Theodoric, met the Romans as they were starting. He had
with him a priest of the barbarians, whom the Romans call
a presbyter, to give him surety of safe conduct. Taking this
man with them, they hastened forward to Lychidnus. The
men of that city, both the citizens of rank (for this city
was formerly wealthy and fortunate) and others, met them
and they entered the place.

Adamantius sent to Epidamnus again, ordering Theodoric to come to one of the places around Lychidnus with
a few followers to discuss the matters with him about
which he had sent a message, or, if he wished Adamantius to
come to Epidamnus, to send Soas, his general, and Dagistheus
as hostages to Lychidnus, to be retained until he returned.
The Goth sent these men, but ordered them to remain at
Scampia and send forward a man to bind Sabinianus by
oath to deliver the hostages unharmed when Adamantius
returned safely.

But Sabinianus refused to swear the oath. In former
times, he said, he had sworn to nothing, nor would he
now lay aside one of his old notions. When Adamantius
said that it was necessary to conform to the occasion or
the embassy would be fruitless—for he said he would not
go unless he received surety of his safety—Sabinianus was
not persuaded. He said the other knew what he should do,
but that he himself would do nothing contrary to his own
custom. Thereupon, Adamantius, being at a loss, took
two hundred soldiers and set out in the evening through
inaccessible hills and on a narrow and unused road, not
known to many. They said it was then traversed by cavalry
for the first time. He went by a circuitous route and came
to a fortress near Epidamnus, situated on a steep hill and

otherwise impregnable. Under it was a deep ravine through which flowed a swift river.

He summoned Theodoric to this place, and he came obediently, posting the rest of his army far off and reaching the river with a few cavalry. Adamantius, having stationed his soldiers in a ring around the hill so that there would be no encirclement on the part of his opponent, went down to a rock from which he could be heard and ordered the barbarian to dismiss the others. They conversed alone. When Theodoric had taken his stand he accused the Romans—justly, as it seemed—saying, "I myself chose to live completely outside Thrace, far off toward Scythia, and by remaining there I did not think I would disturb anyone. I was ready to obey the emperor in whatever he commanded. But you summoned me as though to a war against Theodoric, son of Triarius, and first promised that the general of Thrace would meet me at once with his forces. He never appeared. Then you promised that Claudius, the treasurer of the Gothic funds would come with our mercenaries' pay.[15] I did not see him. And, third, you gave me guides for the roads, who left the easier ways toward your enemies and took us by a steep path and under overhanging crags. As I went among these with my cavalry and wagons and all the camp equipment, I might have been almost completely wiped out along with my whole band, if the enemy had suddenly attacked us. I was forced to make an agreement with them, for which many thanks must be given, because though they could have destroyed me—being abandoned by you—they spared me."

Adamantius reminded him of his honors from the emperor: that he had been made a patrician and general—honors among the Romans for those who have toiled especially hard—and that he had been laden with other gifts and wealth. In return for all this he ought never to treat him otherwise than as his father. As a matter of fact Theodoric had been adopted as son-in-arms by Zeno in 474 at the time of Zeno's restoration after the rebellion of Basiliscus.[16] Adamantius also tried to remove the complaints against the emperor (which in my opinion were justified). He said that the Goth had acted intolerably, seizing parts of the Roman Empire under the pretext of an embassy, and that, although they had had him shut in Thrace by mountains and rivers and an encirclement of encamped soldiers, nevertheless, they had freely agreed to his leaving. He could not have moved from that position if the Romans had been unwilling, not even if he had had a force ten times greater than his present one. Therefore, he advised him to act more reasonably toward the emperor, for, in the long run, he would be unable to outdo the might of the Romans who opposed him on every side. If he would trust him, he ought to leave Epirus and the cities there, for it was not to be endured that such great cities should be occupied by him and their own native citizens expelled. He should go to Dardania where there was land—extensive compared with that he was now living on, and beautiful and fertile besides, and lacking settlers. Farming this, he could support his army in complete plenty.

Theodoric swore that he desired this, but that his army would not stand for it because of having suffered so many hardships earlier and of having now barely attained a cessation of them. While they were still not rested, he was unable to lead them on such a journey. The Romans, he said, ought to allow them to winter here now, if they did not go further than the cities they already had or cause additional devastation. And when agreement had been reached on all matters besides these, they should send a man, when spring came, to lead them to Dardania, and they would readily follow. He said that he was willing to put his baggage and host of noncombatants in any city the emperor chose, leave his mother and sister as hostages for his complete trustworthiness, and go as quickly as possible to Thrace with 6000 of his most warlike followers. He promised that with these and the Illyrian and any other troops which the emperor sent he would destroy all the Goths in Thrace on condition that, if he succeeded, he be made general in place of Theodoric, son of Triarius, and be received into the city to live as a citizen in the Roman way. He was even ready, if the emperor so ordered, to go to Dalmatia to restore Nepos to the Western throne.

Adamantius replied that he had no authority to make any agreement with him while he remained in that country, but that the emperor must first consent to the matter. He would, therefore, return, he said, and Theodoric should wait until he had learned the emperor's decision. They separated from one another on these terms.

While Adamantius was busy with these negotiations, Roman forces had assembled at Lychidnus in accordance with the orders of the general. Someone reported to Sabinianus that the barbarians were leisurely descending from Candavia—scorning danger—both those with the baggage and most of the wagons and those in the rear-guard, including Theodimundus, the brother of Theodoric, and the mother of the two, and that there was a good chance of conquering the greater part of them. Sabinianus was to go with the cavalry himself, and he sent a considerable body of infantry in a circuit through the mountains, telling them when and where they should make their appearance. Then he dined and set out with his army during the evening. At daybreak he attacked the Goths, who were already on their way. Theodimundus and his mother quickly fled at the attack, slipping down to the plain and at once destroying the bridge over which they crossed. This spanned a deep gully in the middle of the road and its destruction made pursuit impossible. They also, however, made escape impossible for some of their own men, so that, though they were few, in sheer desperation they came to close quarters with the cavalry. When the infantry appeared over their heads according to plan, they were defeated. Some died attacking the cavalry and some attacking the infantry. Sabinianus captured their 2000 wagons, more than 5000 soldiers, and no little booty. He burned some of the wagons in the mountains—since it was too much work to drag them through difficult craggy country—and returned to Lychidnus.

He found Adamantius returned from the meeting with
Theodoric, for Theodoric had as yet learned nothing of
what Sabinianus had done in the mountains. Sabinianus
placed the nobly born warriors under guard and distributed
the others among his soldiers with the booty. He had
ordered the cities to prepare many wagons for the use of
his army, but when he had captured the wagons he told
the cities not to trouble themselves further, since he had
enough. After this Adamantius wrote to the emperor, as
he had promised, about the discussion between Theodoric
and himself. Sabinianus and Joannes, the prefect, also
wrote about what had happened, boasting mightily and
asserting that it was unnecessary to make any agreement
with the barbarian, since there was hope of driving him
away from the country by force, or of wearing him down
if he remained.

When the emperor received these messages and considered that war was better than a shameful peace, he
summoned the embassy home, ordering that no agreement
be made yet with the enemy. He told Sabinianus and Gen-
ton, a Goth married to a Roman woman from around
Epirus and who had some influence there, to direct every
effort toward the war, since he had no intention of making
an agreement with the enemy. Adamantius summoned
his soldiers, praised them for their eager spirit, and, like
their fathers, ordered them to continue to act nobly, and
read them the emperor's command. Having encouraged
them with high hopes that the emperor never dismissed
any man's zeal without reward, he gained great praise and
was sent away with honor. He left, doing nothing more.

M.fr.19   Theodoric was held in check in Epirus by
Sabinianus until 481, but Constantinople was afflicted by
another civil war in these years when, towards the end of
479, Marcian rebelled. After violent fighting in and around
Constantinople Marcian was temporarily taken into custody.
Theodoric, the son of Triarius, learning of these events,
considered the time ripe to attack the city and the emperor himself. Straightway he raised all his barbarian force

and came with the pretence that he desired to guard the
emperor and the city, although it was abundantly clear
what he was actually coming for. When the emperor
heard the news he sent a cavalryman to him with a royal
letter, praising him for his zeal but ordering him to depart
—there no longer being need of him—lest he again in-
volve the city, just calmed down from such a great disturbance, in further suspicion and stir up the usual dis-
quiet to a worse outbreak.

The Goth replied that he would himself obey the emperor, but could no longer turn his host back—such a large
body having been collected and no small part of it being
unruly. He thought that no one would oppose him under the
walls—no parapets or towers having been set up—and that
all the populace would side with him on his arrival out of
hatred of the Isaurians. This was the very thing Zeno
feared, and he sent Pelagius with much money and many
promises of gifts for Strabo himself and for the whole
Gothic force. Pelagius persuaded them to go away, partly
by threats, partly by promises, and partly by no small sums
of money, tempting their naturally greedy character.

He considered that this removed an alarming threat
from the city, for if the Goth had entered there would
have been internecine warfare and a conflagration of everything. The Isaurians, determined not to be driven out
tamely, had prepared beforehand long poles with linen
and sulfur bound on their ends. If they had been attacked,
they were ready with these to set the whole city on fire.

Thus Strabo departed. The emperor, however, often sent
him messages, demanding Procopius, Marcian's brother,
his attendants, and Busalbus, and asking him to show in
this way evidence of his good will and obedience. The Goth
replied that he would obey the emperor in all respects, but
that it was not right for Goths, any more than for other
men, freely to hand over suppliants and persons demanding
safety to those who wished to arrest them. He, therefore,
asked the emperor to leave them alone, since they were
men who would in no way be troublesome, except insofar

as they lived. And so they lived with Strabo, farming a
small tract of land.

J.A.fr.211(4)   Alarmed and angered by this fresh show of
independence by the Goth, the emperor deprived Theodoric, the son of Triarius, of his office, and appointed Trocundes in his place, and set Aëtius over the forces in
Isauria. . . . Strabo then renewed an alliance with Theodoric and this union of the two Theodorics again disturbed
the affairs of the Romans, for they pillaged the cities
throughout Thrace, so that Zeno turned to the Bulgarians
who were then first summoned to an alliance. Theodoric
himself, being still in Epirus, was probably a silent partner
in this attack on the empire.

(5)   When Theodoric, the son of Triarius, met
the Huns [or Bulgarians rather, for these terms are constantly confused] and defeated them in battle, he advanced
against the city of Constantinople and would easily have
taken it, if Illus had not occupied the gates first and
guarded it. From there he crossed to the place called
Sycae and again failed in his attempt. Finally, he went over
to Near Hestiae and Losthenium so-called, and tried to
ferry across to Bithynia. But he was beaten in a sea fight
and went back to Thrace. From there he marched against
Greece with his son, Recitach, his two brothers, his wife, and
about 30,000 Scythians, but he was killed at the so-called
Stable of Diomede. While mounting his horse early one
morning, it threw him onto an upright spear standing at
the side of his tent. Some contended that the blow had
been aimed by his son, Recitach, who had been beaten
by him. His wife, Sigilda, who was present, buried him
by night. Recitach, his son, became ruler of the tribe with
his uncles on his father's side. A little later he slew them
and ruled the land of Thrace alone, performing more outrageous acts than his father.

J.A.fr.213   Strabo died in 481, and the next year Zeno,
having previously slain Sabinianus, the commander of Illyricum, by craft,[17] sent Joannes the Scythian and Moschi-
anus, generals, against the other Theodoric, who had again

rebelled and was ravaging both the Roman Empire and in particular the neighboring districts of Greece.

These generals were not the equals of Sabinianus, and Zeno was forced to come to terms with Theodoric in 483. Lands were assigned him and his followers in Moesia and along the Black Sea coast. He was made a master of soldiers [18] and consul for 484, and Zeno made plans to use him against the rebellious Illus. Theodoric before setting out eastward demanded the death of Recitach, since he could not leave a possible rival free scope in Europe during his absence.[19]

J.A.fr.214(3)   When Zeno saw that Recitach was hostile out of jealousy of Theodoric, he contrived to have him killed by the son of Valamir, who was his cousin, but who had an old grudge against him since he had killed his . . . .[20] He murdered Recitach in a suburb called Bonophatianae, when he was going from a bath to a feast, by striking him in his side.

(4)   Zeno sent Theodoric to the war against Illus, but when he reached Nicomedia he faithlessly recalled him, though the Gothic troops continued the war.[21] Then he sent some of the so-called Rugians under Ermenaric, the son of Aspar, against Illus. He also sent out an expedition by sea and appointed Joannes, Basiliscus, and Paul to be admirals, the latter having risen from slavery to become his bursar. The identity of these men is uncertain. Joannes the Scythian had replaced Illus as master of soldiers in the East, but it is hard to say whether he is meant. Paulus may be the former attacker whom Illus had spared or possibly his slave.[22]

(7)   A new breach between Theodoric and Zeno followed, and in 486, in the consulship of Longinus, who was appointed in the following period, when Theodoric again revolted and plundered the Thracian lands, Zeno turned the Rugian race against Odovacar, since he knew that this man was preparing for an alliance with Illus.[23] Odovacar and his army crowned themselves with a glorious victory in 487, and also sent gifts of the spoils to Zeno.

He anticipated the attack of the Rugians by attacking them in their own land beyond the Danube and utterly destroying their power. *Zeno then rejected these allies of his and rejoiced in what had been done.*

(8)   *In the next year Theodoric, returning from Novae, encamped at Regium, so-called, and attacked the neighboring lands—in particular Melantias about eighteen miles from Regium.*[24] *Being willing to give way to him, Zeno sent him his own sister, whom he had held living with the empress, with much money, while he was still waging war. He gave him whatever he wanted with the idea in mind that he might remain friendly.*

So for six years after the death of Strabo, Theodoric vibrated between peace and war with the empire. Then by a brilliant stroke of diplomacy Zeno and his advisers saw how they could at once rid themselves of the Ostrogothic menace and at the same time punish the barbarian usurper on the Western throne. Theodoric was commissioned to proceed to Italy against Odovacar. He left Moesia with his people in 488 and in the next year fought his way into Italy. Within two years almost all of Italy had been conquered and Odovacar, decisively beaten in the field, blockaded in Ravenna. This siege persisted for another two years, until finally under the urging and mediation of the local bishop the two rivals were induced to sign a compact in February 493.

J.A.fr.214a   *Theodoric and Odovacar agreed in a treaty with each other that both should rule the Roman Empire, and thereafter they talked together and frequently went to see each other. But ten days had not passed when Odovacar was at Theodoric's headquarters and two of the latter's henchmen came forward as though suppliants and grasped Odovacar's hands. Therewith those hidden in ambush in the rooms on either side rushed out with their swords. They were panic-stricken at the sight of their victim, and when they did not attack Odovacar, Theodoric himself rushed forward and struck him with a sword on the collarbone. When he asked "Where is God?" Theodoric answered, "This is what you did to my friends." The fatal blow pierced*

Odovacar's body as far as the hip, and they say Theodoric exclaimed, "There certainly wasn't a bone in this wretched fellow." Sending the corpse outside to the meeting places of the Hebrews he buried it in a stone coffin. Odovacar had lived sixty years and ruled fourteen. His brother was shot down with arrows on his allotment of land as he was fleeing, and Odovacar's wife, Sunigild, was arrested along with his son Ocla,[25] whom he had appointed Caesar. Theodoric sent this boy to Gaul, and when he returned to Italy he put him to death and had the wife stoned to death while in prison.

With this piece of barbaric treachery he established himself as sole ruler of an Ostrogothic kingdom in Italy. He lived until 526 and left behind him one of the most golden reputations for statesmanship, nobility, and honor.[26] This kingdom was eventually destroyed by Justinian.

The history of the next century differs in many ways from that of the fifth. The chief threats to the Eastern Empire no longer were to come from the north but from the traditional enemy—Persia—in the east. The empire was to maintain all her frontiers with relative ease and, under the great Justinian, was even to take the offensive and to win back North Africa, Sicily, Italy, and parts of Spain from the Germans. But from our point of view the greatest difference appears in reading about these events. In place of the dim and disjointed flickers of light thrown on events of the tragic fifth century by fragmentary or miserably inadequate chronicles, we have, for the sixth, great beacons of information in the magnificent and complete works of Procopius and the almost equally complete and illuminating writings of Joannes Lydas, Agathias, Menander Proctector, to say nothing of the huge compilation of laws and legal writings made under Justinian. If no other century of Roman imperial history after the first is so completely documented as the sixth no other (except possibly the third) is so poorly recorded as the fifth. But we can in the murk still discern the outlines of the Greek tragedy. The century started with barbarians dominant at the courts and in the army; it ended with half the empire having passed completely out of Roman control but with the remainder at last really independent of the foreigners and savages and so strengthened for another nine and a half centuries of civilized life.

Appendix A

Dates and Sources of Translated Fragments

Not all the extant fragments of Olympiodorus, Priscus, Malchus, and Joannes Antiochenus have been translated for the text. The omitted ones deal with mythology, personal adventures of the authors, people of no interest to political history or are repetitions of fragments already translated. Some minor fragments from Suidas only illustrate the use of certain words. It can be taken that every scrap from our authors that has the slightest bearing on political events has been translated.

In the following tables it will be noted that some fragments are undatable and even those to which a date has been assigned are not certain in all cases. The figures under the column headed *"De legationibus"* refer to the order in the two halves of that work. Priscus' fragments in the *De legat. Rom.* are to be found in Niebuhr on pages 166–228 and in the Paris edition on pages 47–76; those in the *De legat. gent.* are to be found on pages 140–65 and pages 33–46. Niebuhr notices many of the fragments from other sources too. Malchus' fragments in Niebuhr are on pages 244–68 (*De legat. Rom.*) and 231–43 (*De legat. gent.*), and in the Paris edition on pages 78–91 and 91–97. Here again Niebuhr has noticed many fragments from other sources. In many cases the fragments from Suidas are not specifically assigned to Priscus or Malchus, but the tradition of authorship seems very likely though it has been disputed in some instances. The page references under the heading "Translation" are to the text of this book. If present in more than one context I have listed the pages in the order in which they originally occurred.

OLYMPIODORUS

All translated fragments are from Photius' summary.

Fragment	Date	Translation
2	395–408	25–26
3	410 (Or 408?)	34
4	408	32
5	407	30
6	408	32
7		7
8	408–17	37
9	406	30
10	411	35
11		7
12	407–09	30–31
13	410–17	32–34
14	410	37–38
15	410	35
16	410	36–37
17	412	39
18	412?	59
19	412–13	39
20–21	413	40
22	414	40
23	414	38
24	414	40–41
26	414 or 415–18	41–42
29		22
30	408–10	36
31	416	42
33		17–18
34	417	43–44
35	418	43
37		16–17
39		44
40	423	44–45
41	423	45
42		45–46
43		23
44		22–23
46	425	46–47

CANDIDUS

Fragment 1 comes from the summary of Photius and fragment 2 from Suidas. The latter refers specifically to events of 468, but the rest covers the whole reigns of Zeno and Leo (457–91). Most of fragment 1 is translated on pages 132–33, 141–43, 128, 143; and fragment 2 on page 121.

PRISCUS

Fragment	Date	De Legationibus Rom.	Gent.	Other Sources	Translation
1	433	1			59–61
1a	441?			Peri Strategikes in Wescher, Poliorceticis, p. 304	61–62
1b	late 441			Ibid., pp. 305–6	63–65
2	441		1		62–63
3	443		2		65
3a	441			Chron. Pasch., pp. 588.4 (Bonn) s.a. 450	69–70
4	443	2			65
5	443		3		65–68
6	443–48		4		68–69
7	early 448		5		70–72
8	448–49	3			72–101
9	448				101
10	448			Jordanes xxxiv. 178–79	93, 57–58
11	448			Ibid., xxxv. 183, xxiv. 123–28	96
12	early 449		6	Suidas	101–2
13	449	4			102–3
14	449	5			103–4

15	450	7			105–6
16	450	8			106
17	452			Jordanes xlii. 222–23	108
18	452		6		109
19	452	9			109
20	451	10		last part Suidas	14
21	451	11			18–19
22	452				19–20
23	453			Evagrius H.E. ii. 5	109–11
24	455–56	12	7	Jordanes xlix. 254–58	115
25	465–66	13	8		11
26	465–66				11–12
27	457–60		9		116–17
28	461		10		158
29	460–61	14			118
30	462–63	15			118–19, 133–34
31	464		11		120, 8–9 (mingled)
32	464		12		120, 9
33	465				9–11
34	465–66	16			12
35	470	17			158
36	467	18			134
37	467	19			12–13
38	467	20			134–35

Fragment	Date	De Legationibus Rom.	De Legationibus Gent.	Other Sources	Translation
39	467 or 471		21		135–36
40	467	13			120
41	468		22		13
42	468			Theophanes, pp. 178–79 (Bonn)	120–21
Uncert.	?			Suidas	51
MALCHUS					
1	473		1		14–16
2	471–74		2		159–60
2a				Suidas	131–32
3	474–75	3			124–25
4	474–75	4			161
5	474–75			Suidas	161
6	475			Suidas	141
7	474–77			Suidas	145
8	475–77			Suidas	145–46
8a	475–77			Suidas	147
8b	475–77	5			146

	various			source	
8c	various			Suidas	147
9				Suidas	147, 139–40, 140–41
10	477				127–28
11	478	3			162–63
12	?	6	4		140
13	478		5		125–26
14	478	7			163–64
15	478	8			164–66
16	478		6		166–68
17	478	9			168–69
18	479	1			169–70
19	479	2			178–80
20	478 f			Suidas	150–51
21	484 f			Suidas	155–56

JOANNES ANTIOCHENUS

		source	
191–92	408 f	De Virtute, pp. 849–50	27
193		Ibid.	27
194		Ibid. and Suidas	27–28
195	423–25	De Insidiis, p. 70	47
196	425	Salmasian, pp. 399–400	47–48
198		De Insidiis, p. 71	70
199	449–50	Ibid.	104–5

Fragment	Date	De Legationibus Rom.	Gent.	Other Sources	Translation
200	454–55			Salmasian, p. 400	50–51, 52, 53–54
201	454–55			De Insidiis, p. 72 f	51, 52, 50, 52–53, 113–14
202	456			Ibid.	116
203	460–61			Ibid.	117
204	46of			Ibid.	119–20
205	467			Ibid.	136
206	469–70			Ibid.	137
207	470			Ibid.	122
208				Ibid.	138
209	472–74			Ibid.	122–23
210	475			Ibid.	144
211	477–81			Ibid.	147–50, 180
213	482			Ibid.	180–81
214 (1–7)	484–87			Ibid. p. 83	152, 181, 152–53, 181–82, 153–54
(7–12)	487–88			De Insidiis, but from another ms., the codex Escorialensis Ω I, 11	154, 182, 154, 13–14, 154–55
214a					
493				Ibid.	182–83

De Virtute is the Codex Turonensis; *De Insidiis* is the Codex Parisinus 1666; Salmasian is the Codex Parisinus 1763 named after its editor Salmasius.

Appendix B

The Historians

CANDIDUS

Candidus the Isaurian is known to us only from what Photius tells us, and his work is preserved (apart from one passage in Suidas) only in the summary of that man. It is, however, highly likely that many passages in Joannes Antiochenus dealing with Isaurian affairs derive from him, as well as some passages from Suidas more usually assigned to Malchus and others. He seems to have written shortly after 491, when he left Constantinople and was therefore a contemporary and possible eyewitness of much he tells us. Even allowing for a natural pro-Isaurian bias he must be considered a primary source of foremost importance for the whole story of the Isaurian ascendancy under Leo and Zeno.

JOANNES ANTIOCHENUS

There were probably two men whose work is now combined into one work under the name of John of Antioch, one of whom lived in the seventh and the other in the tenth century. The former is probably the author of the passages dealing with the fifth century. He seems to have made use of the best authors, Zosimus, Socrates, Priscus, and Candidus among them, and this wealth of contemporary history makes Joannes particularly useful for this century.

MALCHUS

Malchus' history is variously reported to have covered the whole period from Constantine to Anastasius or to have been restricted to the years 473–80. The earlier books must have been condensed summaries, and certainly all that has survived pertains to the narrow range of seven years. Apparently, he continued Priscus' chronicle, maintaining his high standards of accuracy and vividness in narrative. His interests are almost purely political and military, and, while he is reported to have followed "a religion not outside the Christian church," his

interest in ecclesiastical affairs was minimal. He was almost
certainly a contemporary of the events he describes.

OLYMPIODORUS

The original twenty-two books of the history of this man are
preserved only in Photius' summary. He came from Thebes in
Egypt, but seems to have traveled widely in the West as well
as in the East, and many of his fragments preserve the results
of personal observation. His work covered the years 407 to 425.
He apologized for his style to his contemporaries, calling his
work "source material," but the things the ancients criticize in
him are the very things we praise. He is extremely careful about
his use of technical terms, even if these were not acceptably
literary or even Greek, and his bald factual reporting, stripped
of all vague elegances of fashionable style, and his passion for
statistical, geographic, and chronological accuracy have proved
most valuable for historians of his own day as well as of ours.
He was certainly used by Zosimus and most probably by
Socrates, Sozomen, and Philostorgius, so that our knowledge of
events of the first quarter of the century depends more on
Olympiodorus than might be suspected from the extent of the
fragments.

PRISCUS

The history of Priscus of Panium was without doubt the
most readable and most reliable produced in this century, and
its loss the most regrettable. It originally covered the period
from 433 to 474. Priscus had many of the faults usual to Byzantine historians—a desire to be elegant at the cost of accuracy and preciseness and a dislike of statistics of all kinds,
of careful chronology, and of geographic detail. He has been
accused of bias in favor of the privileged landed classes and even
of such slavish imitation of the great classical historians that he
sacrifices truth to literary merit. On the other hand he knew
many high government officials and took part in several of
the episodes he records. And any reader can judge for himself
his ability as a vivid storyteller; the eighth fragment is justifiably
famous and of all these fragments the only one frequently
translated. The ancients uniformly praised him, and other historians—Joannes Antiochenus, Jordanes, the author of the
Paschal Chronicle, Evagrius, and Theophanes—made wide use
of him in compiling their works. J. B. Bury, in his *History of
the Later Roman Empire* (1923, I, 279–88), and A. J. Toyn-

bee, in *Greek Civilization and Character* (Library of Greek Thought Series, pp. 130–36), have translated or paraphrased most of the eighth fragment. C. C. Mierow in his translation of Jordanes gives, of course, those fragments of Priscus found in his author.

Notes

CHAPTER 1

1. Magistros when not further specified always means the master of offices in Greek writers. On this office Cf. *Not. Dig. Or.* vi. 52, and A. E. R. Boak, *The Master of the Offices in the Later Roman and Byzantine Empires* (University of Michigan Studies, 1924).
2. E. A. Thompson, *The History of Attila and the Huns* (Oxford, 1948), p. 99, n.
3. Cf. p. 19 and J. B. Bury, *Later Roman Empire* (1923), I, 37 n., who summarizes the evidence.
4. Cf. p. 166.
5. Procopius' usual name *Bell. Pers.* I. iii. 1 and etc. From his description they hardly seem of the same race as Attila. Cf. n. 13.
6. The text has "Constantine" here and in frag. 32 (first mention) but "Constantius" elsewhere. The text says third "consulship" in frag. 32, but he was only consul once—in 457. He was praetorian prefect.
7. Compare the story in Herodotus iii. 1.
8. As assessor according to Valesius, p. 538 (Bonn).
9. Cf. Ch. V, n. 5.
10. The text is corrupt, and I have adopted Tillemont's conjecture here. Classen's guess that machen here and below indicates the name of the leader of the Souanni is possible but by itself does not explain this passage. The word sematos without a capital in the text is here supposed to be the name of the leader of the Lazi.
11. I.e., the expedition against the Vandals in 468, cf. p. 120.
12. Müller emends the wrong "7" to "sixty." The date of Perozes' death is determined by an eclipse (Procopius *Bell. Pers.* I. iv). Cabades or Kawad did not succeed till 487–88, and I have changed the "one year" of the text to "four years." Balas, Perozes' brother, ruled in this interval.

13. But Ed. Drouin in *Le Museon*, xiv (1895), 143–44, distinguishes the Kidarites from the Ephthalite or White Huns. Cf. A. Cunningham, "Ephthalite, or White, Huns," *Transactions of Ninth International Oriental Congress* (London, 1892), and Bury, *op. cit.* (1923), II, 5–8 and notes.

14. Cf. Socrates vii. 20, and Sozomen ix. 4.

15. The Greek is ambiguous as to who received the picture. The last clause is omitted by Müller and, if Niebuhr is correct, should be.

16. Theophanes 5990 A.M.

17. Smaragdos in Greek was a green precious stone, but there is doubt whether it was what we call an emerald.

18. Herodotus iii. 26, and again iv. 181; cf. W. W. How and J. Wells, *Commentary on Herodotus* (Oxford, 1928).

19. E. A. Thompson, "Olympiodorus of Thebes," *Class. Quart.*, XXXVIII (1944), 44, is wrong in identifying Siwah here.

20. Procopius *Bell. Pers.* I. xix. 32–33; Jordanes *De success. regn.* mentions Florus in this connection and calls him procurator of Alexandria.

21. Priscus' (?).

22. *Later Roman Empire* (1923), I, 50 n. Cf. also Tenny Frank, *Economic History of Rome* (Baltimore, 1920), pp. 80–83.

23. *The History of Attila and the Huns*, p. 74.

24. Anon. Vales. 73.

25. Cf. pp. 42–43.

26. Reinesius and Niebuhr emend this name to Olybrius, and Müller (index) implies this was the emperor of fifty years later (472). This is impossible, and, though Thompson, *op. cit.*, p. 50, adopts this name, I can find no basis for the emendation beyond the reputation of the Olybrii for wealth. The Olympius may be the same as the minister of Honorius (frag. 2 and frag. 8). Samuel Dill, *Roman Society in the Last Century of the Western Empire* (London, 1898), pp. 126 and 127 n., seems to identify this Probus with Symmachus' friend, the consul of 371. This is obviously wrong, but possibly he was of the same, the Anician, family, which was famous for its wealth.

CHAPTER 2

1. This sympathetic picture surely comes from another source than that used for frag. 194. Could it be Olympiodorus? Nearly the same words are found in Socrates vii. 22, who we know used Olympiodorus.

2. The rest of this passage from Suidas, *s.v.* Theodosius ho mikros is almost word for word the same as the end of the previous paragraph. Niebuhr assigns it to Priscus.

3. Zosimus v. 26; 29, 14.

4. Justinianus and Neviogastes, in Zosimus vi. 2.

5. The poems of Claudian are the best sources for the career of Stilicho, though full of the most abject flattery of his hero.

6. This was, at any rate, Stilicho's argument though Gratian had given this region earlier to the east (Zosimus v. 26, 2).

7. Jordanes xxx. 157.

8. Prosper *s.a.*

9. Müller has sakkois and translates *saccis*, "with sacks," an idea completely unintelligible to me. Dindorf has sokkois "lassoes."

10. This could mean New Carthage (Cartagena) in Spain. Schottus suggested an emendation to Ravenna which has not been accepted. Bury, *op. cit.* (1923), I, 195 n. 2, without evidence thinks the heads of Constantine and Julian had been set up at Cartagena, but those of Jovinus and Sebastian were sent to Carthage in view of the revolt of Heraclian there in this year.

11. If this is the eastern *comes domesticorum*, mentioned in frag. 46, pp. 46 f., as the indices of Müller and Dindorf both imply, he must have given this advice to hurt Honorius, as part of the continuing friction between the two courts of Constantinople and Ravenna.

12. Orosius vii. 42.

13. Modii probably; a modius was about a quarter bushel.

14. From Socrates vii. 23–24; cf. Philostorg. xii. 13.

15. The Greek has "Goths."

16. E. A. Freeman, "Aëtius and Boniface," E.H.R., II (July 1887), 337, n. 2. and Bury, *op. cit.* (1923), I, 245, discredit this whole episode on the (unproved) grounds that Aëtius was then in Gaul.

17. Cf. p. 28.

18. Valens in the Greek. Thompson, *Class. Quart.*, XLI (1947), 65, denies that this passage from Suidas, *s.v.* Thladias ("eunuch") comes from Priscus. Müller attributes it to Joannes Antiochenus. Aëtius died in 454 (Marcellinus *s.a.*). The end of the passage (not given here) is almost the same word for word as the end of J. Ant. frag. 200 (1).

19. A back to front way of putting it. The next sentence is also corrupt.

20. Something is missing from the text.

CHAPTER 3

1. xxxi. 2, 11.

2. Dindorf and Müller too cautiously suppose that Jordanes' use of Priscus ends here, but they give no reason. Since I believe the whole passage is based on Priscus, I have here translated it. There is certainly no indication in Jordanes that he has ceased to use his source and some reasons to believe the opposite (see n. 3 below).

3. The same tribes are mentioned in Priscus frag. 1. with slight variations in spelling, but there the first and second are grouped together as Amilzouri. Possibly a marginal correction has crept into Jordanes' text here. This coincidence of names shows that Jordanes is here still following Priscus as also does his use of the Greek word ephebi for "youths" below.

4. Marcellinus *s.a.* 427.

5. Not after 408 as Bury, *History of the Later Roman Empire*, I (1889), p. 126, says. Uldin was then in the West serving with Stilicho.

6. Sozomen ix. 5; cf. Socrates vi. 1.

7. Zosimus v. 22 f.; Philostorg. xi. 8; Marcellinus *s.a.* 406; Orosius vii. 37, 12.

8. Socrates vii. 43; Prosper *s.a.* 423 and 425; Renatus in Gregory of Tours ii. 8; Philostorg. xii. 14; Prosper Tiro *s.a.* 423; cf. E. A. Freeman, "Aëtius and Boniface," *E.H.R.*, II (July 1887), 454. E. A. Thompson, *The History of Attila and the Huns*, p. 64, thinks the cession of Pannonia was by the treaty of 433, but cf. Marcellinus *s.a.* 427.

9. Niebuhr's addition to the text.

10. Thompson, *op. cit.*, pp. 216–17. Epigenes was not actually quaestor till after 438.

11. A hiatus in the text is partly filled by Niebuhr.

12. Jordanes xxxv. 182, possibly from Priscus. Cf. Gibbon, III, 418.

13. E.g., the Altiziagiri and Akatziri of Jordanes v. 37. For Ulmerguri cf. Jordanes v. 26. For the Saraguri and Onoguri cf. below p. 207.

14. Thompson, *op. cit.*, p. 218.

15. *Germ.* 43.

16. Seeck, *Untergang*, VI, 291.

17. An obvious corruption. Naissus, as Priscus himself says (p. 71), is five days' journey from the Danube. Besides, Priscus always calls this river the Ister, and not even elsewhere do we find a form like Danoubas for Danoubios. As Thompson says (*Class. Quart.*, XLI, 61) the difficulty is insoluble and none of the proposed emendations attractive. Nisch is on the Nischava River, the ancient name of which is unknown.

18. Constantine was born and brought up at Naissus and later decorated the city, but he did not found it. Cf. Müller, V, 25 n. for references.

19. The whole bridge story is an obviously bad guess. The Huns would not waste time building a bridge during a campaign, and surely Naissus had a bridge before this. Cf. Thompson, *The History of Attila and the Huns*, p. 83 n.

20. Cf. p. 94.

21. For the second embassy cf. pp. 102 f. On his other offices cf. Theodoret *Ep.* 47, and p. 94. For Zeno cf. pp. 98 f.

22. Bury, *op. cit.* (1923), I, 235 n. and Thompson, *op. cit.*, pp. 192–93 and 282.

23. For the Vandals *cf. Nov. Valent.* III, Tit. ix, dated 440, and Prosper *s.a.* 442. For the Saracens cf. p. 14. For the Ethiopians cf. above pp. 18 f.

24. I am at a loss to explain the meaning of this sentence.

25. J. Ant. frag. 198. For Cyrus cf. also Malalas, p. 361 (Bonn), Theophanes, p. 149 (Bonn), John Lydus *De Mag.* ii. 12, Suidas, *s.v.* Kyros and Theodosius ho mikros which may be from Priscus (Niebuhr, p. 226, and Bury, *op. cit.* (1923), I, 227–28).

26. Marcellinus *s.a.* 447 and 448.

27. T. Hodgkins, *Italy and Her Invaders* (Oxford, 1892), II, 517. Cf. Malchus, pp. 126 f. below, and Anon. Vales. 45.

28. Or Vigilas as many transcribe his name. Cf. Thompson, *op. cit.*, p. 98 n.

29. Socrates vii. 20; *Cod. Theod. Novell. Mart.* Tit. II. 1.7; Gib-

bon, III, 434 n. W. Ensslin has collected the facts about him in "Maximinus und sein Begleiter, der Historiker Priscos," *Byzantinische-neugriechische Jahrbucher*, V (1926–27), 1–9.

30. Cf. p. 71.

31. Pearls? Cf. Thompson, *Class. Quart.*, XLI (1947), 62.

32. Cf. p. 126.

33. So Thompson, *op. cit.*, p. 63.

34. Bury, *op. cit.* (1923), I, 212 n., is quite wrong in saying Müller mistranslates this passage. This refers not to Attila's message (p. 70), as Bury asserts, but obviously to the emperor's letter *to* Attila on p. 73. Thompson, *The History of Attila and the Huns*, p. 106, follows Bury's error.

35. In 443 (above p. 65) or early this same year (p. 70).

36. Cf. p. 97.

37. Cf. p. 83.

38. Thompson, *The History of Attila and the Huns*, p. 64, thinks that Carpileon became a hostage in 433 (cf. note 8 above); Bury, *op. cit.* (1923), I, 291, quoting Cassiodorus *Variae* i. 4, 11, says 425.

39. Akatziri here, but elsewhere (pp. 86, 90, 134, 12) Akatiri and below (p. 81) Katziri. The same tribe is mentioned by Jordanes v. 36, and probably again xxiv. 126. They are certainly to be grouped if not identified with the tribe of Amilzouri in frag. 1 (cf. n. 3 above). They lived on the shores of the Black Sea (p. 90). On their name, cf. Thompson, *op. cit.*, p. 95 n. and 96.

40. This scheme was later apparently carried out (cf. p. 90). This son's name was Ellac (Jordanes l. 262).

41. This could read "his daughter Escam," but lack of comment by Priscus precludes this possibility, so startling to a Roman and to us.

42. Cf. Thompson, *Class. Quart.*, XLI (1947), 63.

43. A similar custom is recorded by Marco Polo among a tribe dwelling in Mongolia or western China (Everyman edition, ch. 38, p. 107).

44. Valesius proposed for Armiou trapezes to read arguriou trapezes or money exchange. Bury translates "silversmith (or banker)." Armius is unknown.

45. The date is probably 441 or 443 rather than 447, the three years of known Hunnish invasions, since below we have a story about a man captured in this siege who, by the time of Priscus' visit, had built an elaborate bath for Onegesius out

of laboriously imported stone. This would likely be more than a year's work, and it is not recorded as being newly completed in 448. Furthermore, Bleda is mentioned as living after this siege and he was murdered in 444 or 445. Thompson, *The History of Attila and the Huns*, says (p. 81) that Sirmium fell in 441, but he also says (p. 211) that it happened in 443.

46. The text reads "and to ordinary people," which does not accord with what immediately follows. Bury translates "and to others for sacred purposes." Others delete the "and" and so read "ordinary priests." I prefer to read with Müller "and not."

47. Cf. p. 101.

48. Cf. p. 81.

49. Cf. Thompson, *Class. Quart.*, XLI (1947), 63. He draws parallels to this description of hair style from Herodotus iii. 8, 3, and Procopius *Anec.* vii. 10.

50. Cf. p. 63.

51. To stratiotikon siteresion or *annona militaris* (Müller). Toynbee says "Army Food Stuffs Quota." Thompson, *op. cit.*, p. 64, suggests "and they appointed others to collect etc.," involving an unnecessarily great emendation, it seems to me.

52. Marcian's first novel (450) aimed at reforming the bad administration of justice in the provinces and the culpability of local judges (*Cod. Just.* VII. 51, 4, i.e., Novell. Marc. I, 1, 7). This complaint is, therefore, well founded.

53. Hereca, according to Thompson, *op. cit.*, p. 64, was the original name. It is spelled Rhekan on p. 98. The Cerca of Gibbon is in error. She was, of course, only the chief of his harem.

54. Date unknown but possibly 423-25, when Rome and Constantinople were in conflict over the usurper Joannes.

55. The text lacks the number of days. Does the flame from the sea refer to the oil fields of Baku? Cf. Thompson, *op. cit.*, p. 31 and n., and Marquart, *Eranšahr*, p. 97.

56. Cf. p. 65 and pp. 102 f.

57. There were two men by the name of Ardaburius, one the father of Aspar and the leader of the expedition against Joannes in 425 (Olympiodorus frag. 46, p. 46), and the other the son of Aspar (frag. 20, p. 14). Aspar led an

expedition to Libya against the Vandals under Gaiseric in 430 (Procopius *De bell. Vand.* III. iii. 35).

58. Saturnilus in the text but, as Müller translates, Saturninus is undoubtedly the name indicated. He was a *comes domesticorum*.

59. Athenaïs, as she was known before her marriage to Theodosius II, or Eudocia, as she was known after it, had retired in disgrace to Jerusalem in 444 (Marcellinus *s.a.*), and the destruction of the count of the bodyguard occurred there. Zeno was not the future emperor, but had been consul in 448 probably as a direct reward for his activity around Constantinople during the invasion of 447, the "war" mentioned here. It was probable that it was in the same year that he was made master of soldiers in the East in succession to Anatolius (p. 65). The dispute about Constantius' bride had, therefore, been going on for at least four years—since before the death of Saturninus. Rufus was a brother of Apollonius (p. 109) and a consul himself in 457.

60. I would read basilea pseudesthai and make the statement parallel to Constantion . . . diamartein, a simpler emendation than others have proposed.

61. Cf. p. 68.

62. Cf. p. 54.

63. The following begins Bk. IV of Priscus' history.

64. Jordanes v. 33. He disputes the inclusion of Vandals in the Sarmatian federation (ix. 58); cf. also xii. 74. The term is usually applied to an Iranian people.

65. I adopt Classen's emendation in spite of Thompson's argument, *Class. Quart.*, XLI (1947), 64, that it is unnecessary. But Thompson is undoubtedly right in his interpretation of the 100 pounds of gold mentioned here. Fifty pounds of this was the original bribe offered to Edeco (p. 72, the sum referred to on p. 103 is not this bribe as Thompson says) and the other fifty is the ransom for Bigilas (p. 101 and again p. 103) which, in fact, he did not yet have.

66. Cf. p. 61.

67. But cp. p. 70 and n. 25 above. Joannes summarizes this whole episode.

68. Cf. p. 65 and n. 59 above.

69. He must have succeeded Martialus, possibly because of the latter's association with the plot against Attila.
70. Cf. p. 60.
71. The Vandals are probably meant and the expedition that of 441, or perhaps 430, though the latter would make his widow rather old.
72. Cf. n. 59 above.
73. Flavius Bassus Herculanus was not consul until 452.
74. Malalas xiv, p. 366 (Bonn).
75. Probably the semimythical king Merovech who united the Salian Franks into a strong kingdom (c. 440–50), though Gibbon, III, 455, thinks Clodion, his father, is here indicated.
76. Or, adopting Niebuhr's emendation, "when I was on an embassy at Rome."
77. Sir Edward Creasy, for instance, includes it, under the title of the Battle of Chalons, in his *The Fifteen Decisive Battles of the World.*
78. Jordanes and Idatius, respectively. The other sources for the war are listed in Gibbon, III, 458, n. 33.
79. Gibbon, III, p. 466.
80. Jordanes xl. 221.
81. Thompson, *The History of Attila and the Huns,* pp. 147–48. The last part of this fragment is not usually included among the preserved works of Priscus, but in Jordanes whence this quotation is taken there is no indication of where he ceases using his source. Other sources for this episode are *Chron. Pasch.,* pp. 587–88 (Bonn), and Malalas, p. 359, 4 (Bonn).
82. On pp. 98 and 103 she is called the daughter of Saturninus.
83. Marcellinus *s.a.* 454.
84. Müller only includes in Priscus' fragments the passage to "true evidence." Dindorf's text ends here, but he adds that the rest of the story from Jordanes here included is possibly from Priscus too. I concur.

CHAPTER 4

1. Majorian passed a law to preserve the buildings of Rome (*Nov.* 4), probably as an outcome of Avitus' vandalism.

2. Gregory of Tours *Hist. Franc.* ii. 11.
3. Hodgkin, *op. cit.*, II, 426–27.
4. So Bury, *op. cit.* (1923), I, 332, n. 1. The first two sentences of this fragment (omitted here) repeat verbatim the first two of Priscus frag. 27.
5. Idatius *s.a.* Cf. Anon. Cusp. and Marcellinus for these years.
6. Sidonius *Carm.* II. 348 f. and below frag. 30. Theophanes wrongly dates the treaty restoring the royal ladies in 457 (cp. Idatius *s.a.* 462). Cf. Procopius *De bell. Vand.* I. v. 6.
7. Cf. Priscus frag. 40, p. 120.
8. Suidas *sub* Markellinos.
9. Jordanes xlv. 236 dates this attack in 467; Anon. Cusp. gives the year 464 (Cf. also Cassiodorus, Marcellinus, and Paulus Diac. *s.a.*). Only the first and second last sentences of frag. 31 are quoted here.
10. The first two sentences repeat verbatim the last two of frag. 31. The last sentence is on p. 9.
11. The text has 100,000, but I accept Müller's emendation (followed by Dindorf). Cedrenus says 1113, p. 613. (Bonn).
12. Reading arkountōn with Müller and Valesius, but otherwise Dindorf's text. Müller translates the last clause "since expenses were abundantly available, partly from the public funds," etc. Bury. *op. cit.* (1923), I, 337, n. 3. adopts this reading too. Procopius *De bell. Vand.* I. vi, tells the whole story of this expedition.
13. He is not unlikely the same man as in Priscus, frag. 8, p. 83, since in the earlier period he was a military man, and *magister* here could mean *magister militum*, though when he occupied that post or where is unknown.
14. The Greek has "nine," but cf. below.
15. The Greek has Gundoubandus first and Gundubales here and calls him first Ricimer's brother, then his nephew. But they are both the same Gundobad in the German forms. Ricimer's sister had married the Burgundian King Gundioc, and this was their son, now in Roman service and later to succeed his father as king of the Burgundians.
16. An anonymous chronicle quoted by Clinton, *Fasti Romani*, *s.a.*, gives the dates of July 11 and August 18. Cassiodorus gives the interval of 40 days. The anonymous chronicle

gives the date of Olybrius' death as October 23, but cf. Bury, *op. cit.* I (1923), 340, n. 6. All other sources give the figure of seven months for Olybrius' reign.

17. Victor Vitensis i. 17, and Procopius *De bell. Vand* i. 7.

18. There had been a peace made with Byzantium in 475 (frag. 3) and with Rome under Romulus Augustulus (Paulus Diac. xv. 7). The war may be the war with Euric, concluded in 475, in which the Vandals sided with the Visigoths (Jordanes xlvii), but this hardly concerned Byzantium. Unless we go back to 468 there was no war "just finished," arti kathistamenon, with the East. But that means a very generous interpretation of arti ("lately") and calls for an explanation as to why these present matters were not settled by Severus in 475.

19. Cf. Victor Vitensis ii. 3 f.

20. Bury, *op. cit.*, p. 405.

21. Odovacar had a brother named Onoulph (Onulf or Hunulph) (frag. 8c, p. 147 and J. Ant., frag. 209). Jordanes liv. 277, mentions an Edico, or Edica, and a Hunnuulf, *primates* of the Scyri, but Hodgkin, *op. cit.*, II, 517, n. 1, and III, 23, n. 1, thinks that this resemblance of names to Odovacar's father and brother is purely accidental and disputes Gibbon's identification of the men (ed. Bury, IV (1909), 53). If the Onoulph of frags. 8a and 8c is Odovacar's brother, as J. Ant., frag. 209 (1), specifically states, Odovacar was half Thuringian and half Scyrian. J. Ant. (*loc. cit.*) says he was "of the nation of the Scyri." Cf. also Anon. Vales. 45, and above pp. 70, 74.
On Odovacar's name cf. Hodgkin, *op. cit.*, II, 516, and III, 150.

CHAPTER 5

1. Cf. p. 14.

1a. Zonaras xiv. 1 *init.*

2. Or Tarasicodissa of Rusumblada according to E. W. Brooks, "The Emperor Zenon and the Isaurians," *E.H.R.*, VIII (1893), 212, n. 12.

3. But Marcellinus *s.a.* 471, and Evagrius ii. 16 (quoting Priscus) say Patricius was killed at this time.

4. The Greek says "not being present with his son" (phynti, an obvious error for physanti, "father").

5. The Saraguri, possibly the same as the Sadagarii of Jordanes l. 265 who at least lived in the same region, reappear as a threat to Persia in frag. 37 (pp. 12 and 62). They are also mentioned by Zachariah of Mitylene, p. 328. The Onoguri are certainly the Hunnish Hunuguri of Jordanes v. 37, where the Sabiri are also mentioned. Cf. frag. 1a (p. 62).

6. This passage in parentheses is from Suidas, *s.v.* Abaris, and inserted by conjecture of Classen, since Suidas repeats, *loc. cit.* and *s.v.* Akatiroi and Saragouroi, much that is also recounted here. Thompson, *Class. Quart.*, XLI (1947), 64, points to a close imitation of Herodotus in this passage. It is therefore interesting to note that in iii. 116 Herodotus also discusses griffins. Thus, there is another parallel strengthening Classen's conjecture and probably nullifying the emendation to "vultures" proposed by Hemsterhuis.

7. Cf. p. 61. Marcian had probably discontinued it.

8. In 469 at any rate according to Bury, *op. cit.* (1923), I, 320, n. 4. This friend of Aspar later served with Strabo, son of Triarius (John Malalas xiv, p. 371, (Bonn) and Theophanes *s.a.* 5964).

9. Suidas, *s.v.* Indakos and Cherreos. The last part may pertain to events recorded in frag. 214(5) below.

10. Suidas, *s.v.* Epinicus. He calls him "prefect of the city under Basiliscus," but since he was in office in 478 and obviously held power in the provinces these statements are mistakes. This passage is probably from Malchus (so Müller) or Candidus; cf. p. 148. Joannes Lydus *De Mag.* iii. 45 also tells of financial mismanagement and administrative inability in this reign.

11. Also variously called Harmatus (Suidas) and Armatus (as here).

12. Theodore Lector i. 20.

13. Epinicius in this passage.

14. On this theological dispute cf. Theodore Lector i. 32–33, p. 182 (ed. Migne).

15. Apollinaris Sidonius, "Panegyric on Avitus," 1, 323.

16. Brooks, *op. cit.*, p. 218 f. and Hodgkins, *op. cit.*, III, 51 f. straighten out these events.

17. The text is corrupt here. The date is from Marcellinus *s.a.*, though Theophanes says 478, the year after Zeno's return!

18. Cf. pp. 150 f., where Thebes is given as his birthplace.
19. Cf. p. 178. Marcian was Verina's son-in-law.
20. There is a hiatus in the text here.
21. Was this the murderer of Valentinian now serving in the East? Dionysius probably commanded the palatini not the scholae. He was praetorian prefect in 479–80, and possibly the envoy to Lazica in 465 (p. 12).
22. For additional information on Pamprepius cf. J. Ant., frag. 211(2), Candidus, Damascius *ap.* Photius, Eustathius, frag. 4, and Suidas, *s.v.* Saloustios (from Damascius probably). He was, according to this last reference, "a writer of epics, flourishing in the reign of the emperor Zeno. He wrote a rendering of Etymologies and an Isaurian Catalogue," which were probably prose works. Suidas, *s.v.* Pamprepios (also possibly from Damascius), also says he was from Panopolis in the Thebaid and was of dark skin; he was possibly a Negro. There is an excellent article on him by J. R. Asmus, *B.Z.,* XXII, 320 f. "Pamprepios," which also discusses the pagan influence of his period.
23. Also called Lingis (Suidas, *s.v.* biaioi), Ninilingis (Theophanes), Indes (Evagrius), and Lilinges (Jordanes *De regn. succ.*). But cp. Brooks, *op. cit.,* p. 226.
24. He was not an Isaurian (Josh. Styl. 14) and so cannot have come from the Isaurian Dalisandus.
25. Cf. p. 181.
26. The Greek "shield-bearer" often indicates a chamberlain, but here probably something like an adjutant.
27. Theophanes, A.M. 5976.
28. Toumbikas for *tu vincas.*
29. Who this Conon or the men called Longinus are is unknown. Neither Longinus is the one from Kardala mentioned above. In Mommsen's text, *Hermes,* VI (1872), 330, the son is unnamed, and even Müller thinks it is a gloss. In that case the unnamed son might be the just-mentioned Conon. Cf. Brooks, *loc. cit.*

CHAPTER 6

1. J. Ant. frag. 206, p. 138 and Jordanes lii. 268–71.
2. Hodgkin, *op. cit.,* pp. 15 and 16 n.
3. Jordanes l. 265; lii. 275; xlvi. 242.
4. Jordanes liii. 276.

5. L. Schmidt, *Geschichte der deutschen Stämme*, I, 127, n. 3. In this case anepsios (J. Ant. frag. 214 (3)) represents a loose description of the relationship. To avoid confusion I consistently use the name Strabo for this man unless our authorities specify him as the son of Triarius. Often they simply call him Theodoric.

6. No man of this name is known. Niebuhr suggests either Pelagius (cf. frag. 19) or Eulogius (frag. 2a). T. Hodgkin, *op. cit.*, III, 76, says Pelagius.

7. *Magister equitum et peditum praesentalis.* Brooks, *op. cit.*, p. 216, thinks this is correct in spite of J. Ant. frag. 210, who says he was *magister militum per Thraciam.* Heracleius held that post (frag. 4).

8. Cf. p. 144.

9. The text is corrupt. Müller translates "*et venerint, ut aurum modio admetiantur,*" which is far too loose, even wrong. Hodgkin, *loc. cit.*, p. 87, has "and the time hath been when these penniless wanderers would use a bushel to measure their *aurei,*" a free translation, but I prefer Hoeschler's emendation as here translated. A *medimnus* is just over one and a half bushels.

10. Hodgkin, *op. cit.*, p. 88 n.

11. The great wall of the city was built by Anthemius in the minority of Theodosius II and rebuilt after an earthquake in 447, but the wall normally called "The Long Wall" was not built till 497, under Anastasius—Bury, *op. cit.* (1923), I, 435, n. 5. Malchus, writing after this, probably uses this anachronistic term to describe the limit of Theodoric's advance, but there was no wall there to hinder the Goth. Or perhaps the Goths actually penetrated to the city wall, though from his words the historian's contemporaries would not understand that.

12. Cassiodorus *Var.* i. 43.

13. Only Gaiseric had touched this coast; cf. p. 124.

14. Marcellinus *s.a.* Cf. J. Ant. frag. 213, p. 180.

15. The *Gothicum* must be, like the old English Danegeld, a special fund for dealing with the Goths; the *xenicon*, a fund for paying mercenaries as distinct from regular legionaries (Hodgkin, *op. cit.*, III, 104).

16. Jordanes lvii. 289.

17. Marcellinus *s.a.* 481.

18. Marcellinus *s.a.* 483.
19. So Brooks, *op. cit.*, p. 223.
20. Something is missing from the text. Bury, *op. cit.* (1923), I, 421, n. 3, thinks that Recitach's murder of his uncles (frag. 211 *fin.*) was the cause of the blood feud, but this surely could at best have only been a pretext, since the slain men were more closely related to Recitach than to Theodoric.
21. Cf. para. 214 (6), p. 153. Theophanes makes Theodoric take part in the war, and Brooks, *op. cit.*, p. 228, disallows the truth of this recall.
22. Cf. pp. 148 and 154.
23. But cp. p. 152.
24. Marcellinus *s.a.* 487.
25. Thela in other sources; this is doubtless an error. Marcellinus wrongly dates Odovacar's death in 489.
26. The chief ancient sources for his life and career apart from those translated are Ennodius *Panegyric on Theodoric*, Evagrius, Jordanes, Marcellinus, Procopius, Anonymus Valesianus, Anonymus Cuspianus, and Eugippius *Vita Severini*. Cf. Hodgkin, *op. cit.*, III, chaps. VI to XII *ab initio*. Of modern works Ensslin's *Theodorich der Grosse* is the standard reference.

Selected Bibliography

This does not pretend to be a list of works which have been consulted or used in the preparation of these translations, much less a complete listing of works dealing with the historians or with the history of their period. For more comprehensive bibliographies the student can do no better than refer to those included in Vol. I of the Cambridge Mediaeval History. This list merely includes ancient sources and modern works frequently referred to in the notes.

TEXTS OF THE TRANSLATED HISTORIANS

Bekker, I, and B. G. Niebuhr, in Corpus Scriptorum Historiae Byzantinae (quoted as Niebuhr, the editor of this volume).
All authors in same volume. Bonn, 1829.
Olympiodorus, pp. 447–71: notes by P. Labbaeus, pp. 557–78.
Priscus, pp. 139–228: notes by H. Valesius, pp. 533–39.
Malchus, pp. 231–78: notes by H. Valesius, pp. 539–45.
Candidus, pp. 472–77: notes by P. Labbaeus, pp. 578–89.
Dindorf, L. Historici Graeci Minores (quoted as Dindorf), Vol. I. Leipzig, 1870.
Olympiodorus, pp. 450–72.
Priscus, pp. 275–352.
Malchus, pp. 383–424.
Candidus, pp. 441–45.
Müller, C. Fragmenta Historicorum Graecorum (quoted as Müller or F.H.G.), Vols. IV and V. Paris, 1868 and 1870.
Olympiodorus, IV, 57–68.
Priscus, IV, 69–110, V, 24–26.
Malchus, IV, 111–32.

Candidus, IV, 135-37.
Joannes Antiochenus, IV, 612-21, V, 27-28.

COLLECTIONS OF ANCIENT AUTHORS

Corpus Scriptorum Historiae Byzantinae, ed. I. Bekker and B.
    G. Niebuhr (CSHB, quoted as Bonn). Bonn, various
    dates.
Historiae Romanae Epitomae. Amsterdam, 1630. (HRE.)
Monumenta Germaniae Historica (MGH). Berlin, various dates.
Patrologia Graeca ed. J. P. Migne. Paris, 1857-1905. (MPG.)

INDIVIDUAL ANCIENT AUTHORS

Anonymus Valesianus in Ammianus Marcellinus, Vol. III, ed.
    J. C. Rolfe. Harvard, 1939. Loeb Classical Library
    (LCL).
Cassiodorus in HRE.
Chronicon Paschale in CSHB, ed. L. Dindorf. Bonn, 1832.
Evagrius, Historia Ecclesiastica, ed. Bidez and Parmentier.
    Paris, 1898. Trans. anon. London, 1854.
Joannes Lydus, De Magistratibus, ed. R. Wuensch. Leipzig,
    1903.
Joannes Malalas in CSHB, ed. L. Dindorf. Bonn, 1831.
Jordanes, De Origine Actibusque Getarum, ed. C.A. Closs.
    Stuttgart, 1866. Trans. C. C. Mierow. Oxford, 1915.
    Regni Romanorum successio in HRE.
Justianus, Corpus Iuris Civilis. Berlin, 1912-22, Vols. I and
    II, Digest, ed. T. Mommsen; Vol. III, Novellae, ed. R.
    Schoell and W. Kroll.
Marcellinus Comes in MGH, Vol. XI, ed. T. Mommsen.
    Berlin, 1894.
Orosius, Historia contra Paganos, ed. C. Zangemeister. Leipzig,
    1889. Trans. I. W. Raymond. New York, 1936.
Paulus Diaconus in HRE.
Philostorgius, Historia Ecclesiastica in MPG, Vol. 65. Trans.
    E. Walford. London, 1855.
Photius, Bibliotheca, ed. I. Bekker. Berlin, 1824-25.
Procopius, Works, ed. H. B. Dewing. Cambridge, Mass., 1914-
    40. Loeb Classical Library.
Prosper in Migne's Patrologia Latina, Vol. 51.
Sidonius Apollinaris, Works, ed. P. Mohr. Leipzig, 1895.

Letters, trans. O. M. Dalton (Oxford, 1915); Poems, trans. W. B. Anderson (London, 1936), Loeb Classical Library.

Socrates, Historia Ecclesiastica in MPG, Vol. 67. Trans. A. C. Zenos in The Nicene and Post-Nicene Fathers, Second Series. Oxford, 1890–, Vol. II.

Sozomen, Historia Ecclesiastica in MPG, Vol. 67. Trans. C. D. Hastranft in The Nicene and Post-Nicene Fathers, Second Series. Oxford, 1890–, Vol. II.

Suidas, Lexicon, ed. I. Bekker. Berlin, 1854.

Theodore Lector in MPG, Vol. 66.

Theophanes, Chronographia in CSHB, ed. J. Classen (Bonn, 1839).

Victor Vitensis, De Persecutione Vandalorum in MGH, Vol. III, ed. C. Halm. Berlin, 1879.

Zonaras, Epitome historiarum, ed. L. Dindorf. Leipzig, 1868–71.

Zosimus, Historia Nova, ed. L. Mendelssohn. Berlin, 1887.

MODERN WORKS

Brooks, E. W. "The Emperor Zenon and the Isaurians," English Historical Review (E.H.R.), VIII (1893), 209–38.

Bury, J. B. A History of the Later Roman Empire. London, 1889 and 1923.

Cambridge Mediaeval History, Vol. I.

Clinton, H. F. Fasti Romani. Oxford, 1845–50.

Dill, Sir Samuel. Roman Society in the Last Century of the Western Empire. London, 1898.

Ensslin, W. "Maximinus und sein Begleiter, der Historiker Priskos," Byzantinische-neugriechische Jahrbücher, V (1926–27), pp. 1–9.
    Theoderich der Grosse. Munich, 1947.

Freeman, E. A. "Aëtius and Boniface," English Historical Review (E.H.R.), II (1887), 417 f.

Gibbon, Edward. The History of the Decline and Fall of the Roman Empire, ed. J. B. Bury. London, 1909.

Hodgkin, T. Italy and Her Invaders, Vols. II and III. Oxford, 1892 and 1896.

Mommsen, T. "Bruchstücke des Joannes von Antiochia und des Joannes Malalas," Hermes, VI (1872), 323 f.

Pauly-Wissowa (A. Pauly, G. Wissowa, and W. Kroll) (P.-W.). Real-Enzyclopadie d. klassischen Altertumswissenschaft.

Schmidt, L., Geschichte der deutschen Stämme bis zum Ausgange der Völkerwanderung. Berlin, 1910.

Thompson, E. A. The History of Attila and the Huns. Oxford, 1948.

"Notes on Priscus Panites," Classical Quarterly (C.Q.), XLI (1947), 61–65.

"Priscus of Panium, Fragment 1b," C.Q., XXXIX (1945), 92–94.

"Olympiodorus of Thebes," C.Q., XXXVIII (1944), 43–52.

Toynbee, A. J. Greek Civilization and Character. London, 1924.

Geographical Names

In the translations I have retained the ancient place names (except in the case of the Danube River, Spain, and one or two others), but elsewhere, especially in the case of names occurring only once or twice, I have sometimes used the modern names. This list only includes ancient place names that require identification for the modern reader (and where this is impossible I have so said) and one or two names of infrequent use today.

Adrianopolis—Edirne in European Turkey
Ankyra—Ankara
Aquileia—west of Trieste on the Adriatic
Arcadiopolis—probably the ancient Bergulae, renamed modern Bergas between Constantinople and Adrianople (Edirne)
Arelate—Arles
Asemus—mentioned again by Theophylactus, vii. 3, in the reign of Maurice. Gibbon tries to identify it with the fortress of Esimontou mentioned by Procopius *De Aed.* iv. 11, and located near Anchialus (modern Anhialo in Bulgaria) on the Black Sea. This does not agree with the location specified in P. frag. 5, and Thompson, *op. cit.*, p. 85, says it was where the Osma River (ancient Asemus) flows into the Danube nine miles east of Vid (ancient Utus)
Azestus—unknown
Balaam—unknown
Bithynia—province on north central coast of Asia Minor
Blachernae—a suburb west of Constantinople. There was a church of St. Maria there
Boane—*see* Nicomedia
Bononia—Boulogne
Bonophatianae—unknown
Bruttium—in the toe of Italy

Caesarea
   (in Cappadocia)—modern Kaisari in Turkey
Calchedon
   (less correctly, Chalcedon)—across the Bosporus from Constantinople, now Kadiköy. Site of fourth Oecumenical Council
   in 451
Candavia—a mountain range between Lychidnus and Dur-
   razzo (Epidamnus or Dyrrachium)
Cappadocia—province in central Asia Minor
Carsum—probably the Carso of Procopius De Aed. IV. xi. 20,
   described as in the interior of Moesia. Cf. Itin. Ant. 224.
   4 (Wesseling). Modern Harsova in Romania
Caspian Gates—see Iouroeipaach
Cherris—see Dalisandus, also called the hill of Papirius in
   J. A. frag. 206 (2). Müller thinks it not far from Caesarea
   in Cappadocia (note to frag. 214 (10)), F.H.G., V, 28
Chersonese—Gallipoli
Chiris—possibly for Tzitzis, modern Debod
Cilicia—province along southeast coast of Asia Minor
Colchis—a country to the East of the Black Sea, also called
   Lazica from the inhabitants
Corycus—Korgos in southern Turkey
Cos—see Knidus
Dacia—now applied to a province south of the Danube
Dalisandus—one of the numerous hill towns or forts in Isauria,
   like Cherris, which are unidentifiable now. There was an-
   other Dalisandus in Lycaonia farther west. Cf. Bury, A
   History of the Later Roman Empire, I, 394, n. 2
Dalmatia—roughly modern Yugoslavia
Dardania—a district near Sofia and probably the equivalent of
   Pautalia
Drecon R.—see Tigas
Dricca R.—see Tigas
Dyrrachium—see Epidamnus
Edessa—Vodena in Macedonia, not the same city as in Priscus
   frag. 32 (p. 173)
Edessa—Urfa in eastern Turkey (p. 9)
Epidamnus—or Dyrrachium, modern Durazzo
Epirus—also called Epirus Nova, roughly modern Albania
Galatia—in central Asia Minor, or Gaul (usually Western
   Galatia)

Gangra—or Germanicopolis, Kiankari, Tschangri, or Cankiri north of Ankara in Turkey

Gorga—unknown but presumably on the northern Persian frontier

Hadrianople—*see* Adrianople

Haemus Mts.—modern name

Hellespont—Dardanelles

Heraclea—formerly Perinthus, modern Eregli on the Sea of Marmora. In Malchus frag. 15 the Heraclea in Macedonia (modern Monastir) is not indicated (pp. 132, 164)

Heraclea—Monastir (in Malchus frag. 18). It was an important administrative and military center on the Egnatian Way between the Aegean and Adriatic seas, commanding passes of the Balkans and the great Central plain of Macedonia (pp. 170–72)

Hestiae—*see* Sycae

Iberia—not Spain but a country to the east of the Black Sea between the Roman and Persian empires

Illyricum—roughly modern Yugoslavia, Albania, and parts of Hungary and northern Greece

Iouroeipaach—also called Biriparach or Biraparach by John Lydus (*De Mag.* iii. 52–53). In the Dariel Pass between Baku and Derbent; often carelessly called the Caspian Gates. Cf. Bury, *op. cit.,* II, 6.

Isauria—in south central Asia Minor

Italies—Italy and the islands of Sicily, Sardinia, and Corsica

Jotabe—Iaboa (Jobeb) in the northern Red Sea, an important trading center on the sea route to India and a Roman customs station

Knidus (Cnidus)—a city on the modern Cape Krio on the Turkish Aegean coast and Cos the adjoining island, now Stanco

Losthenium—*see* Sycae

Lychidnus—Ochrida on the northern edge of the lake of the same name, where an isolated cliff dominates the surrounding country. There is still a castle there

Maeotis—Sea of Azov

Marcianopolis—Shumba

Margus—Dubrovica at the mouth of the Morava R. in Yugoslavia

Massilia—Marseilles

Moesia—two provinces along the Danube toward its mouth

Moguntiacum—Mainz. It was plundered by the Germans in
407

Mysia—province of west central Asia Minor

Naissus—Nish, a very important city and site of an arms factory

Narbo—Narbonne

Neapolis—*see* Caesarea

Nedao—unidentified river in Pannonia

Nicomedia—Ismit on the Gulf of that name opening off the
Sea of Marmora. There are two sizable lakes fairly near it,
but they were called Sumonensis and Ascania. Which of
these is referred to under the name of Boane, if either, cannot be determined

Nicopolis—in Epirus (Müller) on the northern peninsula en-
closing the Gulf of Arta

Noricum—roughly modern Austria

Novae—Vardim near Svishtov on the Danube in Bulgaria.
Also called Eustia by Jordanes xviii. 101

Novidunum—Isaccea in Romania near the mouth of the
Danube, not Novigrad on the Colapis R., a branch of the
Upper Save in ancient Pannonia as Müller, V, 24, says

Oasis—El Kargeh (cf. p. 18)

Odessus—Varna on the Black Sea in Bulgaria

Pannonia—(Paeonia in Greek), western Hungary

Paphlagonia—central Turkey

Papirius (hill of)—*see* Cherris

Patavio—Pettau or Ptuj on the Drave in Yugoslavia

Pautalia—or Pantalia, a little south of Sofia (Sardica)

Pegai—a suburb of Constantinople, also called Selymbria. The
word means "springs"

Pergamum—Bergama in n. w. Turkey

Philae—100 miles south of Thebes on the Nile. It was at the
southern boundary of Roman territory at the First Cataract

Philippi—Filibah in Bulgaria

Philippopolis—Plovdin in Bulgaria

Phoenico—a town of this name lay east and slightly north of
Thebes, but cannot be meant in Olympiodorus frag. 37.
There is either a textual error, or another unidentifiable town
is meant

Placentia—Piacenza

Prima—Toski or Toshka in Egypt

Propontus—Sea of Marmora

Ratiaria—Near Akchar below Viddin on the Danube in Bulgaria (Bury in Gibbon, III, 425 n. and Thompson, *Attila and the Huns*, p. 83). It was the capital of Dacia Ripensis and the site of an arms factory (*Not. Dign. Or.* xlii. 43; xi. 38)

Regium—Reggio in Italy (p. 35)

Regium—a western suburb of Constantinople (p. 182)

Rhaetia—Tyrol and south Bavaria

Rhodope Mts.—modern name

Salona—also called Spalato, modern Split

Sardica—Sofia. It was destroyed in the invasion of either 441, 443, or 447

Saus R.—Save

Scampia—Elbassan

Scardus Mts.—modern name

Sebasta—(or Augusta in Latin), Sevasti in Turkey

Selymbria—*see* Pegai

Singidunum—Belgrade

Sirmium—either Mitrovica or Sabac on the Save in Yugoslavia

Sondis—unknown. Valesius' conjecture, Succi, is a pure guess (Hodgkin, *Italy and Her Invaders*, III, 86, says this is Manso's guess)

Stable of Diomede—on the Egnatian Road, possibly to be identified with Cellae (the name means "storehouse"), modern Kailari

Stobi—near Gradsko in southern Yugoslavia

Suania—a country in the Caucasus

Sycae—just across the Golden Horn from Constantinople. Hestiae and Losthenium, other suburbs of the city are farther north

Syene—or Soene in Greek, Aswan near the ancient Philae in upper Egypt

Talmis—Kalabshu

Thapis—possibly for Taphis, modern Tafa

Thebes—a very large and ancient city near modern Karnac on the upper Nile in Egypt

Thessalonica—Salonika

Tibisia R.—*see* Tigas

Tigas R.—the Tisia of Jordanes xxxiv. 178 (frag. 9, p. 101 and V, 33 and the modern Theis. The Tiphesas R. is the Tibisia of Jordanes, *loc. cit.*, or sometimes Tibiscus and the modern Temes. The Drecon of p. 81 and p. 103, called the Dricca by Jordanes, *loc. cit.*, can hardly be the modern Drave as some have supposed. First, the ancient name of the Drave was Dravus or Draus, and second the river referred to on p. 81 is north of the Danube, which Priscus had already crossed (p. 75). The different orders in which the rivers are mentioned on p. 81 and p. 101 and the fact that in both places the Theis is mentioned before the Temes, when Priscus must have reached and crossed the latter first, shows that he makes no attempt to name the rivers in the order with which they were met. This makes the identification of the Drecon difficult, but probably either the modern Bega, Maros, or Koros, all of which flow from the east into the Theis, is meant. The former seems most likely, since no ancient name is recorded for it, whereas the others are known elsewhere as the Marisus (or Marisia) and Crisia (or Gerasus). Any of these three would accord well enough with a journey toward the northwest from a Danube crossing near Margus (Dubrovica). Possibly, the *Geographus Ravennae* IV. 14, refers to this river under the name Drica. Cf. Closs, note to Jordanes xxxiv p. 127, and the inconclusive note of Thompson, *op. cit.*, pp. 221–22 with the references there

Tiphesas R.—*see* Tigas

Tisia R.—*see* Tigas

Trapezus—Trebizond

Valentia—Valence

Varanus—or Ouanarus, part of Constantinople

Viminacium—Kostolacz (or Kostolatz) near Margus downstream on the Danube. Procopius *De Aed.* IV. v. 17 says of this town that "long ago it was destroyed to its very foundations"

Index of Persons, Tribes, and Official Terms

Honorius, 1, 7, 25, 28, 30–34, 36–40, 42–45
Huneric (Honoric, son of Gaiseric), 50, 114, 118–19, 125
Huns, 8–10, 12, 26, 29–30, 45, 47–49, 54, Chap. III
    passim, 134–37, 143, 147, 157

Illus (general and rebel), 129, 138, 142–44, 146–55, 164,
    166, 180–81
Illus (slave of above), 154
Indacus Kottounes, 137–38, 153–55
Isaurians, 8, 26, 69, 98, 132–33, 137, 139, 141–56, 159, 179
Itimari, 58–59

Joannes (father of Jordanes), 137
Joannes (prefect of Illyricum), 169, 171, 178
Joannes (the Scythian), 152, 154, 180, 181 (?)
Joannes (usurper), 22, 43, 45–47, 54, 59
Jovian (or Jovius, Honorius' general), 32–33, 37
Jovinus (usurper), 39–40, 59, 198
Julian (s. of Constantine the usurper), 31, 37, 39
Julianus (envoy of Zeno), 167
Julianus (primicerius), 33
Justinus (Justinianus(?), general of Constantine), 31

Kadisenes, *see* Ephthalites
Katziri, *see* Akatiri
Kidarites (*see* Huns), 9–13, 197
Kottomenes, 153, 155
Kottounes, *see* Indacus

Lazi, 11–12
Leo I, 12, 14–15, 54, 117, 120–21, 123, 125–26, 131–39,
    141, 145, 158–59, 166
Leo II (son of above), 133, 139, 141
Leo (Pope), 108
Leontius (Illus' puppet), 143, 152–55
Leontius (steward of Placidia), 44
Longinus (brother of Zeno), 146, 152, 155–56, 181
Longinus (of Kardala), 153, 155

magister equitum, 6, 36
magister militum (unspecified), 3, 6–7, 55, 92, 181
magister militum
    per Galliam, 119
    per Illyricum, 6, 74, 147, 158
    per Italiam, *see* magister utriusque militiae